Reputation and Civil War

Of all the different types of civil war, disputes over
self-determination are the most likely to escalate into war and resist
compromise settlement. *Reputation and Civil War* argues that this
low rate of negotiation is the result of reputation building, in which
governments refuse to negotiate with early challengers in order to
discourage others from making more costly demands in the future.
Jakarta's wars against East Timor and Aceh, for example, were not
designed to maintain sovereignty but to signal to Indonesia's other
minorities that secession would be costly. Employing data from
three different sources – laboratory experiments on undergraduates,
statistical analysis of data on self-determination movements,
and qualitative analyses of recent history in Indonesia and the
Philippines – Barbara F. Walter provides some of the first systematic
evidence that reputation strongly influences behavior, particularly
between governments and ethnic minorities fighting over territory.

BARBARA F. WALTER is Professor of Political Science in the
Graduate School of International Relations and Pacific Studies
at the University of California, San Diego. She is the author of
Committing to Peace: The Successful Settlement of Civil Wars
(2001) and co-editor of *Territoriality and Conflict in an Era of
Globalization* (Cambridge, 2006) and *Civil Wars, Insecurity and
Intervention* (1999).

Reputation and Civil War

Why Separatist Conflicts Are So Violent

BARBARA F. WALTER

University of California, San Diego

CAMBRIDGE UNIVERSITY PRESS
Cambridge, New York, Melbourne, Madrid, Cape Town, Singapore,
São Paulo, Delhi, Dubai, Tokyo

Cambridge University Press
The Edinburgh Building, Cambridge CB2 8RU, UK

Published in the United States of America by Cambridge University Press,
New York

www.cambridge.org
Information on this title: www.cambridge.org/9780521747295

First published 2009

Printed in the United Kingdom at the University Press, Cambridge

A catalogue record for this publication is available from the British Library

Library of Congress Cataloguing in Publication data
Walter, Barbara F.
  Reputation and Civil War : why separatist conflicts are so violent /
  Barbara F. Walter.
      p.   cm.
  Includes bibliographical references.
  ISBN 978-0-521-76352-3 (hardback)   1. Civil war.   2. Insurgency.
  3. Autonomy and independence movements.   4. Political violence.   I. Title.
  JZ6385.W35 2009
  303.6′4–dc22
  2009023523

ISBN 978-0-521-76352-3 hardback
ISBN 978-0-521-74729-5 paperback

To Zoli and Lina

Contents

Figures

Tables

Maps

Acknowledgements

This book began during dinner with Rui de Figueredo in San Francisco. I had just finished a book on civil wars and was left with a puzzle for which I had no clear answer. Of all the civil wars over the last sixty years, the most intractable ones were the ones fought over territory. The two of us talked about this until Rui inquired: "what about the problem of entry-deterrence in economics? Have you thought about that?" So began the book.

It's been a number of years since that dinner and many people have stepped in to help along the way. Tanisha Fazal, Jim Fearon, Hein Goemans, Ted Hopf, Patrick James, Miles Kahler, Andy Kydd, David Laitin, Bob Powell, John Ruggie and Ken Schultz read early versions of the project and gave serious and helpful feedback. Participants at seminars at Yale, Columbia, University of Southern California, University of California, San Diego (UCSD), the University of Chicago, Dartmouth, Princeton, Washington University in St. Louis, and the University of Washington generously read parts of the project and gave additional advice. Kristian Gleditsch patiently and rapidly answered all queries related to data, Langche Zeng made sure the empirical work had no glaring errors, and Tom Palfrey was an early and crucial proponent of the experiment. Thanks also to John Haslam at Cambridge University Press as well as two anonymous reviewers who liked the manuscript and helped improve it even further.

This book required an enormous amount of data collection which I could not have completed without generous funding from the National Science Foundation (grant # 03576670), the Carnegie Corporation of New York, and the Academic Senate at UCSD.

These grants allowed me to focus more heavily on the project and hire terrific research assistants including Shannon Eliot, Kathleen Gallagher Cunningham, Stephanie McWhorter, Mike Pisa, Chad Rector, and Idean Salehyan.

Writing is never easy, yet two nurturing work environments helped ease the burden. The first and most important has been the Graduate School of International Relations and Pacific Studies at UCSD. Anyone who knows my colleagues knows that they are not only talented but big hearted. Thank you Lawrence Broz, Peter Cowhey, Erik Gartzke, Peter Gourevitch, Steph Haggard, Gordon Hanson, Miles Kahler, David Lake, Megumi Naoi, Branislav Slantchev, and Chris Woodruff for all of our interactions and for making it enjoyable to go to work every day.

Much of the final version of the book was written during the year I spent at the Niehaus Center for Globalization and Governance at Princeton University. My time there was a scholar's dream – a year filled with engaged colleagues, stimulating seminars, and lots of quiet time. There I met Dustin Tingley who, as a first year Ph.D. student, showed a natural instinct for social science and made chapter three possible. I also had the great good fortune to interact with Bob Keohane on an almost daily basis. His deep interest in the project, as well as his lengthy correspondence, made the final stages of writing exciting. Thanks also to Joanne Gowa for always checking in on me, and to Helen Milner for working her institutional magic to make it all happen.

Despite this, the book would never have been finished without the endless support of my family. The writing of this book corresponded to the first six years of my daughter's life. Despite her sometimes distracted Mom, Lina was a happy and easy child, choosing only to interrupt me when a favorite toy was missing or a boo-boo required an immediate kiss. She filled our house with love and laughter, and was my antidote to the often dismal world of civil war. The person who shouldered the biggest burden, however, was my husband Zoli. Not only did he read and comment on every chapter, but he also made sure that the bills were paid, that Lina got to school on time, and that I had uninterrupted time to write when I needed to write. I could not do what I do without the thousands of little things he does for me and Lina every day. His love and generous spirit continuously astound me.

Part I **Theory**

I Introduction

This book seeks to answer one of the central puzzles surrounding civil war. Of all the different types of disputes that can occur within states, self-determination disputes are the most likely to escalate to war and the most likely to resist compromise settlement.[1] More than half of all civil wars in 2008 were fought between ethnic minorities and their central governments over greater autonomy or independence. Moreover, wars in Sri Lanka, Sudan, Georgia, the Philippines, Kashmir, and Chechnya have lasted for years and have shown little sign of settlement. Muslims in southern Philippines have been seeking independence for over thirty-five years. And India has been fighting to retain Kashmir since 1989. The pervasiveness of these types of wars has made them the chief source of violence in the world today.[2]

Self-determination disputes are also the most intractable type of civil war.[3] Between 1955 and 2002, only 25 percent of all separatist groups were given independence or autonomy and most of these concessions were granted only after lengthy fights.[4] Moscow has been fighting a bloody war against the Chechens rather than grant them any degree of autonomy or independence. Georgia has

---

[1] Since 1980, almost half of all armed conflicts have been fought between governments and ethnic minority groups seeking self-determination. See Marshall and Gurr (2003).

[2] See the Minorities at Risk project for data comparing political, economic, cultural, and autonomy civil wars.

[3] In fact, between 1940 and 1996, governments were 70 percent less likely to negotiate with groups seeking self-determination than with groups seeking any other goals. See Walter (2002).

[4] Source: Center for International Development and Conflict Management's (CIDCM) 2003 report on self-determination movements. See Chapter 4 of this book for greater details.

refused to grant South Ossetians and Abkhazians greater self-rule even if it means a war with Russia. India has come to the brink of a nuclear confrontation with Pakistan in order to retain Kashmir. And Sri Lanka has vowed "never, ever" to cooperate with the Tamils despite a seemingly endless war.[5]

The fact that self-determination disputes tend not to end in negotiated settlements is puzzling for at least three reasons. First, if war occurs, these types of conflict tend to be long and costly to the government involved. The average civil war between 1940 and 1992 (excluding separatist wars) lasted a little over five years. The average independence war during this same time lasted almost eight years, killing significantly more people.[6] Given the costs, why are governments not settling? Second, governments have multiple ways to peacefully end these disputes without giving up territory, including granting greater political, fiscal, and/or cultural autonomy. Disputes over territory, in fact, should be easier to resolve than disputes over government control where many of the key positions – like the presidency – cannot be easily shared. Third, maintaining a large territory is becoming less important in an age of increasing globalization, yet leaders continue to fight hard to maintain their existing territorial boundaries. What, then, explains the decision not to settle?

CONVENTIONAL EXPLANATIONS
The standard explanation for why wars so frequently occur over territory has to do with the value of land.[7] According to conventional

---

[5] Interview with US State Department official stationed in Sri Lanka.
[6] Civil War Resolution Dataset. See Walter (2002).
[7] I am not the first scholar to notice that territorial disputes are particularly difficult to resolve short of war. A similar pattern has already been discovered in disputes between states. Luard (1986), Holsti (1991), Goertz and Diehl (1992), and Vasquez (1993) each found that territorial issues are one of the most frequent sources of interstate wars, and the least likely to be resolved peacefully. While Hensel (1996) found that territorial disputes between states are more likely to escalate, to produce a greater number of fatalities, and be more conflictual than

accounts, states are less likely to negotiate because land often contains important natural resources, serves a vital security function, or plays a critical role in the identity of a country.[8] Anecdotal evidence about separatist regions seems to support this. Many contested regions contain precious minerals, fertile agricultural zones, or critical tax bases that are vital to the well being of the central government. Most of Nigeria's agricultural revenue, for example, and almost all of its petroleum came from the secessionist region of Biafra. Congo's Katanga corridor, site of numerous secession attempts, holds important mineral deposits. East Timor lies just north of potentially significant deep-sea oil reserves. And Moscow relies heavily on Chechen oil.

Many separatist regions also appear crucial for maintaining the security of a state.[9] The Golan Heights, for instance, sheltered Israel from Syrian rocket attacks and gave it a valuable listening post to Syrian army movements. Serbia's only access to the Mediterranean Sea was through Bosnia and Montenegro. And Kashmir contains the Himalayan mountains – an important buffer between India and Pakistan. It is not hard to believe, therefore, that the value of these strategic assets makes compromise unlikely.

Some pieces of territory, such as Kosovo and the West Bank, also hold great symbolic value because they represent the historical homeland of a people or play a critical role in the identity of a country. As Isaiah Bowman wrote in the aftermath of World War II: "there is a profound psychological difference between a transfer of territory and a change in a trade treaty or pact of international cooperation. Territory is near and plain and evokes personal feelings and group sentiments ..."[10] If two groups hold the same strong attachment to the same piece of land, the stakes could

---

non-territorial confrontations. For whatever reason, territorial disputes, whether within or between states, tend to end in war.

[8] See especially Gilpin (1981), Doyle (1986a, 1986b), and Van Evera (1998).

[9] For a summary of this view see Jack Snyder (1991: 24–5).

[10] Bowman (1946: 177). See also Toft (2003).

easily be defined in all-or-nothing terms, making compromise unlikely.

These arguments, however, cannot explain two puzzles associated with what are often lengthy and painful separatist wars. First, they cannot explain why governments would not offer ethnic groups a deal short of independence that would satisfy both sides. Governments could offer ethnic groups significant political autonomy, where the government retains sovereignty over the land, while the ethnic group makes decisions about governance. Governments could transfer fiscal power, allowing the group to tax individuals and businesses in their region and then determine how the money will be spent. Or governments could offer to create a federation where power is decentralized down to the regional level. All of these solutions would enable the center to retain control over a piece of territory while avoiding war.[11]

Second, existing theories cannot explain the many cases where governments have chosen to fight for territory that has little economic, strategic, or symbolic value or give up territory that does. East Timor's alleged oil reserves are far less than the hundreds of millions of dollars Indonesia has spent trying to hold on to this region.[12] The former Soviet Union, for example, was willing to grant independence to the Kazakhs, Kirghizs, Moldavians, Tadzhiks, Ukrainians, and Uzbeks even though each of their territories contained valuable strategic features.[13] And, the Israeli government

---

[11] Some governments, although not many, have opted to make these concessions without first fighting a war. Canada awarded the Quebecois a series of political provisions designed to address their drive for independence. Nicaragua, Ecuador, Panama, Peru, and Bolivia have granted various degrees of autonomy to indigenous groups unhappy with years of discrimination and neglect. And the Czech Republic peacefully granted independence to the Slovakians.

[12] This point was acknowledged by a member of Indonesia's House of Representatives (2004–7) in an interview with the author, May 2008. See also Di Giovanni (2000).

[13] This coincides with findings on interstate territorial conflicts. According to a widely cited study by Paul Huth, governments are only 6 percent less likely to compromise with another state if the territory under dispute is strategically important. See Huth (1996b).

negotiated away the Sinai, parts of the West Bank, and will, I believe, eventually agree to a division of Jerusalem. A land's value may explain government behavior toward some separatists some of the time, but it does not explain the many cases where governments fight over land that holds little obvious value, or do not fight over land that does.[14]

THE ARGUMENT OF THE BOOK

What, then, explains why so many leaders in so many countries fight? I argue that leaders fight not because territory is so valuable, as many people have assumed, but because fighting helps them to deter other groups from seeking secession in the future. Think for a moment about two cases where governments have been willing to grant independence without first going to war: Canada and the former Czechoslovakia. On the surface these two countries appear to have little in common, yet they share a trait that helps answer the question posed above. Unlike most countries in the world, Canada and Czechoslovakia are ethnically relatively homogeneous. Canada contains concentrated ethnic minorities in Quebec and in northern Canada where native Americans and Inuit live, but few additional groups with any serious desire to secede. Czechoslovakia contained only two concentrated minority groups – the Slovaks and Hungarians – both of whom occupied territory in the secessionist region of Slovakia.[15] The fact that so few potential separatists existed in both countries allowed leaders to negotiate with one group without triggering multiple additional challenges. Canada and Czechoslovakia had the luxury to negotiate with their ethnic minorities because so few additional ones existed.

---

[14] The many disputes over small and insignificant islands in Northeast Asia, as well as the war between Britain and Argentina over the Malvinas or Falkland Islands, are two examples of this phenomenon between states.

[15] In 1991, ethnic Czechs represented 62.8 percent of the population, Slovaks 31 percent, and Hungarians 3.8 percent. Hungarians lived predominantly in the soon-to-be-created Slovakia. Source: Library of Congress Country Studies.

In what follows, I argue that the low rate of negotiation is the result of reputation building, where governments are refusing to negotiate with early challengers in order to discourage others from making even more demands in the future.[16] Jakarta's wars against East Timor and Aceh were not designed solely to maintain sovereignty over these two tiny regions, but to signal to Indonesia's many other minorities that secession would be costly. As one Indonesian general argued in 2000, giving independence to Aceh "could set off a violent Balkans style breakup of Indonesia."[17] Fighting a war against one challenger is the price governments are willing to pay in order to deter additional challengers later on.[18]

In Chapter 2 I develop this theory by describing how uncertainty and repeated play create strong incentives for governments to invest in reputation building.[19] I argue that a contributing factor in the outbreak, duration, and resolution of these conflicts is a government's private information about its willingness to negotiate with separatists, and the incentives a government has to misrepresent this information when numerous potential challengers exist. Governments, especially those presiding over multi-ethnic populations, would very much like ethnic groups living within their borders to believe that obtaining self-determination will be costly and counter-productive. Would-be separatists, on the other

---

[16] Although this book focuses only on self-determination movements, the reputation theory should apply equally well to territorial disputes between states. As long as governments expect a neighboring country or countries to launch a series of demands for territory, incentives should exist for the defending state to be tough, at least against early challengers.

[17] *New York Times*, April 21, 2000, p. A13.

[18] The idea that states might fight hard for useless territory in order to signal to future secessionists has been discussed in the literature, but not developed or tested. See Van Evera (1998), Saideman (1997), and Toft (2003) for some examples.

[19] Note that there are other types of reputation, such as a reputation for reliability, or a reputation for honesty, that I do not analyze in this book. I focus on a reputation for resolve because it is the concept most often cited by both policymakers and scholars seeking to explain certain behaviors related to international security.

hand, would very much like to determine if the government will make deals in the face of a violent challenge. The result is a complex strategic interaction where governments are actively seeking to deter separatists, and separatists are carefully trying to uncover if and when the government will grant concessions. As one Russian political scientist aptly observed: "The fighting in Chechnya was not just against the Chechen rebels, it was against movements all around."[20]

REPUTATION BUILDING IN INTERNATIONAL RELATIONS

I am not the first person to suggest that reputation building may affect how governments respond to threats and challenges. In fact, reputation has been one of the most talked about yet puzzling concepts in international relations for the last forty years. Foreign policy leaders and scholars such as Henry Kissinger and Thomas Schelling have long argued that governments must cultivate a reputation for using force in order to deter future aggressors, even over issues seemingly not worth the costs of war. "We lost thirty thousand dead in Korea," Thomas Schelling famously wrote, "to save face for the United States and the United Nations, not to save South Korea for the South Koreans, and it was undoubtedly worth it."[21]

The idea that reputations matter, however, has lost favor in international relations because little empirical evidence has been found to support its usefulness, at least until recently.[22] Studies on interstate disputes by Huth and Russett, Hopf, Mercer, and Press uncovered scant evidence that a reputation for toughness had

---

[20] Ellen Barry, "Russia's Recognition of Georgia Areas Raises Hopes of Its Own Separatists." *New York Times*, October 9, 2008, 6.

[21] Schelling (1966: 124).

[22] Although the literature arguing against reputation is fairly large, few empirical studies exist that attempt to test the theory. These include Huth and Russett (1984, 1988), Huth (1988b), Shimshoni (1988), Huth *et al.* (1992, 1993), Orme (1992), Fearon (1994), Hopf (1994), Lieberman (1994, 1995), Mercer (1996), and Press (2001).

any positive effect. Huth and Russett, for example, found that the past behavior of the defending country had no significant impact on whether an aggressor backed down once it had threatened to attack.[23] Hopf found that Moscow did not infer anything about America's likely behavior in Europe or Northeast Asia based on how it had behaved in more peripheral states.[24] And Press found that the Kennedy administration did not change its assessment of how the Soviets were likely to behave in Cuba based on how the Soviets had behaved in Berlin.[25] These findings have led many international relations scholars to reject reputation building as a useful tool for explaining behavior. As John Mearsheimer recently concluded, "[r]eputation is an overblown concept."[26]

This statement seems premature for three reasons. For one, it is hard to believe that so many leaders in so many contexts could be wrong. If reputation building consistently fails to deliver the desired outcome, why would leaders continue to invest in it?[27] Even critics of reputation building arguments – such as Mercer – acknowledge that most of the leaders they examined seem to truly believe that reputation building works. "My three case studies," admits Mercer, "provide ample evidence that Russian, British, French, German, and Austrian decision-makers were concerned with their reputations for resolve."[28] It is puzzling, therefore, that so many leaders would continue to invest in reputation building if it did not work.

Second, formal models in economics reveal that reputation building *does* influence behavior at least under certain well-specified conditions. Both Milgrom and Roberts (1982) and Kreps and

---

[23] Note that this study comprised fifty-four cases of extended deterrence between 1900 and 1980. Huth and Russett (1984).

[24] Hopf (1994).

[25] Press (2001).

[26] From the back cover of Press (2005).

[27] Leaders could be mistaken, but leaders who wish to remain in power generally wish to avoid pursuing bad policies, especially those that are economically and politically costly.

[28] Mercer (1996: 21).

Wilson (1982) show that reputation building tends to emerge "in any situation where individuals are unsure about one another's options or motivation and where they deal with each other repeatedly in related circumstances."[29] And experimental evidence has supported various implications of these models. In an experiment on product markets, for example, Miller and Plott (1985) found that sellers developed reputations for selling high-quality products, and that these reputations allowed them to command premium prices.[30] Roth and Schoumaker (1983) found that past histories of players affected outcomes in bargaining experiments.[31] And Ebay has shown that buyers rely heavily on information on the past conduct of sellers when determining from whom to buy.

Finally, evidence for reputation building is also beginning to emerge in studies on international diplomacy and lending. In work on crisis bargaining, Anne Sartori has found that leaders benefited from developing reputations for honesty when engaged in relatively costless verbal negotiations.[32] Michael Tomz found that countries could gain reduced interest rates from international lenders by building reputations for reliably repaying their debts.[33] These studies suggest that reputation building can be a powerful theoretical tool for explaining certain types of behavior. The challenge is to determine where and when it applies.

CONDITIONS CONDUCIVE TO REPUTATION BUILDING
One of the reasons I believe international relations studies have found only limited evidence for reputation building is because the theory has frequently been applied to the wrong types of

---

[29] Milgrom and Roberts (1982: 304).
[30] DeJong et al. (1985) found similar results in an agency setting, and Daughety and Forsythe (1987a, 1987b) found reputation building in experimental duopolies.
[31] See Camerer and Weigelt (1988) for a more detailed discussion of these results.
[32] Sartori (2005).
[33] Tomz (2007).

cases. This study, therefore, starts by outlining the conditions under which reputation building should emerge and explains why self-determination movements are such a good fit.[34] As mentioned earlier, formal models in economics by Milgrom and Roberts (1982) and Kreps and Wilson (1982) show that two features of the strategic environment create strong incentives to invest in reputation building: repeated play and incomplete information. Parties must believe that they will deal with each other in related circumstances over time, and they must be unsure about how each is likely to react in those circumstances.[35] "If the situation is *repeated*," wrote Kreps and Wilson, "so that it is worthwhile to maintain or acquire a reputation, and if there is some *uncertainty* about the motivations of one or more of the players, then that uncertainty can substantially affect the play of the game."[36]

Economic models, however, remain frustratingly vague about what is meant by repeated play.[37] Does it matter whether a government encounters the same challenger again and again, or if it encounters a series of different ones over time? If the situation includes a series of different players, how similar must each of the players be in order for inferences to be drawn? And does it matter how many interactions a defender anticipates? Will reputation building materialize only when many repetitions are expected, or can a few suffice?

A similar set of questions can be asked about the sources of uncertainty necessary for reputation building to emerge. If incomplete information is critical, as Kreps and Wilson and Milgrom and Roberts claim, what types of uncertainty are most likely to cause governments

---

[34] There has been a limited attempt in the economics literature to specify these conditions. See Kreps and Wilson (1982). The one attempt in the political science literature is Downs and Jones (2002).

[35] Milgrom and Roberts (1982: 304).

[36] Emphasis added. Kreps and Wilson (1982).

[37] This is because economists have applied the theory almost exclusively to a single well-defined context: situations where a monopoly firm seeks to deter a number of smaller firms from entering a lucrative market. The appropriate context in international relations, however, is less clear.

to try to signal resolve? Is it uncertainty over a defender's preferences (such as the value it places on land), or is it some other factor not yet uncovered? In what follows, I develop these two concepts in an attempt to determine where reputation is likely to apply.

Repeated play: the first critical feature necessary for reputation building to take place is repeated play. For a situation to be considered part of a repeated game, it must contain three elements. The first is *repetition*. A government must believe that it will engage in the same type of interaction a number of times. Governments may interact with the same party repeatedly, as the United States has done with North Korea over nuclear weapons since the early 1990s. Or it may interact with a series of different parties sequentially, as Israel has been doing with different terrorist organizations since the early 1980s.

The second feature is *issue specificity*. For reputation building to be rational, individuals must also interact in ways that are sufficiently similar such that parties can identify the correct set of cases from which to draw inferences.[38] Israel, for example, is engaged in a series of disputes with neighboring parties over access to water, a clearly defined issue area that determines the set of related and comparable cases. Reputation building should not have a consistent effect when one looks across different issue areas, but it should have a strong effect when one looks at similar players, fighting over similar issues, against the same opponent over time.[39]

The fact that reputations are likely to be context-specific means that governments can develop different reputations depending on the issue under dispute. The United States, for example, has developed a reputation for being quite resolute against terrorists, but relatively cowardly when faced with peacekeeping duties. As Downs and Jones have observed, "[o]ver time, states develop a number of reputations,

---

[38] Milgrom and Roberts (1982: 304).

[39] The few studies that have limited the context in which reputation took place found strong reputational effects. In interstate disputes, when players interacted in the same region over time, reputations did appear to form on the basis of past behavior. See Huth *et al.* (1992), Shimshoni (1988), Lieberman (1994, 1995), and Evron (1987) in their studies of Arab–Israeli relations.

often quite different, in connection with different regimes and even with different treaties within the same regime."[40] This helps explain why countries might have a poor reputation for compliance in one area (e.g., environmental agreements), but an excellent reputation for compliance in another (e.g., trade).[41]

But reputational dynamics will still fail to emerge if potential challengers cannot observe how a defender behaved in the past in order to determine how the defender is likely to behave in the future. The third and final feature of repeated play, therefore, is *observability*. A government's behavior must be visible and public; it cannot act clandestinely or under conditions of limited verification. Saddam Hussein, for example, made no attempt to hide atrocities directed against Kurdish separatists. In fact, his most famous attack, the chemical gas attack on Halabja in March 1988, killed an estimated 5,000 villagers whose bodies were captured in brutal photographs published around the world. Hussein's policies drew the condemnation of the international community, but provided clear information to other Iraqi citizens that rebellion would be costly.

Incomplete information: repeated play, however, is not sufficient to cause governments to care about reputation building in the absence of private information about preferences. For governments to benefit from investments in toughness, there must also be uncertainty about how much a government values the stakes over which it is fighting. If ethnic groups, for example, knew for sure that

---

[40] Downs and Jones (2002: 97).

[41] Critics might argue that issue specificity is too strong an assumption to make. It is possible, for example, that a government may accommodate one group that seeks control over a small piece of territory and then successfully argue that it would fight any group seeking a larger piece of land. Or that a government could accommodate a powerful rebel movement, but then refuse to accommodate a weak one. If this were true, governments could develop two different reputations even if the disputes were over the same issue. What we see in Chapters 4 and 5 is that issue specificity does matter. Governments that made concessions to one challenger over territory triggered significantly more challenges even when the demands and the capabilities of the challengers were held constant.

a government would relinquish control over a piece of land, they would always challenge. If they knew the government would never concede, they would remain quiet. It is uncertainty over how the government is likely to react that makes the game of reputation building possible.

WHY SELF-DETERMINATION MOVEMENTS?

The conditions outlined above bring us back to self-determination movements. Leaders in countries with many disgruntled minorities face a strategic environment perfectly suited for reputation building. First, multiple challenges over self-determination are possible if not likely. Thus, the opportunity for a repeated game exists. Second, the issue under dispute – greater territorial autonomy or independence – is easy to identify and relatively consistent across groups.[42] This makes inferences straightforward to make. Third, ethnic groups live in close proximity to one another, making it easy for potential separatists to observe and monitor each other's behavior. Observability, therefore, is likely to be fairly good. Finally, the government is likely to have private information about the value it places on controlling its territory. Thus, the element of uncertainty necessary for reputation building exists.

But why would governments invest more heavily in reputation building over territory than over any other issue? Theoretically, governments should engage in reputation building whenever a particular stake is valuable and frequently contested. The more valuable the stakes and the greater the number of anticipated challenges, the more important deterrence becomes, and the more incentives governments have to signal toughness. In the case of self-determination movements, land is highly valued; governments cannot make too

---

[42] One of the challenges in studying reputation building is to determine what the comparable set of cases will be from which governments and challengers draw inferences. Self-determination movements are a particularly good phenomenon to study because the criteria for judging similar players and similar issues are so clear.

many deals over territory without eventually negotiating themselves out of business. Land is also heavily disputed. Since 1980, governments have received seven times more challenges over territory than over any other issue.[43] It is because governments anticipate more disputes over self-determination than over any other issue that reputation building becomes so important.[44]

RESEARCH DESIGN

This chapter asked why governments often fight ethnic groups seeking self-determination rather than offer a compromise settlement. It argued that governments facing multiple potential separatist challengers are in a strategic situation that strongly encourages reputation building. War is the costly signal governments use to deter multiple ethnic groups from seeking separation.

In the next chapter I explore the causal mechanism by which reputation building in separatist conflicts works. To do this I rely heavily on theories of entry deterrence in the economics literature, and in particular the chain store paradox. This theory, with its emphasis on incomplete information, helps to lay out the logic by which reputation building deters ethnic challengers. If the theory is correct, we should observe that leaders with many concentrated ethnic minorities occupying important pieces of land invest heavily in reputation building. We should also see that reputation building works to discourage ethnic groups from challenging the state. All else equal, governments that are tough toward one group should face fewer self-determination movements than those that are not. Ethnic groups, conscious of the incentives governments have to invest

---

[43] See the Minorities at Risk project for data comparing political, economic, cultural, and autonomy grievances.

[44] Some readers may wonder why secessionist challenges are so frequent given that governments are working so hard to deter them. The simple answer is that ethnic minorities seek self-rule for many reasons, many of which are unrelated to whether or not it will actually be granted. For a more in-depth look at ethnic nationalism see Sambanis and Milanovic (2004).

in reputation building, should also be more inclined to challenge governments that have granted concessions, and to challenge at those times when weak governments have few incentives to bluff.

Chapter 3 tests the logic of the chain store model in a series of laboratory experiments. These experiments serve two purposes. The first is to see if, in a perfectly controlled environment, individuals respond to the strategic incentives in ways predicted by the theory. The experiment will reveal the theory's strengths and weaknesses, and disclose whether the theory needs to be re-evaluated or revised before going to the field. Laboratory experiments also allow me to answer an important question regarding repeated play. We know that defenders have increasing incentives to invest in reputation building as the number of repetitions increases, but is there a critical number at which these incentives kick in? Do defenders still invest in reputation building when the number of iterations is low? We see that subjects engage in reputation building behavior, but in ways not completely predicted by the model.

Chapter 4 tests the hypotheses against data on all self-determination movements between 1955 and 2000. Here I focus on government behavior and ask whether governments behaved as the theory expected. Is a desire to deter future challenges and future losses critical in government decisions to fight or accommodate ethnic separatists, or do they focus more heavily on present interests and capabilities? We see that government accommodation is not only influenced by the number of ethnic groups in a country, but also by the costs a government is likely to incur if future challenges arise. Governments that face a larger number of potential future challengers who occupy vast territories and control valuable land, are far more likely to fight than governments that face fewer challengers. These findings confirm that governments believe that a tough reputation will help them reduce future conflicts, and that this investment pays out.

Chapter 5 looks more closely at ethnic group behavior and, therefore, addresses one of the main criticisms of reputation building: that it does not work. A third test of the theory, therefore, looks specifically at ethnic groups and tries to determine if they consider a government's reputation when deciding whether to challenge. Are ethnic groups more likely to challenge if they observe governments making concessions to other ethnic groups? Do they launch challenges during those times when governments have fewer incentives to be tough? Here, a second dataset is used to analyze ethnic group behavior, one that includes information on every ethnic group in every country from 1940 to 2000. We see that ethnic groups are significantly more likely to seek self-determination if the government made concessions to an earlier challenger, and if the government was unlikely to encounter additional challengers in the future. These findings confirm that reputation building, at least in the world of government–ethnic minority relations, worked quite well.

Chapter 6 and 7 analyze decision making in two individual cases: Indonesia and the Philippines since 1945. These cases allow me to disaggregate my unit of analysis down to individual leaders to better assess elements of the theory presented in Chapter 2. I have three objectives with these chapters. The first is to determine whether reputation building plays any role in ethnic group decisions to seek self-determination and government decisions to fight or negotiate. The second is to assess more closely the impact of rival explanations. The third goal is to identify new variables that might be significant determinants of behavior, and to see which factors best reflect what is really happening on the ground. What we see is that government and ethnic group leaders are heavily motivated by concerns about reputation, but that other factors such as domestic politics, a loss of political autonomy, and a lucrative resource base influence them as well.

The book ends by reflecting on the main findings and contributions of the book. We see the value of using a range of empirical tests to explain an important problem in international security, namely why separatist disputes are so violent. Using laboratory experiments, quantitative analysis, and detailed case studies, I show that governments are refusing to compromise in order to deter additional challenges, and that this strategy frequently succeeds. Thus, in at least one particular domain – ethnic minorities challenging their central government for self-determination – governments care a lot about their reputation and it is quite rational for them to do so.

2 Reputation building and self-determination movements

This chapter applies the chain store model on reputation and entry deterrence to self-determination disputes in an attempt to explain why they are so difficult to resolve short of violence.[1] What we will see is that the reputation theory helps explain why some ethnic minorities seek self-determination while others do not, why some groups delay making demands, and why some governments are willing to negotiate while others are not. In the process, it underscores the amount of strategizing that occurs between governments and ethnic groups, and the ways in which private information shapes how governments and ethnic groups choose to behave.

The chapter is organized into three sections. The first walks the reader through the logic of reputation building, explaining how repeated play and incomplete information create strong incentives for governments to fight early challengers. In section two I describe how governments would behave if the theory were correct, and draw out a number of hypotheses for testing. In section three, I shift the focus to ethnic minorities and discuss how these groups are likely to respond to reputation building strategies being used by some governments. These hypotheses will then be subjected to a range of tests in the remaining chapters.

THE LOGIC OF REPUTATION BUILDING
Information asymmetries and signaling dynamics are key to understanding why self-determination disputes are so difficult to resolve

---

[1] See especially Spence (1973), Rosenthal (1981), Kreps and Wilson (1982), Milgrom and Roberts (1982), Dixit (1982), Schmalensee (1981, 1983), and Kennan and Wilson (1993). There is also a long literature on reputation and deterrence in political science. See especially Schelling (1966), Lebow (1985), Alt *et al.* (1988), Nalebuff (1991), Mercer (1996), Hensel (1996), and Toft (2001).

peacefully and why governments and ethnic minorities behave the way they do. To understand how reputation building works, assume that a country contains only one minority group, and that this minority group must decide whether to challenge the government for greater self-rule or accept the status quo.[2] If the group chooses to challenge, then the government must decide whether to accommodate these demands or resist them.[3] If the government accommodates, it gets peace in return for some territorial concessions. If the government chooses to resist, it has a chance to maintain full control over its territory, but it must then pay the costs of fighting.[4]

When governments face only one challenger the logic of how to respond is fairly straightforward. Since there is little value in paying the costs associated with developing a reputation for toughness, strong incentives exist to accommodate.[5] This does not mean that the government will always give in when faced with a single challenger.[6] It does mean, however, that fighting under these circumstances will not have the added benefit of discouraging other ethnic groups from challenging the state.

The situation is more complicated when a government believes it could face a series of potential challengers over time. Here, a

---

[2] By challenge I mean an explicit threat to use military force in the event that the government does not acquiesce to the demand.

[3] In reality, governments can pursue a variety of mixed strategies in response to ethnic separatists that are not reflected in the game theoretic framework I use. I have chosen to reduce the choices available to both the government and the ethnic groups down to two, to simplify both the theoretical and empirical analysis. I attempt to correct for this simplification in the case studies presented in Chapters 6 and 7 by tracing the range of different strategies both governments and ethnic groups have chosen to pursue.

[4] "Fighting" represents a continuum from group repression to outright war. The fact that governments choose to fight, however, does not mean that they are not also dangling concessions short of independence or autonomy to the rebels.

[5] This assumes that the government will face this one challenger only once. If the government expects to face a single challenger multiple times (i.e., an ethnic group challenges repeatedly for increasingly higher stakes) the game would take on the dynamics of a repeated rather than a single-shot game, and incentives to build reputation would emerge.

[6] Some governments may refuse to concede because accommodation in this one case may itself be too costly.

government has to consider that the game could be repeated as many times as there are separatist groups and that its behavior in the first period could affect decisions by other separatists later on. For example, when the predominantly Muslim republic of Dagestan sought independence in 1999 President Yeltsin and the new prime minister, Vladimir Putin, vowed to relentlessly protect "the links in the chain" that make up the Russian Federation.[7] How often the game is likely to be repeated, therefore, fundamentally affects the incentives to fight or accommodate.

Repetition, however, is not sufficient to bring about reputation building behavior in the absence of uncertainty. In order for reputation building to make sense, ethnic groups must also be unsure of how the government will respond when challenged. To understand the importance of incomplete information, assume that governments come in one of two types. A government can either be conciliatory and thus willing to part with some territory in return for peace, as the Swiss were willing to do with the canton of Jura in 1979. Or a government could be more extreme – unwilling to compromise at almost any cost – as Yeltsin and Putin have been with the Chechen Republic. One can think of this as the value a government places on maintaining a state's territorial integrity. If ethnic minorities knew what type of government they were facing their behavior would be predictable. Faced with a government known to compromise, ethnic groups' optimal strategy would always be to challenge. Faced with a government known to fight, their optimal strategy would be to remain quiet. Either way, you would observe peace.

In reality, ethnic groups can never be sure what type of government they are facing and this is why we sometimes get war. As long as ethnic groups are uncertain about the government's value for fighting versus acquiescing, conciliatory governments have incentives

---

[7] Holmes (1999: 3).

to behave as if they were tough – at least toward early challengers. Chinese leaders, for example, have long asserted that they will crush any moves toward secession. As one top official announced, "we will never tolerate 'Taiwan independence.' We will unswervingly oppose and curb secessionist forces and their activities."[8]

Ethnic groups, of course, understand that governments have incentives to behave strategically and will, therefore, attempt to challenge only when they believe they are likely to face a government likely to make concessions. The trick for ethnic groups is to figure out the *likelihood* that they are facing a government that is not only conciliatory, but also has no incentive to bluff at a particular point in time.[9] These are the times when an ethnic group's demands are most likely to be rewarded with a deal.

The theory discussed above reveals how two features of the strategic environment (repeated play and incomplete information) encourage reputation building and thus affect incentives to cooperate and fight. This provides a starting point to understand the conditions under which conciliatory governments are likely to fight against an ethnic group and the ways in which reputational dynamics affect each side's behavior. In what follows, I analyze the specific strategies each of the parties is likely to pursue as a result of these dynamics, and develop a series of corresponding hypotheses to test.[10]

---

[8] Annual speech by Jai Qinglin, China's top political advisor, to the National Committee of the Chinese People's Political Consultative Conference, as published on chinadaily.com.cn, March 4, 2006.

[9] Ethnic groups are likely to assign a probability that they are facing a conciliatory or non-conciliatory type. All else equal, the greater the probability that they are facing a conciliatory type, the greater incentive a group has to challenge.

[10] Note that these hypotheses verbally elaborate on the chain store model but do not directly follow from it. I have chosen not to take the implications of the model too literally for two reasons. First, the relationship between governments and domestic ethnic groups differs in certain important ways from firms described in the chain store model. Second, certain data limitations (described in Chapters 4 and 5) make it impossible to test the full implications of the model.

*Implications for government behavior: factors affecting
the decision to fight*

Governments should be more likely to invest in reputation (i.e., fight a particular ethnic separatist) when the expected value of deterrence is high. At least three factors are likely to affect this calculation: the number of challengers a government expects to face, the value of the land these challengers occupy, and the costs the government would have to pay to fight for these lands. The more valuable future lands and the more costly it will be to fight for them, the more cost effective reputation building becomes.

The number of future challenges: as discussed above, reputation building makes no sense unless a game is likely to be repeated. The greater the number of potential future challenges, the greater the value associated with deterrence is likely to be, and the more likely a government is to fight. As Boris Yeltsin asserted in the summer of 1994, "[w]e cannot stand idly by while a piece of Russia [Chechnya] breaks off, because that would be the beginning of the collapse of the country."[11] In the case of self-determination movements, governments can estimate the number of future challenges in at least three ways: the absolute number of ethnic minorities in a country, the number of ethnic minorities that have not yet challenged, and the number of years a leader expects to be in office.

An important first step in determining who is likely to challenge and how much land is likely to come under dispute is to determine which groups have the possibility to mobilize against the state. One rough but easily observable measure is the number of ethnic groups in a country. Self-determination movements are almost always launched by ethnic minorities, and in particular concentrated ethnic minorities, that reside within a given country. All else equal, the greater the number of ethnic minorities in a country, the greater the number of self-determination movements

[11] Yeltsin (2000: 58–9).

a government can expect. This simple measure gives us our first hypothesis to test:

> $H1_{gov}$: a government's decision to accommodate a group seeking self-determination will be inversely related to the number of ethnic groups in that country.

Governments interested in reputation building, however, are likely to distinguish between ethnic groups that have already challenged and those that have not. This is because fewer incentives exist to invest in toughness against later challengers, even if the absolute number of ethnic minorities in a country remains the same. Gorbachev, for example, was far more willing to negotiate with Estonia on independence, after Georgia, Azerbaijan, and Lithuania had already declared independence. This gives us our second hypothesis to test:

> $H2_{gov}$: governments should be increasingly willing to accommodate ethnic groups as the number of remaining challengers declines.

The number of ethnic groups in a country and the number of remaining challengers are not the only factors that are likely to determine how many separatist challenges a leader is likely to encounter. A leader's tenure in office should also make a difference.[12] Leaders who expect to be in power for long periods of time, such as President Marcos of the Philippines or President Suharto in Indonesia, can expect a larger number of challengers than those who expect to rule only briefly. The shorter a leader expects to be in power, the fewer challengers he or she is likely to encounter, and the less important reputation building becomes. The effect of a leader's tenure, therefore, gives us a third hypothesis to test:

---

[12] The fact that leaders change and that different administrations may represent different types of leaders should not fundamentally affect the way the game is played; conciliatory administrations will still face strong incentives to invest in reputation and thus behave *as if* they were committed.

$H3_{gov}$: a leader's decision to accommodate self-determination demands should be inversely related to the length of time he or she expects to be in office.[13]

The value of future stakes and the costs of fighting for them: counting the number of challengers, however, does not address what is likely the main concern of governments. Reputation building is only important if the land that could come under dispute is valuable and the costs of fighting to keep this land are high.[14] A government that expects to face future separatists who occupy relatively worthless land may have little interest in paying the costs to deter these groups. In this case it may be in the government's interest to grant concessions to all or most of the groups in order to avoid the costs of war. Similarly, a government that expects to face a series of weak opponents should be less concerned about building reputation than a government that expects to face a series of more powerful and costly opponents. It makes no sense to fight the tough in order to deter the weak, if the weak are cheap and easy to defeat.[15]

This logic gives us two additional hypotheses to test:

$H4_{gov}$: a government's decision to accommodate separatist groups will be inversely related to the cumulative value of all the land within its borders that could come under dispute in the future.

---

[13] Although the theory predicts that most leaders will feel this way, some may not. Some individuals may care more about their historical legacy and will resist giving up territory even if they know they are likely to be in office only a short time.

[14] Why include the number of challengers at all? One of the challenges in testing reputational effects in civil wars is that data on the value of land occupied by ethnic groups are often rough and poorly measured. Including the number of ethnic groups, therefore, is a reliable proxy for the amount of land that could come under dispute, and therefore, the relative value of different pieces of territory to the government.

[15] Work by Triesman (2004), for example, has argued that governments with limited resources may have strong incentives to appease early challengers in order to conserve sufficient resources to deter others.

H5$_{gov}$: a government's decision to accommodate will be inversely related to the costs of fighting all groups that could challenge in the future.

One of the conclusions to draw from the preceding analysis is that the reputation theory both complements and extends theories that emphasize the value of land as well as relative capabilities. Boris Yeltsin, for example, cared about the Chechen pipelines that carried oil from Central Asia to the Black Sea, and these interests almost certainly influenced his statement about "standing idle." What the reputation theory emphasizes, however, is that Yeltsin also likely factored in the potential for future losses in Uzbekistan, Tajikistan, Tatarstan, and Turkmenistan as well.

Implications for ethnic group behavior: determining if and when to challenge

If it is true that governments consciously invest in reputation building, then it must also be true that ethnic minorities understand this and adjust their behavior accordingly. In what follows, I argue that ethnic minorities are likely to rely on four markers to determine when governments are likely to be tough. If the theory is correct, these four factors should strongly determine if and when groups challenge.

The past behavior of the government: the most obvious way ethnic groups can attempt to gauge a government's response is to observe how it has behaved in the past.[16] A government that has granted independence or autonomy to one group has revealed itself

---

[16] A distinction needs to be made, however, between concessions being made before a war has been fought, and concessions made after a war has been fought. Theoretically, it is those cases where a government has not been willing to go to war – where it has made concessions without paying the costs of fighting its opponent (such as the Czech Republic) – that signal a lack of resolve. Governments that are willing to fight a war, whether they are forced to make concessions in the end or not, signal clearly to future challengers that self-determination will be costly and their reputation should not suffer as much as a result. This point is brought to light in Chapter 6 in terms of Habibie's

to be conciliatory and is likely to make peace again in the future. President Habibie provided considerable information to other minority groups in Indonesia in 1999 when he agreed to a referendum in East Timor. According to one activist in Aceh, "[i]f East Timor [is] granted the right to vote on its future, then there is no reason Aceh should not be next."[17] A single act of accommodation, therefore, can provide substantial information about a government and have dramatic effects on ethnic group behavior. This simple observation gives us our first prediction about ethnic group behavior:

> $H1_{eg}$: ethnic groups should be more likely to seek self-determination if they observe government accommodation toward an earlier challenger.[18]

But past accommodation is not the only way ethnic groups can collect information about a government's likely future behavior. Ethnic groups can also estimate a government's response based on the conditions under which conciliatory governments have fewer incentives to bluff. As discussed above, conciliatory governments have decreasing incentives to fight: (1) the fewer the number of potential future challengers, (2) the lower the value of future land, and (3) the weaker the future challengers. These are the times when at least partial concessions are likely to be made.

The number of potential future challengers: ethnic groups know that conciliatory governments only have incentives to fight

---

decision to grant independence to East Timor but only after years of costly fighting.

[17] Lekic (1999: 9).

[18] One possible counter-argument is offered by both Robert Jervis and Daryl Press in their work on reputation building. They speculate that a government that concedes may have an incentive to redouble its effort in the future in an effort to recoup whatever reputational capital it has lost. If governments behave this way, then ethnic groups would be less likely to seek self-determination after observing government accommodation toward an earlier challenger, not more. This argument, however, is refuted by the empirical findings in Chapter 5 that show that ethnic groups are more likely to challenge after observing such concessions, not less.

if they believe numerous additional challengers exist, all of whom are waiting to see if the government will reveal itself to be irresolute. Basque leaders, for example, have consistently acknowledged that Madrid is unlikely to agree to a self-determination referendum not because they are fundamentally opposed to concessions for the Basques, but because this would "lead to similar demands from other autonomous regions, like Catalonia and Galicia."[19] Potential separatists, if they are forward looking, should be aware of the incentives governments have to behave strategically and be more inclined to challenge when additional challengers are few or absent. This logic gives us our second hypothesis about ethnic group behavior:

> **H2$_{eg}$**: the greater the number of potential future challengers, the less likely ethnic groups are to seek self-determination.

The number of future challengers, however, is also likely to be affected by a leader's time in office.[20] Ethnic groups should also be less likely to seek self-determination against leaders who are expected to have lengthy terms in office. While President Suharto of Indonesia expected to be in power for decades and thus face numerous disputes over self-determination, President Habibie expected to be in power for less than a year. Reputation building under the conditions in which Habibie operated was less important and ethnic minorities should know this.

This additional distinction gives us one more nuanced hypothesis for testing:

> **H3$_{eg}$:** the shorter a leader's expected tenure in office, the more likely an ethnic group is to seek self-determination.

---

[19] Anderson (2001: 43).

[20] This assumes that government leaders care more about their own individual reputation than the reputation of their party or the government as a whole. It also assumes that leaders are not motivated to be tough in order to preserve their historical legacy.

The order in which the challenge is made: just as conciliatory governments have greater incentives to fight early opponents, so too do ethnic groups have incentives to challenge late in the game. Ethnic groups understand that each successive group that challenges a conciliatory government reduces the government's value for reputation building and increases the chances of accommodation. Ethnic groups, therefore, who wish to maximize the likelihood of gaining concessions, should delay their challenge until other ethnic minorities have chosen to act. This gives us a fourth hypothesis to test:

$H4_{eg}$: the fewer the remaining ethnic groups, the more likely any ethnic group is to challenge.

This strategy, however, creates a dilemma. If ethnic groups are likely to benefit by challenging late, who would ever choose to move first? Theoretically, ethnic groups can solve this problem in one of two ways. First, they can coordinate their attacks, transforming the repeated nature of play into a one-shot game. Conciliatory governments facing a single coordinated attack would gain little by investing in reputation building and have more incentives to make a comprehensive deal with all groups. If the theory is correct, therefore, we should observe a clustering in the timing of attacks, with numerous ethnic groups choosing to challenge the government at the same time.

There is, however, a potential problem with this strategy that may reduce its practice in the real world. Clustering may solve the problem of early entry, but creates a second problem of coordination. Ethnic groups who wish to synchronize their challenges with other ethnic groups must do so despite living in different regions, following different customs, and often speaking different languages. Moreover, the government will almost certainly be working to thwart such cooperation. A simultaneous attack, therefore, might be ideal in theory, but difficult to manage in practice.

A second, more realistic option for ethnic groups would be to wait until the more committed separatists moved first. As will be discussed below, some ethnic minorities are likely to place a higher value on obtaining autonomy or independence, making them more willing to challenge despite lower odds of success. The Ibos of Nigeria and Uzbeks in Afghanistan had been seeking independence since colonial times and were the first groups in their respective countries to challenge their governments. Some ethnic groups may be more committed to independence because they have suffered greater discrimination, making the status quo unbearable. Other groups may find themselves with a strong patron willing to finance their challenge but unwilling to wait until the government is more likely to negotiate. Finally, a group may suddenly lose autonomy as a result of historical events; East Timor demanded independence as a result of being abruptly abandoned by Portugal in 1975. Thus, ethnic groups will always exist that are willing to challenge first because their value for self-governance is so high.[21]

How valuable is deterrence?: Finally, ethnic groups should also calculate a government's expected utility for deterrence over time. If the costs of fighting exceed any benefits to be gained by deterring additional entrants then reputation building will not be a rational strategy for the government to pursue and ethnic groups should act. Self-determination movements, therefore, should be more numerous when the value of future stakes is low, and when the costs the government would have to fight for these stakes is high. This logic gives us two final hypotheses for testing:

H6$_{eg}$: ethnic groups should be more likely to seek self-determination when the value of all land that could come under dispute in the future is low.[22]

---

[21] The theory of reputation has nothing to say about which groups are apt to move early in the sequence and which are likely to fight longer and harder for their goals. This question is addressed in much greater detail in the large literature on ethnic mobilization and rebellion. See for example Sambanis and Milanovic (2004) and Fearon and Laitin (2003).

[22] Note that a more literal interpretation of the model would offer a slightly different prediction. According to the model, ethnic groups should be more

H7$_{eg}$: ethnic groups should be more likely to seek self-determination when the costs of fighting all potential future challengers is high.

Explaining the outbreak of war

A key question, however, remains unanswered. If governments are consciously seeking to deter challenges, and ethnic minorities are actively seeking to avoid fighting, why would we ever observe war? Wars continue to occur because the information ethnic groups are able to collect is neither complete nor perfect. First, ethnic groups will never be able to perfectly assess when they are facing a conciliatory government willing to negotiate because governments have incentives to hide this information. Ethnic groups know that conciliatory governments have declining incentives to fight wars as the number of potential separatists declines, but they do not know exactly when these incentives will disappear. Ethnic groups may challenge, believing they are likely to be met with concessions, only to find that the government is committed, or not yet willing to concede. It is during this transition period – when the gains from reputation building are increasingly dubious – that mistakes are most likely to be made.[23]

Wars may also occur because of numerous information gaps. Ethnic groups, for example, can never be certain how long a leader will be in power, or when he or she will be replaced. This is especially true in countries with no set term limits or constitutionally established elections. The first four prime ministers of India, for example, ruled for widely different periods. Prime Minister Nehru ruled for

---

likely to seek self-determination when the government's expected value for future conflicts is low. Here expected value would weight the value of land by the probability of winning a fight against the challenger and the probability of a challenge. I do not use this interpretation of the model because data on the probability of winning are not available.

[23] The unique sequential equilibrium shows that governments should fight against early challengers, play a mixed strategy in the middle, and then consistently acquiesce to the final challengers.

seventeen years, while his successor, Prime Minister Nanda, ruled for thirteen days.[24] Similarly, Prime Minister Indira Gandhi ruled for eleven years while her successor was in power for just two years. Anticipating which leader is likely to have a particularly long time horizon, and therefore greater incentives to fight, is difficult to do under these circumstances. New administrations are likely to bring greater uncertainty and a higher likelihood of war.

Third, ethnic groups can also miscalculate the government's expected utility for fighting in any particular case. A group may overestimate its strength, or underestimate the value a government places on a piece of territory. The result would be a situation where the ethnic group expects a government to benefit from conciliation, but where the incentives to invest in reputation are still strong. The Ibos, for example, overestimated the amount of outside assistance they would receive in their fight against the Nigerian government, and therefore overestimated their capabilities.[25] Government behavior is influenced by a variety of factors that are difficult for would-be separatists to gauge, such as the costs and risks a government believes it would pay for future fights. Governments, for example, might choose to acquiesce to one strong challenger in order to conserve resources so that they can better fight a series of lesser opponents in the future.[26] Even under the best conditions, therefore, ethnic groups cannot know exactly how a government will respond to any given challenge.

The fact that ethnic groups cannot always correctly anticipate how a government will react does not mean that information gathering has no value or that it will not influence decisions to seek self-determination. Information about how a government behaved in the past, and how many challengers it is likely to encounter in the

---

[24] Prime Minister Nanda served as interim prime minister of India after the death of Jawaharlal Nehru and was not expected to serve very long. He was followed by Lal Bahadur Shastri, who ruled from June 1964 until January 1966 when he died in office.

[25] See Stremlau (1977).   [26] See especially Triesman (2004).

future, may not be a perfect predictor of how the government will behave. But any information that reduces doubt about how a government will respond will also reduce the likelihood of war and be of great value to ethnic groups operating in an otherwise uncertain environment.

Additional implications

Until now, we have analyzed the conditions under which governments have incentives to invest in reputation building, and the conditions under which ethnic minorities have incentives to challenge. We have also discussed those situations where ethnic minorities are most likely to miscalculate: in the middle of the sequence when it is not clear exactly when conciliatory governments will stop bluffing, in countries where an executive's tenure in office may vary widely, and in information poor environments – environments when it is difficult for ethnic minorities to obtain information about the relative strength of the government and the relative value the government places on the territory under dispute. We have still not explained, however, a class of cases that does not fit any of these situations: self-determination wars that occur in seemingly information-rich environments.

The logic of the reputation theory implies that ethnic groups should almost always challenge a government that has shown itself to be conciliatory; a single act of conciliation should trigger a host of additional challenges. Conversely, ethnic groups should almost never challenge a government that has consistently refused to grant concessions in the face of multiple challenges; such a government is likely to be truly resolute. Yet, empirically we know that a number of groups have done the opposite. The Zomis, Mons, Shans, Kachins, and Karens of Burma have all launched armed challenges against a government that has granted no meaningful concessions to any of its many ethnic opponents. And the Chechens have been fighting a lengthy war against the Russians with no sign that Moscow will eventually concede.

These anomalies reveal limitations of the theory presented above. One of the simplifying assumptions made by the theory is that incomplete information is one-sided; only governments have private information and incentives to misrepresent this information. In reality, governments are likely to be equally uncertain about the type of separatist group they are facing. I believe that adding two-sided, incomplete information to the theory helps explain this seemingly irrational behavior by some groups.

Just as there are committed and uncommitted governments, there are also likely to be resolute and irresolute challengers.[27] One can think of "resoluteness" as the expected value ethnic groups place on gaining self-determination, which in turn is likely to be affected by factors such as the group's commitment to self-rule, the value it places on the stakes over which it is fighting, its capabilities, and the costs it is willing to bear in order to attain its goals. Ethnic groups that are particularly resolute will be more willing to challenge despite low odds of success; their high value for gaining independence offsets the greater costs they are likely to incur. Less resolute separatists will require more certainty that the government is conciliatory before they will be willing to take action.

Ethnic groups know whether they are resolute, but the government does not. If a government knew for sure that it faced a resolute challenger, it would have fewer incentives to fight, and concessions would be more likely. Knowing this, ethnic groups may have incentives to exaggerate just how committed they are and to attempt to signal that they are willing to absorb high costs to obtain independence.

Ethnic groups can signal this commitment by launching challenges when the government is more likely to fight. This could be early in a leader's tenure, early in a sequence of challengers, or

---

[27] There is a large literature in comparative politics, anthropology, and sociology arguing that the strength of some group identifications, and the resulting nationalism, is stronger in some groups than others.

after observing brutal behavior by the government against another separatist group. A challenge under these conditions is apt to be interpreted as signaling resoluteness, and may convince a more conciliatory government to grant concessions earlier than it otherwise would. Thus, ethnic minorities could potentially be making three calculations when determining whether or not to challenge: (1) how much they value the benefits of independence, (2) how likely the government is to be tough, and (3) how signaling resoluteness might help their cause. The result is that different groups are likely to have different incentives to move early or late.

An interesting conclusion to be drawn from this analysis of ethnic group behavior is that the effectiveness of reputation building is never as perfect as governments (or ethnic groups) might wish. Governments can invest in reputation building, but the effectiveness of this strategy will be somewhat reduced because ethnic minorities anticipate this type of behavior. Conciliatory governments can choose to fight early opponents, but this reputational investment will not serve to deter as many opponents as they would like. Many ethnic groups will still choose to challenge knowing that this type of bluffing is occurring and that an early challenge may convince a government that it faces a particularly determined challenger. Similarly, the effectiveness of ethnic group strategizing will also be reduced by the government's ability to anticipate their behavior and not concede. Because governments know that irresolute types may have greater incentives to move early, governments are more apt to fight these groups. What this means is that any effect that we do see in the empirical chapters offers particularly strong evidence for reputation building.

One final question has not been answered. If wars over self-determination occur because there is uncertainty about both government and the ethnic group resolve, why do conflicts last as long as they do? Once it becomes clear that both the ethnic challenger and the government are resolute, a deal should be struck that allows both sides to avoid the additional costs of war.[28] Part of the answer, I believe, lies with additional information gaps that exist between the two combatants, in particular information that is impossible to obtain without first engaging in battle. Just as there is incomplete information about resolve, so too is there incomplete information over a host of other factors critical to the outcome of war, such as the financing of war, or cost tolerances of each side.[29]

A second part of the answer lies with problems both sides are likely to face credibly committing to a compromise settlement.[30] Governments may offer to transfer political and economic control to a particular province as part of a compromise settlement, but ethnic minorities will have little power to enforce this deal in the absence of a continued military threat. Ethnic minorities, on the other hand, may promise not to seek independence if greater territorial autonomy is granted, but may have difficulty convincing the government that they will not escalate their demands in the future. In cases where the terms of settlement create large opportunities for post-treaty exploitation, a decisive military outcome may be the only solution.

CONCLUSION

This chapter reveals the analytic power that comes from applying a relatively simple model from economics to a complicated problem in international relations. It also demonstrates the power of looking beyond the immediate structural conditions surrounding secessionist movements and analyzing the larger game that is being played between the government and its many ethnic groups over time.

---

[28] See especially Fearon (1995).
[29] For an excellent discussion of information that is likely to be revealed during war see Slantchev (2003).
[30] For a sample of the growing literature on commitment problems in civil wars see Fearon (1995), Walter (2002), and Powell (2006).

In the next chapter I investigate the theory more closely using incentivized laboratory experiments. I do this for three reasons. First, lab experiments allow the researcher to manipulate the decision environment in specific ways. Instead of relying on observational data from historical cases (which can be highly unreliable), these experiments allow me to alter the values of specific variables while carefully controlling other parts of the decision context. Thus, I can determine the boundary conditions in which specific behaviors should be observed. Second, experiments allow the researcher to obtain unambiguous evidence about causation. If the predicted relationships do not emerge in the context of a highly controlled (and properly constructed) environment, then the assumptions about how individuals process information and react to incentives are likely to be wrong. Finally, experiments also reveal deviations from purely rational behavior, opening a window for additional theorizing about different patterns we may see in the real world. Subjects in the laboratory did appear to follow most of the predictions made by the reputation theory discussed above, but not all.

Part II **Empirical tests**

3 An experimental study of reputation building and deterrence

(co-authored with Dustin Tingley)

This chapter uses a series of laboratory experiments to test whether individuals react to incentives to build reputations in the way the chain store model predicts.[1] We include this chapter because experiments offer a unique opportunity to adjust or improve the theory before it is tested against the complex and often messy data on self-determination disputes, and because it offers an unambiguous way to determine causality. If subjects adhere to the predictions of the theory in the controlled environment of the laboratory, then we know that people are at least capable of making the strategic decisions outlined in Chapter 2. If subjects deviate from the predictions, then we know there could be a gap between the theory and behavior that should be flagged before testing the theory in the real world.

Still, the strength of laboratory experiments lies in their ability to test the logic of a theory, and not their applicability to more real-world settings. Showing that undergraduate students at Princeton begin to build reputations in response to strict incentives offered in the laboratory does not mean that government leaders will do the same in the more complex arena of domestic politics. Determining the relevance of the theory to actual disputes between governments and minority groups requires a different set of tests, which will be presented in Chapters 4 through 7.[2] Because different empirical approaches all have significant weaknesses, our research design

[1] For an excellent overview of experimental methods in political science, including their strengths and weaknesses, see McDermott (2002).
[2] See Morton and Williams (2007) and Shadish *et al.* (2002).

draws on multiple methodologies and tries to triangulate across these approaches.[3]

A final reason we include this chapter is that two of the more recent and prominent criticisms of reputational theory in international relations draw from laboratory experiments to help buttress their claims. Both Mercer, and to a lesser extent Press, claim that experiments in psychology laboratories give credence to their claims. But the experimental studies they cite were not designed for testing the type of reputational arguments we have in mind. Moreover, a number of *incentivized* experiments they do not cite suggest reputation building does matter. To maintain a consistent methodological approach with these more recent studies, we designed an experiment that focuses on the key elements of reputational theory outlined in the previous chapter.

THE EXPERIMENT AND ITS OBJECTIVES

This chapter attempts to assess two important aspects of the chain store model.[4] The first is whether the past behavior of the defender affects decisions to challenge, and if so in what ways. According to the model, entrants should be far more likely to challenge if they observe even a single act of accommodation, and these challenges should begin immediately after accommodation is observed. The laboratory experiments, therefore, allow us to determine whether this temporal relationship exists.

This chapter also seeks to determine whether the number of future challengers can cause defenders and entrants to change their behavior. We know from the model that repeated play creates

---

[3] See Kinder and Palfrey (1993), McDermott (2002), and Bueno de Mesquita (2002).

[4] We are not the first scholars to design experiments to test the chain store model. A number of experiments have tested different implications of the model. See Bolton and Ockenfels (2007), Brandts and Figueras (2003), Camerer and Weigelt (1988), Jung et al. (1994), Neral and Ochs (1992), and Sundali et al. (2000). We are the first to explore experimentally a particular comparative static of the equilibrium model – changing the number of entrants a defender faces.

incentives to build reputation, but we do not know how many players are needed before this occurs.[5] We also do not know whether players significantly alter their behavior based on the number of iterations they expect to encounter.

The experiment reveals that subjects do engage in reputation building behavior in a repeated game with incomplete information, and that reputation building deters future challenges under these conditions. As will be discussed in greater detail below, conciliatory defenders do choose to fight against early challengers in order to signal toughness even though they could potentially pay heavier short-term costs as a result. Similarly, entrants are significantly more likely to challenge after they have observed accommodation. Thus, in a controlled laboratory environment where the amount of information and the number of repeated plays can be controlled, reputation building emerged as an important variable influencing behavior.

But the experiments also suggested two ways in which behavior deviated from the expectations of the model. The first has to do with the number of repetitions necessary for reputation building to emerge. Subjects invested in reputation building even against a relatively small number of challengers. Thus, depending on the payoffs, a game need not be repeated as often as theory might predict for reputation building to emerge. The second deviation has to do with entrant and defender behavior in the very early rounds of the game with a large number of entrants. Entrants challenged much sooner, and defenders accommodated these early entrants much more than the theory predicted. These results suggest that at least three additional hypotheses regarding government and ethnic group behavior need to be added. We discuss these findings in more detail below.

---

[5] One exception is Richard Selten (1978) who suggested that reputation building was unlikely to occur in games 1–4, would begin to break down around games 5–8, and would certainly not occur at game 20, but these critical thresholds have never been empirically tested.

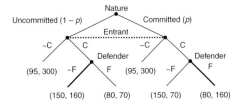

FIGURE 3.1 The structure of a single-shot play

THE STRUCTURE OF THE GAME

Figure 3.1 shows the structure of a single-shot play of the game we were attempting to test as well as the payoffs each of the players knows it will receive for the different outcomes.[6]

The game is the same repeated version of the entry–deterrence game with incomplete information used in Chapter 2.[7] The game begins with nature randomly choosing whether the defender is committed or uncommitted to fighting a challenge. If the defender is committed, the entrant should prefer not to challenge. If the defender is uncommitted, the entrant should prefer to fight. The entrant, however, does not know what type of defender it faces. If the entrant decides to challenge, the defender then chooses whether to fight this challenger or make the concessions that are necessary to avoid a fight. Once the defender chooses whether to fight or accommodate, a second entrant then chooses whether to challenge, after which the defender again decides whether to fight or accommodate. As

---

[6] Note that the Defender's (D) payoffs depend on his or her type. If the entrant chooses to challenge, a committed defender receives a higher payoff from fighting, while an uncommitted defender receives a higher payoff from backing down. Payoff parameters are the same as those used by Jung *et al.* (1994).

[7] The standard set-up of this game – which gives rise to the so called "chain store paradox" – assumes one-sided incomplete information because the entrants in the model (firms) are assumed to be homogeneous. This is not the case in many situations in the real world. Some entrants may put up more of a fight than others, and defenders may not have perfect information about the "type" they face. Future research is needed to incorporate two-sided incomplete information into experiments (see Tingley and Wang 2008), although we note that working out tight theoretical predictions in such cases with repeated play would be quite difficult.

each entrant plays, they are given information about how previous entrants played against the defender they are currently matched with, and the choice of the defender *if* the previous entrant decided to challenge.[8] The game continues until the defender has faced a commonly known set number of entrants.[9]

In the actual experiment, we used value neutral labels to avoid leading the subjects in any way. Instead of entrant, we used "first-mover," and instead of defender we used "second-mover." In each interaction with a potential challenger, the defender was first asked "if the first-mover chooses 'A1' (enter), what will be your response?" This question was asked because entrants were expected not to enter in early rounds, thus making it impossible to determine how the defender would respond to a challenge at this point. Including this question, therefore, allowed us to collect data both on and off the actual path of play. In the experimental literature this is known as the strategy solicitation method.[10]

In what follows, we explore the sequential equilibrium predictions of this repeated game and then return to a more thorough description of the experiment and our results.

[8] Challengers do not, however, know what payoffs a defender receives from each of his or her decisions. This information is not revealed because it would also reveal the state's type in cases where they challenge entry.

[9] The game could also be played repeatedly between a defender and a single entrant. This would be similar to a situation where a government engaged in a series of continuing disputes with a single ethnic group, where the ethnic group demanded greater and greater concessions over time. The Canadian government's relationship with the Parti Quebecois would be an example of this type of two-player repeated game. In order to simplify the analysis we only analyze repeated play between different opponents. The same dynamics, however, should hold in any situation where a defender expects repeated interactions over time.

[10] This does not mean that our subjects played the simultaneous normal form version of the game, as the defender's strategy choice is only elicited for the conditional case where there is entry. Our empirical results conform to previous experiments on the chain store game that did not use the strategy method, and thus our experiment *appears* to reside in the set of cases where the strategy solicitation method has little effect on strategy choices (Brandts and Charness 2000).

HYPOTHESES

The model presented above has a sequential equilibrium that is (plausibly) unique, meaning that actors are best responding at every sequential stage of the iteration, updating their beliefs with relevant observations. The sequential equilibrium prediction of this game can be summarized as follows.[11] If an entrant observes a defender accommodating one challenger, its belief that the defender is committed is updated to $p=0$. Knowing that the defender is not committed, all subsequent entrants should challenge, and all uncommitted defenders should continue to accommodate. This portion of the equilibrium generates the following hypotheses:

> $H1_E$: *entrants should always enter if they observe accommodation.*
>
> $H1_D$: *weak defenders that have backed down once should continue to back down.*

Not all entrants, however, will observe accommodation in a previous round. If the entrant observes no accommodation, we consider the game in three phases, an early, a middle and a late phase. This is where we should observe differences in behavior based on the number of challengers a defender anticipates. If the number of challengers is sufficiently high, there is a pure strategy period of play where entrants never enter and defenders always fight. This is because entrants understand that even weak defenders have incentives to invest in reputation in these early rounds. After reaching some period, φ^*, defenders have incentives to play a mixed strategy, fighting with some probability, and backing down with some

---

[11] The analysis provided here follows Jung *et al.* (1994) to which we refer the reader for the mechanics of the proof. We note that the sequential equilibrium also prescribes different strategies for entrants depending on whether there was entry by the previous entrant in the immediately preceding period. While technically an important part of the equilibrium, the results below do not change if we break apart the data to accommodate this fact. To simplify our presentation and tighten our focus on reputation building we ignore this feature.

probability. Entrants should respond accordingly. During the mixed strategy period, defenders should fight with a decreasing probability as the end of the round nears. On the last round of play, weak defenders should always back down and challengers should always enter.

This generates the following set of hypotheses in those cases where no previous accommodation was observed:

H2$_E$: *if the period* < φ^* *then entrants should enter with probability 0.*

H2$_D$: *if the period* < φ^* *then weak states should fight with probability 1.*

VARYING THE NUMBER OF FUTURE CHALLENGERS

We investigate two different experimental treatments that vary the total number of future challengers a defender faces. In one treatment, a defender faces eight future entrants, in the other the defender faces four. These numbers were chosen for the following reason. Previous research on self-determination movements found that governments invested in reputation building when faced with as few as four potential separatist challengers.[12] The theoretical model considered here, however, suggests that for the payoffs we use, reputation building should only consistently occur in cases with *more* than four challengers. Our four- and eight-entrant design was chosen to mimic this feature of the real world while also setting up a stark difference in the predictions of our model to test in the laboratory.

According to the model, the sequential equilibrium predictions about play in the four-entrant and eight-entrant cases are different in an important way. In the eight-entrant design there is an initial pure strategy phase described above: entrants should never challenge, and any challenge should always be resisted. The mixed-strategy

[12] See Walter (2006).

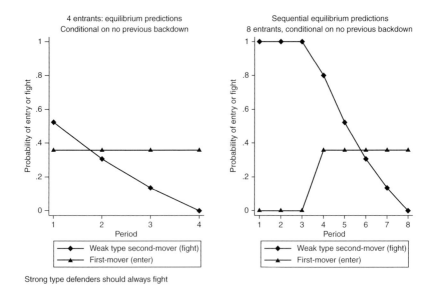

FIGURE 3.2 Predicted probability of entry and fighting in each period

phase of the game should not begin until the fourth round in the eight-entrant design.

When there are four entrants, subjects will be in the mixed strategy phase of play from the very beginning, meaning that much less reputation building should occur in early rounds. Entrants should be much more apt to challenge in the first round of play, and defenders should be more likely to back down. The behavior of the defenders and challengers in this design should mirror the behavior we observe in the last four rounds of the eight-person design.

We can graphically illustrate the equilibrium predictions for different numbers of entrants. Figure 3.2 shows the predicted probability of entry and fighting against each period of the sequence, *given that the defender has not backed down in the past*. Figure 3.2 does not include strong type defenders, as they should always fight in every period.

These graphs illustrate the fundamental difference between the four- and eight-entrant designs, and suggest the following testable hypotheses:

H3$_E$: *in the four-entrant case, we should see more entry in the first, second, and third periods of play compared to the eight-entrant case.*

H3$_D$: *in the four-entrant case, we should see more accommodation in the first, second, and third periods of play compared to the eight-entrant case.*

The intuition behind this result is that in the four-entrant treatment the final round of play is closer, creating fewer incentives for defenders to invest in reputation building in early rounds.

EXPERIMENTAL DESIGN

We recruited subjects through Princeton University's Laboratory for Experimental Social Science (PLESS) using an e-mail solicitation to all Princeton students who had signed up with the lab. Those who responded were accepted until all positions were filled. Students entered the laboratory one by one and were seated at computer workstations that were separated by pull out dividers to prevent interaction between subjects. Instructions were then read to all the participants. During this process, subjects were given the opportunity to make practice decisions and review a set of questions and answers about the experiment. Any questions from subjects were repeated and answered so that all subjects could hear. This was done to ensure that all aspects of the experiment design were common knowledge. A copy of the instructions is included in Appendix 1.

Subjects were randomly assigned to two separate groups, entrants and defendants, which were referred to simply as first movers and second movers. Second movers (defenders) were also assigned a "type" (weak or strong), which we called "type 1" or "type 2." First movers (entrants) were only told that there was some probability ($p = \frac{1}{3}$) that they were facing a strong type of defender. All of the subjects were told exactly how many total defenders or entrants they would face.[13]

---

[13] The fact that the terminal node was known to all subjects does not always exist in the real world. Defenders often do not know exactly how many interactions

Defenders faced a known number of entrants, and each entrant played each defender once within a "run" of the experiment.[14] Entrants were able to see the history of the defender they were paired with, which included how all previous entrants had played, and how the defendant had responded.

The experiment proceeded as follows. Entrants were asked to choose between A1 and A2 (entry and not entry). Defendants were asked to select a strategy based on what an entrant might do: "if the first mover enters I will choose B1 or B2" (not fight or fight). In the next period entrants were matched with a new defender. Each entrant would observe what happened in this defender's earlier periods. As a result of this matching procedure, each entrant made one decision with no available history (in the first period), one decision with information on how their defender played in the first period with a different entrant, and so on. After each entrant had played each defender once, subjects saw a screen with their decision history, the decisions of the subject they were paired with in each period, and their own payoffs. Subjects were allowed to write these payoffs down to compare with future runs. Payoffs were expressed in points which were then translated to US dollars at the end of the experiment.

The experiment was repeated four times in order to take into account the effects of learning and to generate sufficient data for the analysis. The precise number of times the subjects would repeat the experiment was unknown to them. Subjects were paid one by one at

they are likely to have. Governments, for example, might be able to reasonably estimate how many ethnic separatists they are likely to encounter, but they are unlikely to know when the last challenge will be. The fact that the final round of play is unknown, however, does not mean that reputation building will not occur. In fact, this uncertainty is likely to create greater incentives to invest in reputation building, since defenders know they have declining incentives to invest in reputation as the terminal node nears.

[14] Subjects were informed of their roles at the beginning of a run; first and second movers kept their roles throughout the entire experiment, but the second mover "type" could change from one repetition of the experiment to another.

the end of the experiment with money earned in the experiment and a guaranteed $10 "show-up" fee. The experiment was programmed and conducted with the software z-Tree (Fischbacher 1999). Appendix 1 covers our design in more detail.[15]

EMPIRICAL ANALYSIS

The model we test is about reputation building, and thus our analysis is crafted in a way that conditions behavior on the history of play by each defender and observed by each entrant. Our basic empirical strategy is to derive empirical probabilities of entry and fight behavior by taking mean values of the dichotomous decision variable *conditional on the history of play experienced by each subject.* Consider first the case where an entrant faces a defender that has not backed down in an earlier period. For each individual period (1–4 or 1–8) we add up the number of enter (or fight) decisions that occur where the defender had not previously backed down in an *earlier* period. We then divide by the total number of observations where the defender had not previously backed down in an earlier period. Because we code our Enter variable as a 1 if Enter (Fight) was chosen and 0 if Not Enter (Not Fight), this gives us the probability of Enter (Fight) conditional on the fact that the defender had not previously backed down in an earlier period. We calculate these values for each period. We perform an analogous calculation for cases where the defender had backed down in an earlier period.[16]

---

[15] Note that our design, instructions, and computer interface went through a lengthy series of reformulations/testing in order to obtain the best possible experimental protocol.

[16] This is the appropriate empirical strategy given that the strategic situation has players using mixed strategies. We do not directly observe the randomization procedure that subjects (presumably) utilize, and thus by aggregating across subjects we assume that each individual uses the same mental randomization device. This is a standard empirical approach when analyzing laboratory (O'Neill 1987) and field data (Walker and Wooders 2001), but also represents an active area of debate in the experimental literature (Ochs 1995). We consider a more individual level analysis below.

RESULTS AND INTERPRETATION

The effects of past accommodation

The results are organized into two sections. First, we look at whether entrants changed their behavior based on the past behavior of defenders. According to the sequential equilibrium prediction, entrants should always enter if they observe a defender backing down in a previous period. This gives us a direct check on whether a failure to be tough makes challenges more likely.[17]

Figure 3.3 shows the average behavior of both the entrant and the defender in cases where the defender backed down in a previous period. What we see is striking. In line with predictions of the model, entrants in both the four- and eight-subject experiments almost always challenged if they had observed prior accommodation. This suggests that challengers updated their beliefs about what type of defender they were facing, almost certainly believing they were facing a weak defender if he or she had acquiesced. In addition, defenders in both experiments consistently chose to continue acquiescing once accommodation had occurred. This is strong evidence that entrants are strongly influenced by the past behavior of the defender. It also reveals that defenders generally do not attempt to rebuild a reputation for toughness once they have lost it.

Figure 3.3, however, reveals some behaviors that warrant closer examination. A small percentage of entrants in both the four- and eight-person experiments chose not to enter after the defender had revealed itself to be weak. In fact, as you can see on the left side of Figure 3.3, the probability of entry declined slightly in both cases after an initially high rate of entry. Because this behavior was quite rare, however, we take the overall results to be very supportive of $H1_E$ and $H1_D$.

---

[17] Each separate experiment session drew subjects from the same population, although subjects that had participated in our experiment previously were not allowed to participate again. Thus we pool across different sessions to generate separate samples for our eight and four entrant designs.

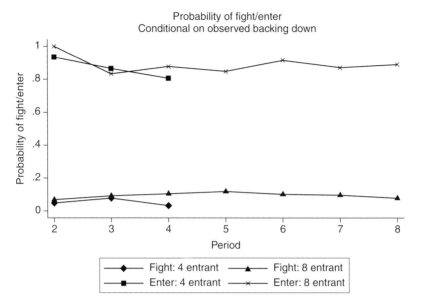

FIGURE 3.3 Probability of fight/enter

The effects of repeated play

Next, we looked to see if subjects behaved differently depending on the number of potential challengers that existed. Here we analyze per period probabilities of entry and fighting in cases where no accommodation was observed, aggregated over four separate "repetitions" of the experiment from each experimental session.[18] Figure 3.4 gives us our first look at whether the comparative static prediction on number of entrants holds in the laboratory.

Figure 3.4 reveals the first real deviation from the model. The model predicted that we should see significantly lower rates of entry in the first two periods in both the four- and eight-person designs than we observed in the laboratory. According to the theory, approximately 36 percent of entrants in the four-entrant design should

---

[18] Such an analysis ignores subject learning but is the appropriate first swipe at analyzing the data.

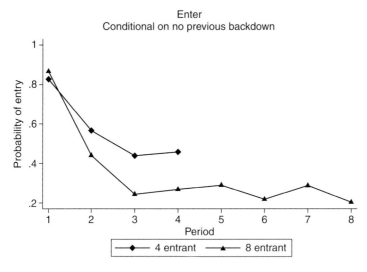

FIGURE 3.4 Probability of enter

enter in each period if there is no observed accommodation. Yet, as Figure 3.4 shows, over 80 percent of subjects in the four-entrant game entered in the very first round. This percentage dropped in the second and third round, but never reached the low rate predicted by the model.

The same is true in the longer eight-entrant game. According to the model, entrants should never enter in the first, second, and third periods of an eight-entrant design. After that, approximately 36 percent of them should enter if no previous accommodation is observed. But as Figure 3.4 shows, challengers again entered at a high rate in the first period, reduced their entry in the second period, and then ended close to the predicted entry rate of .357 by the third period. Thus, while the entry rate is higher than predicted in the first two periods of play, subjects behaved closer to equilibrium predictions during the mixed and final phases of the game.

In both designs, the striking differences between predicted and observed behavior occur in the very earliest rounds. The first three entrants in the eight-entrant design simply *should not enter*. If entrants enter during these rounds, and defenders fight them (as the theory expects them to do), entrants will receive fewer payoffs than if they had not entered. Yet, over 80 percent of subjects in both designs chose to challenge in the very first round.

This behavior is quite puzzling and does not lend direct support to hypothesis $H2_E$. There are at least three possible explanations for this pattern. The first is that early entrants have not yet learned how to play the game, an explanation we explore in greater detail below. A second possibility is that entrants at the front of the pack challenge in order to gather information about defender type that could be valuable to the remaining entrants. This altruistic behavior is not taken into consideration by the model.[19] A third explanation is that entrants bring certain "homemade priors" or beliefs to the game, where they expect certain defenders to concede, making early entry potentially more profitable than the theory predicts.[20] A final explanation, which we investigate below, is that defender responses made these higher rates of entry rational.

We find mixed support for $H3_E$ which predicted that in periods 1–3 there should be more entry in the four-entrant design than in the eight-entrant design. In the first period there was no discernible difference in entry behavior. However, in periods two and three entry was significantly more likely in the four-entrant design.[21] The significant difference in the fourth period is not predicted by our theory, as the probability of entry in both designs should be .357. Our model predicts that in periods one, two, and three, the conditional entry rate should be higher in the four-player design. Thus, in two out of the three periods we find behavior that is consistent with $H4_E$.

Figure 3.5 shifts the focus onto defenders. Our equilibrium model predicted that defenders would fight based in part on whether

[19] For a discussion of considerations along these lines see Bolton and Ockenfels (2007).

[20] Camerer and Weigelt (1988).

[21] Difference in means and difference in proportions both produce significant test statistics with p<.05.

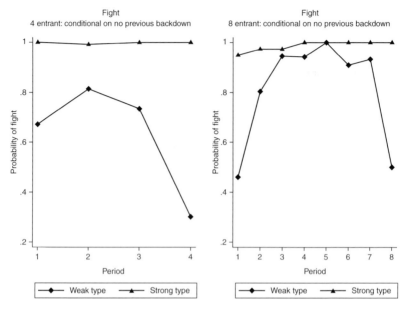

FIGURE 3.5 Probability of fight: four- and eight-entrant designs

they were strong or weak types. Strong types were expected never to back down; weak types were expected to fight a mixed strategy.

Figure 3.5 reveals that strong defenders behaved exactly as the theory predicted. Strong defenders backed down only once out of 492 times in the four-entrant design, and only 8 out of 352 times in the eight-entrant design. This implies that strong types understood the incentive structure for being tough and were behaving exactly according to type.

Weak defenders, however, did not act exactly according to equilibrium predictions. In the eight-entrant design, weak defenders should have fought in periods one, two, and three, and should only have begun to play a mixed strategy in period four. Yet Figure 3.5 shows that only about 45 percent of weak defenders chose to fight in the very first period. Weak defenders acquiesced to very early movers at a far higher rate than they should have to maximize payoffs.

Weak defenders also behaved somewhat differently than expected in the four-entrant design. Here, weak defenders were expected to play a mixed strategy from the very first period, with fight rates declining from .52, .30, .13, to 0 in the last round of play. Subjects, however, did not decrease their willingness to fight until after the second period, with a sizable decline from the third to fourth period. Hence we find mixed support for hypothesis $H2_D$. Weak defenders did not always fight prior to reaching the mixed strategy stage (in the eight-entrant case). The frequency of fighting, however, declined in the last two periods of the four-entrant design and the last period of the eight-entrant design. This suggests that at least at the end weak defenders came to appreciate the declining value of holding on to a reputation for fighting.

Finally, hypothesis $H3_D$ (which predicted that defenders should resist more in the eight-entrant design in periods 1–4) finds mixed support. In period one, defenders are *more* likely to resist in the four-entrant design. In the second period there is no discernible difference, and in the third and fourth periods defenders were significantly more likely to resist. Thus in two out of the four periods we find support for hypothesis $H3_D$, but in one period we find evidence that rejects the hypothesis.

Why did so many weak defenders give in to the first entrant when they knew they were facing eight entrants in total? And why did so many weak defenders choose to fight against the first three entrants even though they knew they would face only four entrants? It could be that defenders care less about the total number of entrants they are facing than about the number of remaining entrants. In both the four- and eight-player games, the most extreme change in defender behavior occurred at exactly the same time – in the final play of the game. This suggests that some weak defenders may be extremely averse to losing their reputation, only backing down when they know this behavior will not be observed by *any* future players. It also suggests that governments are likely to be more interested in the number of remaining ethnic groups than in the absolute number that exist.

This, however, does not explain why so many weak defenders facing eight entrants would choose to accommodate the first challenger. This is the more puzzling behavior revealed by the experiment. One explanation is that defenders, like entrants, require time to figure out how the game is played. If this is true, then these high rates of accommodation should decline as learning takes place. A second explanation is that these findings are caused by a sub-set of weak defenders who choose to accommodate every entrant no matter what. It is possible, for example, that some defenders simply will not engage in deception, or refuse to manipulate fellow participants. If this is the case, then certain individuals are driving the unexpectedly high rate of early accommodation. Both explanations will be explored more carefully below.

LEARNING

Figures 3.6 and 3.7 investigate learning effects that may be taking place in the course of the experiment. Is the high rate of entry by early challengers, and the relatively low rate of fighting by defenders, the result of inexperience? In order to determine this, we disaggregate the data, showing the choices subjects made each time they repeated the experiment. This allows us to investigate whether the subject's increasing familiarity with the strategic context drives behavior toward or away from equilibrium predictions. It also lets us evaluate whether our decision to aggregate these "repetitions" and report them together was an appropriate one.[22]

Figure 3.6 reveals that entrants did not change their behavior significantly across repetitions of the experiment. In both the four- and the eight-entrant design, the general trend was several periods of declining entry rates against a defender who had not yet backed down, leading to relatively stable entry probabilities of around .45 and .2

---

[22] The cost is a smaller sample size that reduces our ability to make tight point predictions from the data. We do not model any sort of learning dynamics in our theoretical model, though it is common practice in the experimental literature to compare the behavior of experienced and inexperienced subjects. Indeed, this reflects the notion that a game-theoretic 'equilibrium' is the result of a learning process (Fudenberg and Levine 1998).

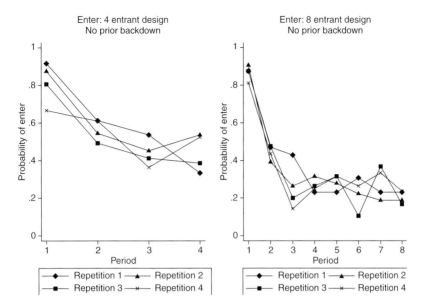

FIGURE 3.6 Probability of enter: four- and eight-entrant designs

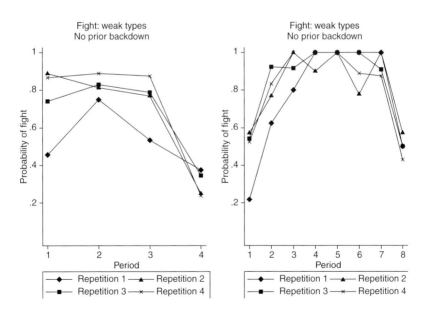

FIGURE 3.7 Probability of fight: four- and eight-entrant designs

respectively. The only significant change is that entrants in the four-person design were notably less likely to enter when they had the greatest amount of experience. This suggests that subjects had learned that defenders in the four-person design frequently chose to fight in the first round but that significant changes in behavior did not occur.

Defenders, however, did alter their behavior as they gained more experience with the game. Figure 3.7 shows how weak defenders behaved across four runs of the experiment. In both the four- and eight-entrant design, weak defenders invested more heavily in reputation over time. This increase took place primarily in the first three periods, with most change taking place between the first and subsequent repetitions of the experiment. Interestingly, this increase was even more pronounced in the four-entrant design. Thus, defenders in both short and long games were learning that fighting early challengers paid off.

Still, it is puzzling why some defenders insisted on backing down to the first challenger even after gaining experience with the game.[23] In an attempt to explain this, we examined two types of individual level data. Since defenders repeated the same sequence of decisions four or eight times, we looked at the percentage of times each subject chose to fight in more than half the periods.[24] Figure 3.8 shows that many weak subjects fell into one of two groups: they either regularly backed down or they regularly fought, with fewer playing a more mixed strategy.

Subjects who were willing to back down in the first period were much more likely to continue to back down in the future. This confirms that a certain type of individual – one who always acquiesces – is at least partly responsible for the unexpected results, making it

---

[23] The previous analysis pools together all subjects and does not consider any individual differences.

[24] This decision to fight, unlike in previous analyses, was unconditional on what the entrant chose and simply represents their decision to fight following the statement "if the first mover chooses (to enter) what will you do?"

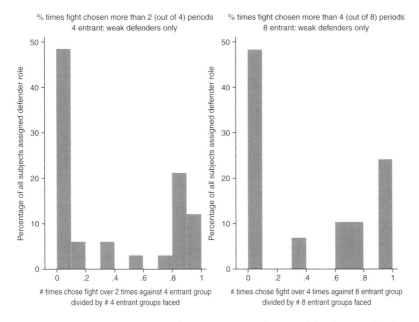

FIGURE 3.8 Percentage of times entrants chose to fight: four- and eight-entrant designs

appear as if all weak defenders are accommodating at a high rate in the very first round when it is actually a sub-set of individuals who are doing so. In the absence of these individuals, the overall rate of fighting in early rounds would be much higher.

Exit interviews also provided insights into why some defenders chose to play consistently sub-optimally. Responses suggest that a certain sub-set of defenders did not appear to understand the strategic logic underlying the reputation building game.[25] The following two responses are indicative of this kind of mistake:

> If you are a weak type, always acquiesce. If you are strong, always fight. It guarantees the most points regardless of what the first mover does. Play the game the same way throughout.

---

[25] This misunderstanding is not entirely surprising since our instructions were designed not to reveal this logic in order to produce a harder test of the theory.

Choose the option that gives you more points. If you are a weak type, acquiesce every move. Even if the first mover chooses not to challenge you can't lose. It will get you more money.

But what about the four-person design? Surprisingly, subjects in the four-person design also invested heavily in reputation building in the second and third round even though they would have benefited by being more conciliatory. Weak defenders in these cases did not appear to learn that the costs of fighting were not offset by future gains for having a tough reputation. Why did subjects in the four-person design move further away from equilibrium predictions over time?

One answer is that weak defenders are more concerned with the number of remaining entrants than with the absolute number of entrants. A closer look at Figure 3.6 reveals that defenders in both the four- and eight-person experiments were fighting at about the same rate against the last four entrants. Thus, weak defenders were learning that there were reputational gains to be made from fighting early entrants even in shorter games. As one subject wrote:

> Fight at the beginning of each four period round to fool the other player into thinking you're tough so they will choose not to challenge, and then revert to acquiescing the following three periods. This can work out better than consistently acquiescing depending on how the first movers react. I didn't think of the strategy of faking out the first mover until about halfway through the experiment.

Weak defenders clearly learned that even entrants in the shorter four-person games could be deterred.

The fact that subjects in the four-person designs behaved increasingly tough over time reveals that reputation building dynamics will emerge even in relatively short games. Four iterations were clearly sufficient to generate incentives to be tough. It also suggests that reputation building might still emerge in situations where only two iterations are expected; weak defenders were willing to continue to invest in reputation building through the second to last play of the game. Additional research will be required to tease out what the critical number of iterations may be for reputation building to become rational in the laboratory.[26]

DISCUSSION AND CONCLUSION

This chapter investigated two fundamental predictions of the chain store model. The first had to do with inferences that were likely to be drawn if a defender backed down against a challenger. The second had to do with the number of challengers and the influence this would have on both defender and entrant behavior.

The experiments reveal that individuals will generally react to incentives to build reputation in the ways the theory predicts. The decision by a defender to grant concessions did appear to send a strong signal to entrants that the defender was weak and did result in a significantly higher number of challenges. Entrants in both the four-person and eight-person designs challenged the defender at a dramatically higher rate if they observed the defender backing down. The defender also seemed particularly worried about sending this signal, often refusing to accommodate until the very last round. Thus, strong inferences were being taken from the past behavior of the defender.

Defender and entrant behavior, however, deviated from equilibrium predictions in two important ways. The most prominent pattern had to do with the willingness of entrants to challenge in early periods, and the willingness of defenders to back down during this time. This was true in both the four- and eight-person games. Although the experiment offers no definitive evidence why individuals behaved this way, individual level data suggest that this result

---

[26] As mentioned in Chapter 2, we believe that this number is likely to vary not only with the number of future challenges, but with the value of their demands and the strength of their forces.

is driven in part by a sub-set of the defenders who chose to remain true to type despite monetary incentives to the contrary. Entrants then exploited these defenders by "attacking" at an unexpectedly high rate early on.

This seemingly "irrational" play by some of our subjects suggests new and productive avenues for future research. Theoretically, much can be learned from the field of behavioral economics where new equilibrium concepts such as quantal response equilibrium (QRE) and cognitive hierarchy equilibrium (CHE) are increasingly being used (Camerer *et al.* 2004, McKelvey and Palfrey 1998). QRE, for example, may help to explain one of the more interesting findings to come from our experiments – why early entrants would challenge at such a high rate. According to QRE, subjects understand that not all players behave perfectly rationally all the time and they take this "irrationality" into account when determining their strategy. This appears to be what we observed with early entrants. Early entrants challenged at a high rate, but this was quite rational given how often defenders were willing to acquiesce to these early movers.[27] Thus, the "best-response" a player can make will not be the unique sequential equilibrium discussed above, but a response that understands that not all players will behave perfectly rationally all the time.[28]

These results suggest two potential modifications to our expectations about how government and ethnic group leaders are likely to behave when engaged in self-determination disputes. First,

---

[27] The high rates of entry in early periods might also reflect social comparison issues. If an entrant does not challenge, they get 95 points whereas the defender gets 300 points. If the entrant enters, the point 'spread' is much smaller whether or not the defender fights, or whether it is committed. Thus entry may serve to equalize earnings for both groups. There was some evidence of this in our post-experiment polls, as some entrants expressed frustration that the experiment favored defenders.

[28] Unfortunately, analytical QRE solutions have only been worked out in much simpler games that do not have the complex repetition and updating dynamic in our model. Computer-assisted numerical approaches are not able to account for the updating central to our interests (e.g., using the software package 'Gambit'). This remains an active area of inquiry.

they suggest that most government leaders will care deeply about building a reputation for toughness, and that they are likely to care even when relatively few ethnic groups exist. The findings also suggest that the number of remaining challengers should be more important to governments than the absolute number of potential challengers, and that most governments should choose to fight all but the last remaining ethnic groups.

Finally, the results also suggest that *some* government leaders will be unexpectedly conciliatory and will accommodate any ethnic group that challenges. Knowing that a certain percent of defenders will always concede should, in turn, encourage more ethnic groups to challenge early in a leader's tenure. This may help to explain why some ethnic groups, such as the Slovenes in the former Yugoslavia, are willing to challenge so early.

In the end, the laboratory experiments confirm important parts of the reputation theory, but also reveal where human beings are likely to deviate from existing expectations about rational behavior. Most individuals do understand the logic behind reputation building and use this strategy to their advantage. But the experiments reveal that some people do not, and it is the behavior of these individuals that behavioral economics is trying to explain. In the meantime, we use the insights garnered from these experiments to modify our expectations of what we should observe in the real world, and use Chapters 4 and 5 to test whether the theory holds up in the more complex world of government and minority relations.

4 Government responses to self-determination movements

The experiments revealed that undergraduate students, for the most part, would invest in reputation building and be deterred by tough reputations in the perfectly controlled environment of the laboratory. What remains to be seen is whether the theory explains government and ethnic group behavior in the real world. This chapter begins this process by testing the theory against all self-determination movements since 1956 and asking whether governments faced with many potential ethnic challengers still behave as the theory would expect.

Recall that in Chapter 2 the theory made three predictions about how governments were likely to respond to self-determination challenges. First, governments were expected to be more likely to accommodate ethnic separatists as the number of future challengers decreases. Second, governments should also be more likely to compromise if the value of future lands and the costs of fighting for these lands are low. Finally, the theory predicted that governments would be penalized for making concessions. Governments that accommodated one ethnic group were expected to face a greater number of challengers than governments that refused. This is the negative effect of compromise that governments are trying to avoid.

The dataset on self-determination movements
In order to test these hypotheses I collected data on every self-determination movement included in the Center International for Development and Conflict Management's (CIDCM) 2003 report on self-determination movements.[1] CIDCM is a group headed

---

[1] Readers should note that CIDCM codes only those ethnic groups listed in the Minorities at Risk dataset and thus may exclude some ethnic groups

by Ted Robert Gurr at the University of Maryland. It defined a self-determination movement as any attempt by a territorially concentrated ethnic group to seek autonomy or independence from the central government using political or military means. The list includes all movements initiated between 1955 and 2002. To qualify as a self-determination movement individual leaders or the organization had to publicly state a desire for greater political autonomy, association with kin in neighboring states, and/or independence. Each self-determination movement represents one case in the analysis and CIDCM identified 146 self-determination movements in total.

Non-violent challenges, as well as violent challenges, were included in the dataset in order to avoid selecting only those cases where the government and the ethnic group failed to resolve their dispute without first engaging in armed conflict. This avoids biasing the results in favor of only the most difficult cases to resolve.[2] It also reflects the fact that initial challenges are often made in the absence of violence (even if it is threatened), and violent challenges are often only observed if the government chooses to ignore the demands. Violence, therefore, may never occur if the government makes a deal in exchange for peace.[3]

in some countries. Readers should also note that CIDCM includes armed self-determination groups from 1955 to 2002, but includes unarmed self-determination groups initiated from the late 1940s until 2003. No explanation was given for this discrepancy. For greater elaboration of the coding rules see Marshall and Gurr (2003).

[2] To ensure that no single country (or a small number of countries) with many potential challengers was driving the results, standard errors for potential non-independence within countries were corrected using the cluster option in Stata. In alternate analysis, I also deleted countries from the analysis in a sequential way. This latter test did not reveal any substantive effects on the results.

[3] Overall, there were seventy violent and seventy-six non-violent cases. To be classified as violent, a movement had to pursue at least a minimum level of violence while seeking self-determination as opposed to conventional politics or protest. Violence ranged from a minimum level (defined as isolated acts of terrorism) up to a maximum level (full-scale civil war). This is the same Rebellion Index used in Minorities at Risk (MAR) Phase IV, and includes the following seven-point scale: (0) no rebellion; (1) political banditry, sporadic terrorism; (2) campaigns of terrorism;

The dependent variables

Two dependent variables are included in this analysis. First, to determine which factors are likely to affect a government's decision to accommodate an ethnic group, I created an ordered categorical dependent variable called *Accommodation*. This variable included four outcomes: no accommodation; some accommodation but not over territory (hereafter referred to as "reform"); accommodation offering some form of territorial autonomy; and accommodation granting full independence.[4] Each self-determination movement was coded at the highest level of accommodation ever offered by the government.[5] Thus, although the Quebecois in Canada were offered various levels of reform during their decades-long battle for autonomy, the case is coded based on the highest level of accommodation offered – the increased territorial autonomy that the Quebecois were offered in 1987. Of the 146 self-determination challenges included in the dataset, 92 (64%) were not granted any accommodation, 11% obtained reform, 22% were given some form of territorial autonomy, and under 4% were granted full independence.

Later, to see if government behavior had the desired effect of deterring additional challengers, I analyze a second dependent variable called *Subsequent challenge*. This was a dummy variable indicating whether a government faced a subsequent self-determination challenge after the self-determination movement under observation

(3) local rebellions; (4) small-scale guerrilla activity; (5) intermediate guerrilla activity; (6) large-scale guerrilla activity; (7) protracted civil war. For specific descriptions of these categories see the MAR codebook. MAR chronologies and the sources identified in Appendix 2 were used to do historical research on the start and end dates of these phases. I thank David Quinn, Amy Pate, Deepa Khosla, and Ted Gurr for their lengthy correspondence on the coding of these variables.

[4] Although these four categories are clearly distinct on a theoretical level, I re-ran all of the subsequent analysis with one or more categories of accommodation collapsed to ensure that each category was in fact empirically distinct. The results indicate that none of the alternate codings led to a significantly better fit than the four category variables used here.

[5] This included every administration between the years 1955 and 2002.

had begun. Details about the coding of each of these variables are included in Appendix 2.

Independent variables – the reputation theory
The reputation theory argued that a government's decision to accommodate would be influenced by the number of future challengers and the costs and value of future lands.

Number of potential future challengers: hypothesis one ($H1_{gov}$) predicted that the greater the number of potential separatist challengers, the less willing a government would be to accommodate a given challenge. Governments would look down the road, determine how many groups could potentially make demands, and plan their strategy accordingly.[6]

Three proxies were used to measure the number of potential separatist challengers. The first two attempt to identify those ethnic groups that were most likely to have the motive and the opportunity to rebel and are taken from the Minorities at Risk (MAR) data project. The first is a measure of the number of *Ethnopolitical groups* in a given country.[7] This measure includes only those groups

---

[6] This hypothesis obviously assumes that governments can determine who the future challengers are likely to be, the extent of their claims, and the resources they are likely to have at their disposal. Although the government can never know exactly how many groups will seek self-determination or the exact future value of territory, governments are likely to have some knowledge about potential troublemakers. Since governments generally control a confined geographical area, with a relatively fixed population, assessing potential challengers should not be too difficult. By examining several different estimates of the number of potential separatist challengers, I hope to show that governments can and do distinguish between different groups to identify the most likely challengers and that, like the chain store model, governments know they face a finite number of players.

[7] Note that this measure, as coded by the MAR dataset, is not trouble-free. Laitin and Fearon (2001), for example, point out that MAR was not systematic in its sample selection procedure. Many African countries with large numbers of ethnic groups, for example, are only coded for one or two groups in MAR, while other more well-known countries are coded for significantly more. Still, this measure should give a rough estimate of whether the number of aggrieved groups in a country is more likely to affect government behavior than simply the number of ethnic groups.

that were systematically discriminated against by the government, and/or mobilized in defense of their interests.[8] The second measure, the number of *Concentrated groups*, includes only those ethnopolitical groups that are geographically concentrated in a single region. Governments are likely to be particularly attentive to both of these groups.

These measures, however, may be endogenous to government policies. Countries with governments that are tough on ethnic separatists will, by definition, have a higher number of groups defined as ethnopolitical. Similarly, particularly tough governments may also cause ethnic groups to concentrate themselves geographically. If this is the case, then any relationship between these two measures and government accommodation would be spurious. In order to address this potential problem I include a third measure: the total number of ethnic groups in each country as identified by the *Encyclopædia Britannica*. This measure included all ethnic, linguistic, or religious groups, as well as all foreign national groups in each country regardless of their level of mobilization or grievance. This more objective measure ensures that any relationship found between government accommodation and the number of groups cannot be a function of government behavior itself. By combining analysis of this more objective measure with the other two measures (which offer a truer assessment of the number of groups that actually pose a threat to the government), I hope to provide a more complete picture of how the number of potential challengers affects government behavior.

Number of remaining challengers: measuring the absolute number of challengers, however, misses a key element of reputation

---

[8] To test for the possibility that the relationship between government concessions and the number of potential challengers is non-linear, various non-linear models and thresholds were tested but all provided a significantly worse or at best similar fit to the linear model presented here. It did not appear that there was a critical threshold beyond which increasing the number of groups no longer affected government actions. Nor did it seem that the impact of the additional potential challengers decreased as the total number increased.

building. Governments will have declining incentives to invest in reputation building with each successive challenge. Chapter 3 revealed that conciliatory defenders are likely to be more concerned with the number of remaining challengers than with the total number of challengers. In order to determine whether conciliatory governments really did have declining incentives, I took the total number of potential challengers (based on the number of ethnopolitical groups listed in MAR) and subtracted the number of self-determination movements that had already been initiated at the time the conflict began.

Leader's tenure in power: hypothesis three ($H3_{gov}$) focused on the effect a leader's tenure in office would have on his or her incentives to accommodate. The less time an uncommitted leader expected to spend in office, the less valuable reputation building becomes, and the more likely he or she would be to accommodate. Leaders rarely know exactly how long they will be in office, but they are likely to have some rough estimation about how long they are likely to last. To get at this, I included a measure that singled out countries whose leaders had an average tenure less than one standard deviation from the average of all countries over a fifty-year period.[9] These cases were considered to have leadership tenures that were short.[10]

In addition to considering the direct effects of tenure, I also considered the relationship between tenure and regime type. As one might expect, analysis of leadership tenure across the countries included in the dataset revealed that leaders in autocracies have,

---

[9] I singled out these extremely short cases because cases with repeated rapid turnover may be the only cases where a leader will have a strong sense of the likely length of their tenure. In most other countries, government leaders and challengers are likely to have a poor sense of how long a particular leader's tenure will last. This is perhaps why alternate specifications using the actual tenure of a leader or a continuous variable with the average tenure of leaders in a country were not significantly tied to government accommodation.

[10] Specifically, I measured the average duration of a leader's tenure in each country in the dataset. Then I created a dummy variable that singled out those countries whose average duration in the second half of the twentieth century was greater than one standard deviation less than the average duration for all countries.

on average, longer and more inconsistent tenures than leaders in democracies. Thus, they generally do not know how long they will be in office but have the potential to hold power for lengthy periods of time. In those circumstances, a leader has an especially strong incentive to appear strong.

The value and costs of fighting for future stakes: the value of reputation is not just a function of the number of potential challengers. Two cases with the same number of ethnic groups might include groups that claim very different types of territory, or have very different capacities to fight. According to H4$_{gov}$, governments have greater incentive to build a reputation for toughness if future challengers lay claim to much of the country's land, population, and resources. They would also have greater reason to invest in reputation if future challengers were expected to be extremely costly to fight (H5$_{gov}$). Thus, even if the number of groups in two countries is identical, the value of deterrence may still differ. The decision to accommodate one challenger, therefore, should be strongly influenced by the combined value of the land future challengers might demand, and the combined costs a government would have to pay to fight for these lands.

The combined value of land was assessed by measuring the economic and strategic value of all land occupied by all ethnopolitical groups in a given country.[11] The *Future economic value* of land was measured using an additive scale that counted the number of marketable resources found in the land area sought by all separatists.[12] While a dollar value might have been preferable, regional estimates of the monetary value of different resources are rarely

---

[11] Note that data were collected on each ethnopolitical group (as defined by MAR) and not on each ethnic group (as defined by the *Encyclopædia Britannica*). This decision was made because sub-national data on ethnic groups are generally not available, while similar data on ethnopolitical groups are.

[12] One potential problem with this measure is that it is quite rough, based on an assessment of the number of resources on a given piece of land, and not the revenue produced by these resources. CIA maps, for example, might show that a given region contains copper, but do not say how much copper exists. It is difficult, therefore, to get a good sense of the value of these reserves.

available and thus could not be included. In an attempt to include a measure that might more closely approximate the monetary value of the resources, in alternate tests I included a variable indicating the number of regions in a country occupied by ethnopolitical groups that included either oil or natural gas. The *Future strategic value* of land was calculated using a six-point additive scale indicating whether a given piece of territory included (1) a sea outlet, (2) a shipping lane, (3) a military base, (4) an international border, (5) an attack route, and/or (6) a mountain range. The number of features contained on the land occupied by all challengers was then summed.[13]

One concern with these two measures is that neither reflects the relative importance of these lands to the government. A square mile of Israel, for example, is worth more to the Israeli government than a square mile of China is to the Chinese. One alternate measure – the *Future proportion of land* – was, therefore, included to give a more accurate assessment of the value governments might place on future stakes. This was a combined measure of the area of all land that could come up under dispute in the future as a proportion of the entire area of a country.

The value of deterrence is also a function of how much it will cost to fight for future stakes if challenges are launched. Future costs, however, are almost impossible to calculate since reliable data on the military capabilities of ethnic groups do not exist. Still, governments are likely to weigh the costs of fighting future opponents when determining how to respond to a given challenge and they are likely to gravitate to the best available measures. I believe that the *Combined population* of all disaffected groups in the country as a proportion of the total population is one rough proxy that governments may use to determine how costly it will be to fight these groups.[14]

[13] In alternate tests I substituted a dummy variable indicating whether a given territory had access to the sea – arguably the most important strategic resource.

[14] Since it is reasonable to assume that the strength of the government would remain relatively constant now and in the future, future costs were calculated

Independent variables – existing accounts

The value of future lands, however, should not be the only factor affecting government decisions. Governments should also care about the parameters of the current conflict, especially the value of the land currently under dispute. To measure current value, the same three measures of economic and strategic value were used. *Economic value* was again an additive scale that counted the number of marketable resources found in the land area sought by separatists. In alternate tests I included a dummy variable indicating whether a given region included either oil or natural gas. The second measure of value, *Strategic value,* was the six-point scale indicating how many strategic features a given piece of territory contained.[15] The final measure, *Land size,* was simply the proportion of all land in the country that was occupied by the current separatist group.

Governments should also care about the relative capabilities of the current challenger and be more likely to fight when it is weak relative to future groups. As mentioned above, relative power is difficult to measure in intrastate disputes. Measures that are available to assess the military capabilities of the government side, for example, are generally not available to assess the military capabilities of various ethnic groups. This will make analysis of this particular variable especially important in the case studies where more detailed information is likely to be available.

Given the absence of any data comparing the relative capabilities of the two sides, I created an amalgam measure, *Relative military capabilities,* that compared the potential military strength of the ethnic challenger (measured as the total population of the group) with the government's actual military forces (measured as

comparing the strength of all challengers that could seek self-determination in the future.

[15] Again, I substituted a dummy variable indicating whether a given territory had access to the sea in alternate tests. The change had no effect on the results.

the average number of military personnel during a challenge). The greater the ethnic group population relative to government military personnel, the greater the incentive to accommodate.

To supplement the meager data that are available on relative capabilities, I included several different indicators of strength for each side. Four indicators were used to measure the potential power of the separatist group. The first measure – the existence of *Neighboring ethnic brethren* – indicates whether the group seeking self-determination was part of a larger ethnic group that extended beyond that country's borders. All else equal, groups with members in neighboring countries were viewed as relatively more powerful than groups with no such outside support. The second measure indicated the *Proportion of the population* represented by the challenging group.[16] The larger the group relative to the population as a whole, the stronger it was assumed to be.[17] A third measure of separatist strength was included to take into account the advantage *Mountainous terrain* could give to rebels.[18] Finally, one measure was added to get closer to the resolve of the separatist challenge. Specifically, cases were coded as either *violent* or non-violent challenges. Challengers who were willing to engage in violence might be viewed as more resolute and potentially more formidable adversaries by governments. To be considered violent a movement had to pursue at least a minimum level of violence defined as isolated acts of terrorism.[19]

---

[16] The size of the group might, of course, also be a measure of the relative value of the group to the central government.

[17] In alternate tests I focused on two different measures of group strength. The first was group concentration. Groups that were more highly concentrated geographically were assumed to be better able to overcome difficult collective action problems and mobilize more effective resistance against the government. The second measure was the presence of a diaspora community in the United States. Ethnic groups with a large proportion of co-ethnics living in the United States were assumed to have access to more remittance money than those that did not.

[18] Fearon and Laitin (2003).

[19] This variable is derived from the Rebellion Index used in MAR Phase I.

A single indicator was used to measure the strength of the targeted government. *Government instability* was a dummy variable indicating whether a country in question experienced rapid regime change at any point during a challenge.[20] Governments experiencing rapid regime change were expected to be weak relative to those that had not. Finally, in alternate tests, I assessed the effects of a range of other measures of government strength including average annual military expenditures of the government during the duration of a challenge, the average annual number of military personnel during a challenge, and the average gross domestic product (GDP) per capita over the course of a dispute. Countries with relatively small defense expenditures and relatively small armies were expected to be more likely to accommodate challengers than countries with large defense expenditures and large armies.

Controls

In addition to this main set of explanatory variables, two control variables were included to ensure that the existence of any afore-mentioned relationships in the analysis were not spurious. A large literature has arisen in the last two decades arguing that democratic regimes are more likely to negotiate with challengers than non-democracies. Democratic governments are thought to face greater domestic constraints on the use of force, be more sensitive to the rights of individuals seeking self-determination, and have a greater range of possible compromise solutions to offer ethnic groups.[21] If this is true, then the type of regime or regimes in power during a challenge will almost certainly affect the likelihood of accommodation.[22] A

---

[20] Countries that experienced a change of three or more points in any year on Polity IV's combined measure of democracy/autocracy were coded 1. All others were coded 0.

[21] See Doyle (1986b), and Morgan and Campbell (1991: 187–211). For a related argument see Goemans (2000).

[22] Democratic leaders are also more likely to have shorter tenures, making them less likely to invest in reputation building.

control variable, *Democracy*, was included to test for this effect.[23] A measure that noted the year the conflict began, *Year begun*, was also included to take into account that some conflicts would have more time to reach a settlement than others simply because they had started earlier.[24]

Finally, it is worth noting that in alternate analyses, I included dummy variables for different regions of the world to ensure that none of the significant variables were proxying for some unmeasured region-specific factor.[25] None of the region dummies were significant and their inclusion or exclusion did not affect the overall conclusions. The exact measurement and coding of all of these variables, as well as details on data sources, are available in Appendix 2.

EMPIRICAL ANALYSIS

Testing conventional accounts

I begin my investigation by testing the effect that present interests and capabilities have on a government's willingness to accommodate separatist demands. This allows me to determine how well existing explanations perform before I include variables associated with reputation. Table 4.1 presents the results of a series of ordered probit regressions with *Accommodation* as the dependent variable. The first model in the table looks only at the present value of the land,

---

[23] To measure democracy, I used the highest level of democracy attained during a conflict as indicated by the Polity IV dataset, assuming that governments would be most likely to accommodate challenges at this point in time. In alternate tests I also used the average level of democracy in a given country. No significant differences were found.

[24] In alternate tests, *Duration* of a conflict was also included to address the possibility that disputes with longer conflict phases would be more costly to governments and therefore more likely to end in some form of accommodation.

[25] A dummy variable indicating whether the conflict was violent was also included in alternate tests to see if the use of force by a separatist group increased the likelihood that a government would accommodate their demands. It was insignificant in all specifications and was dropped from the final model.

Table 4.1. *Ordered probit analysis of factors affecting government responses to self-determination demands – conventional accounts only*[a]

	Level of government accommodation		
	Model 1	Model 2	Model 3
VALUE OF LAND CURRENTLY UNDER DISPUTE			
Economic value	.067 (.033)*	.062 (.040)^	.066 (.047)
Strategic value	−.033 (.091)	−.055 (.104)	−.078 (.094)
Land area	.238 (.691)	.396 (.762)	.074 (.743)
RELATIVE CAPABILITIES: CURRENT DISPUTANTS			
Population of group		−.096 (1.43)	−1.07 (1.53)
Mountainous terrain		−.011 (.007)	−.011 (.007)
Neighboring ethnic groups		−.079 (.106)	−.367 (.341)
Government instability		−.335 (.319)	−.301 (.323)
Relative military capabilities		.066 (.137)	.193 (.117)
CONTROLS			
Average level of democracy			.060 (.028)*
Year conflict began			−.031 (.008)
Violent challenge			.149 (.357)
Constant 1	.489 (.255)	−.082 (.412)	−25.9 (16.6)
Constant 2	.842 (.243)	.280 (.393)	−25.5 (16.6)
Constant 3	2.26 (.350)	1.72 (.446)	−24.0 (16.5)
Pseudo R^2	.014	.044	.111
χ^2	4.09	11.4	24.6*
N	129	103	100

^ $p < .10$, * $p < .05$, ** $p < .01$

[a] Heteroskedastic-consistent standard errors clustered by country.

the second model adds relative capabilities, and the third includes controls for democracy and time.[26]

Surprisingly, the results suggest that few, if any, of the conditions related to the current conflict affect government behavior on their own. Governments appear to be somewhat more likely to accommodate demands for self-determination if the land in question has high economic value. The effect, however, is only marginally significant and fades away in the more complete models in columns two and three. The two other measures of present value (strategic value and land size) showed no sign of affecting government decision making. Governments are no more likely to seek a peaceful settlement when the contested piece of land serves vital security functions or is particularly large than they would if the land did not.[27] Moreover, alternate measures of value fared no better in predicting government accommodation.[28] Isolating regions that held oil reserves reinforced the view that present value plays a marginal role in government actions. Similarly, singling out disputed territories that had access to the sea – arguably the most important strategic resource – also played no clear role in government decisions.

To try to get at the symbolic value of the land under dispute, in alternate tests, I identified disputed territories where the rebel group had been historically autonomous from the central government in the past – thinking that this autonomy might have reduced the government's attachment to the territory. Similarly, I looked at the relationship between the length of time a challenger had resided on the territory – perhaps an indicator of diminishing attachment

---

[26] The total number of cases in the regressions in this table and in the regressions that follow vary because there are missing data for several of the variables.

[27] Even when economic value was dropped from the model, neither of these factors was significant.

[28] When I assessed either economic or strategic value by comparing the value of the land in question to the total value of resources in the country, I found no clear link between land value and government actions. Similarly, logged measures of economic and strategic value were both not significant when introduced into the model.

on the part of the central government – and accommodation. A clear relationship did not exist in either case. Neither the strategic nor the symbolic value of a territory plays a clear role in a government's decision to compromise, at least as measured by existing indicators.

Although the evidence at this point suggests that the economic, strategic, and psychological value of the land under dispute is not a central factor driving government behavior, we should be careful not to over-interpret these results given the weakness of some of the measures. It is quite possible that with better data, we would find a relationship between the current value of land and government behavior. In the meantime, case studies offer an alternate way to determine if and how each of these factors may matter. Chapters 5 and 6, for example, quite clearly reveal that oil and mineral wealth in Aceh and West Papua played an important role in the Indonesian government's decision to fight for those provinces, and that natural resources in Mindanao and the Cordillera brought the Philippine government into conflict with ethnic groups in those regions. The case studies, therefore, revealed that the value of land immediately under dispute did matter, at least in these two cases.

All of the measures of strength that were included in Model 2 were also unrelated to the level of reform or accommodation that a government ultimately offered.[29] Governments were no more or less likely to accommodate separatist groups that made up a larger share of the nation's population, that had the advantage of mountainous terrain, or that had populations that extended into neighboring

---

[29] Goertz and Diehl (1992) had a similar finding on their work on interstate territorial disputes. They found no strong relationship between the balance of military capabilities and the use of armed force in achieving territorial changes from 1914 to 1980. However, in separate studies, Mandel (1980), and Kacowicz (1994), found that armed conflict over territory was more likely between states of roughly equal military capabilities. For a discussion of these differences see Huth (1996: 13–14).

states.[30] Government behavior was also unrelated to the strength of the government itself. Regimes that had experienced rapid institutional change in recent years behaved no differently toward separatists than those that did not suffer such political instability. All other measures of government strength that were tested in alternate models were unrelated to government behavior. Neither military size nor military spending had a significant influence on government decisions to accommodate. Governments with smaller militaries or those that spent a lower proportion of their GDP on the military were no more inclined to accommodate than those that maintained a relatively large number of soldiers or had massive military budgets. Similarly, total government resources, measured by per capita GDP, also did not affect the likelihood of accommodation.

Two other measures of capabilities (relative military capabilities and whether the challenge was a violent one) had more mixed effects on government accommodation. In the model in Table 4.1 neither measure is significant. But in subsequent models when the effects of reputation are added to the model, there are signs that risks and costs of confronting a particular opponent do influence government decisions in at least some cases. Specifically, if we look forward to Tables 4.3 and 4.4, the relative military capabilities of the challenger and the willingness of the challenger to engage in a violent confrontation do appear to shape the level of government accommodation. These more fully specified models suggest that when the size of an ethnic group relative to the size of the military increases, governments become more willing to accommodate. Governments appear to be more willing to offer some form of accommodation if they could lose a battle or pay a high cost for fighting. Similarly,

---

[30] This mirrored two of the findings in Huth's (1996b) study of interstate territorial disputes. He found that the presence of minority groups along the border with ethnic ties to the general population of the challenger had no strong effect on the likelihood of a compromise settlement. He also found that military strength of the challenger was not a necessary condition for the challenger "to remain unyielding in its negotiating position" over disputed territory.

subsequent models indicate that violent challenges are also met with higher levels of accommodation. Again, this likely indicates that separatist demands will come at a heavy price. Given the inconsistent nature of these results, however, more research will need to be undertaken before a definitive account of the relative capabilities story can be told.

One factor in Table 4.1 that has a clear and consistent effect on a government's willingness to give in to separatist demands is the nature of the regime. In all models, more democratic regimes were significantly more likely to accommodate separatist demands than less democratic regimes. In fact, converting the ordered probit coefficients in Table 4.1 into predicted probabilities revealed that democracies scoring an eight on the polity scale were 28 percent more likely to accommodate than autocracies scoring a minus five on the polity measure.[31]

This relationship raises questions about the types of democracy most prone to compromise. In an attempt to determine what it is about democratic regimes that makes them more willing to accommodate territorial demands, I created three additional variables that measured different institutional features. The first was a dummy variable indicating whether a democracy was based on *Proportional representation*, the second measured the degree of *Federalism* within each country, and the third indicated whether or not the government was an *Anocracy*. (See Appendix 2 for a detailed description of each.) Each of these variables was then added separately to the ordered probit model in Table 4.1 to see which of the three democracy measures was most closely linked to government accommodation.

The results (not shown) are interesting but far from conclusive. Two of the three measures, proportional representation and

---

[31] In this case and in all subsequent calculations, predicted probabilities are calculated by varying the measure of interest from the 10th to the 90th percentile, while holding all other variables at their mean values (or modal values for categorical variables). See King *et al.* (2000).

federalism, are positively and significantly related to government accommodation. One could interpret this as indicating that governments are more willing to accommodate demands because they already have a system in place that grants regional autonomy (e.g., federalism) and because minority groups are influential in government decisions (e.g., proportional representation). However, the results are not particularly robust to changes in the specification of the model. Thus, these conclusions should be read with some caution. Moreover, these measures leave several important features of democracy untapped. It is possible, for example, that the constraints imposed by the public's aversion to war increase the likelihood of accommodation. It is also possible that democratic citizens have greater sympathy for the rights of individuals seeking self-determination or a greater variety of concessions to offer. Future research will be required to distinguish which of these alternatives is really at play.

Finally, it is important to note that even when all of these factors are combined, they still have only a small impact on government behavior. As can be seen at the bottom of Table 4.1, the pseudo R^2 reaches a maximum of .11 in Model 3 and only in the last column is the chi squared (χ^2) for the model as a whole significant. The fact that existing models explain only a fraction of government action means that we must look elsewhere if we wish to explain why governments respond to self-determination movements the way they do.

Testing the reputation model

In chapter 2 I argued that reputation building should help explain why governments tend to fight so many ethnic separatists rather than negotiate with them. Governments in multi-ethnic countries often have strong incentives to build a reputation for toughness in order to deter the many ethnic separatists that may exist. To assess the role of reputation building in these self-determination disputes, I start with my main hypothesis. Does a greater number of potential challengers mean less accommodation?

Table 4.2. *The number of potential challengers and the highest level of government accommodation*

Number of groups	No accommodation	Political reform	Territorial autonomy	Full independence	N
Less than 3	40%	20%	40%	0%	10
3–5	55	16	28	1%	69
6–8	69	0	24	7%	29
9 or more	83	10	7	0%	29

The initial answer is yes. Table 4.2 illustrates the relationship between the number of potential challengers that a government could face (as measured by the total number of ethnic groups in the country) and the highest level of accommodation granted by the government to any separatist challenge in that state.

Table 4.2 reveals a clear link between government accommodation and the number of ethnic groups in a country. Governments in more homogeneous countries are significantly more likely to accommodate any separatist movement than governments in more ethnically heterogeneous countries. In countries where the number of potential challengers is very small (less than three), governments generally offer some form of accommodation. In these countries, only 40 percent of the challenges end with no accommodation of any kind. But as the number of groups and potential challengers increases, government behavior changes dramatically. When there are three to five ethnic groups in the country, fully 55% of challenges end with no accommodation. That figure increases to 69% in countries with six to eight ethnic groups. In countries with a lot of potential challengers (nine or more), governments rarely offer any form of accommodation. Here 83% of all challenges are met with no accommodation whatsoever.[32]

---

[32] Theoretically, it is possible that beyond a certain number of ethnic groups more groups in a country makes less of a difference to a government. Once

When governments do accommodate, the degree to which they accommodate is related to the potential number of challengers they face. This is most clearly illustrated by the figures for territorial autonomy in Table 4.2.[33] Governments that face very few potential challengers eventually agree to offer territorial accommodation 40% of the time. That figure declines to 28% in countries with three to five ethnic groups and 24% in countries with six to eight ethnic groups. In countries where the number of challengers tops eight, territorial accommodation is rare; only 7% of the time do these governments offer territorial autonomy.[34] This offers our first evidence that governments do look ahead, choosing to fight if they anticipate multiple challenges in the future.

To test the effect of potential challengers on government behavior more definitively, I include reputation building in a larger regression model presented in Table 4.3. All of the measures of the current value of the land, the relative capabilities of the combatants, and the various controls from the earlier regression models are included. The key addition in the first column is the number of ethnic groups in the country. If governments are concerned about what might happen in the future, their response to any challenge should be strongly affected by this particular variable.

a government has to deal with seven potential challengers, do additional potential challengers substantially increase the incentive to fight? The data in Table 4.2 reveal no obvious non-linearities in government reactions. In alternate regression models I also tested for various kinds of non-linear relationships between the number of groups and government accommodation, but found that the best fit was a simple linear relationship. It appears that each additional ethnic group provides an additional incentive not to accommodate and to develop a reputation for toughness.

[33] Since it may not be clear to either the government or to potential separatist movements whether political reform represents a significant concession on the part of the government, it is not surprising to see that the rate at which governments offer political reform is not closely linked to the number of potential challengers in the country.

[34] Interestingly, governments are exceedingly reluctant to offer full independence, and cases of full independence are rare regardless of the number of potential challengers.

Table 4.3. *Ordered probit analysis of factors affecting government responses to self-determination demands – which groups matter?*[a]

	Level of government accommodation toward any challenger			
	All groups	Concentrated groups	Disaffected groups	Remaining groups
REPUTATION MODEL				
Number of potential future challengers				
Number of ethnic groups	-.137 (.041)**			
Number of concentrated groups		-.176 (.050)**		
Number of disaffected groups			-.185 (.041)**	
Number of remaining groups				-.179 (.053)**
VALUE OF LAND CURRENTLY UNDER DISPUTE				
Economic value	.084 (.053)	.122 (.063)^	.126 (.063)*	.111 (.059)^
Strategic value	-.034 (.096)	-.052 (.091)	-.019 (.094)	-.032 (.087)
Land area	-.187 (.819)	.073 (.746)	.069 (.856)	.266 (.752)

RELATIVE CAPABILITIES: CURRENT DISPUTANTS

Population of group	-2.66 (1.38)^	-2.35 (1.60)	-2.94 (1.49)*	-2.46 (1.45)^
Mountainous terrain	-.011 (.007)	-.012 (.007)^	-.013 (.006)*	-.014 (.007)*
Neighboring ethnic groups	-.073 (.123)	-.063 (.130)	-.127 (.135)	-.033 (.131)
Government instability	-.592 (.343)^	-.379 (.293)	-.540 (.303)^	-.508 (.302)^
Relative military capabilities	.243 (.116)*	.242 (.107)*	.203 (.100)*	.233 (.001)*
CONTROLS				
Average level of democracy	.073 (.024)**	.061 (.023)**	.063 (.023)**	.059 (.023)**
Year conflict began	-.014 (.008)	-.010 (.008)	-.012 (.007)^	-.019 (.008)*
Violent challenge	.648 (.280)*	.323 (.294)	.375 (.262)	-.270 (.276)
Constant 1	-28.3 (15.8)	-21.1 (16.0)	-25.6 (14.6)	-37.6 (15.8)
Constant 2	-27.8 (15.8)	-20.6 (16.0)	-25.1 (14.6)	-37.3 (15.8)
Constant 3	-26.1 (15.7)	-19.0 (15.9)	-23.4 (14.5)	-35.8 (15.7)
Pseudo R^2	.178	.179	.215	.178
χ^2	65.8**	71.7**	54.0**	38.6**
N	100	100	100	100

^ $p < .10$, * $p < .05$, ** $p < .01$

[a] Heteroskedastic-consistent standard errors clustered by country.

The results in the first model of Table 4.3 confirm this relationship. In line with the reputation model, the greater the number of ethnic groups in a country, the *less* likely a government is to accommodate any challenge. Reputation building is not just a significant factor in government decision making, it is also a substantively important one. Converting the ordered probit coefficients in Table 4.3 into predicted probabilities reveals the influence of reputation building on behavior. Governments in countries with a relatively large number of ethnic groups (ten) are 49% less likely to refuse to accommodate at all than those that faced a relatively small number of groups (two). The probability of offering either full independence or territorial autonomy also changed greatly depending on the number of potential challengers involved. Governments in countries with few ethnic groups were likely to offer these major concessions 33% more often than governments in countries with many ethnic groups.

Which groups matter?

So far, the analysis has looked only at the universe of all ethnic groups in a country and not the sub-set of ethnic groups that are most likely to threaten the government. Groups that are more geographically concentrated, are mobilized to pursue particular interests, or have grievances against the state, have greater motivation and opportunity to seek self-determination. Government behavior, therefore, should be more closely linked to these more threatening parties than to the larger population of ethnic groups used in the previous analysis.

In order to see the effect these groups would have on government behavior, I substituted into the analysis three different measures of the number of potential challengers in a country.[35] The second regression in Table 4.3 shows the effect of the number of

---

[35] Due to collinearity between the three measures of potential challengers, including all three in the same model would be suspect.

concentrated ethnopolitical groups on government behavior, while the third regression shows the effect of the number of ethnopolitical groups. Not only are both significantly related to government behavior, but the predicted probabilities suggest that governments are particularly focused on these more troublesome groups. Governments in countries with large numbers of concentrated groups were 58% less likely to offer any form of accommodation than governments in countries with the fewest concentrated groups. Similarly, going from a country with the largest number of ethnopolitical groups to one with the fewest increased the probability of accommodation by 48%. Each of these effects is larger than the effects we saw when we looked at the more general measure of ethnic groups. This suggests that governments are particularly influenced by groups that show real signs of future action.

One problem with summing the total number of ethnic groups or challengers is that it ignores the fact that some groups may have already challenged the government. According to $H2_{gov}$ as well as the results from the lab experiment, the fewer the remaining challengers, the more likely conciliatory governments are to make concessions. To see if this is the case, the final model of Table 4.3 includes a measure of the number of remaining challengers. What we see is that the number of remaining challengers is also highly significant and signed in the correct direction. Governments were significantly less likely to accommodate any ethnic challenger as the number of remaining challengers increased.[36] This is exactly

[36] Yet another set of potentially relevant groups to consider is those with ongoing challenges. Governments may not only want to deter potential challengers from initiating a challenge in the future, they may also want to influence the actions of groups who have already initiated a challenge. By appearing to be tough, governments may be able to get existing challengers to scale back their military efforts, to accept compromises that are more in the government's favor, or even to give up their separatist battle entirely. Alternate tests suggest that this is, in fact, the case. When I added the number of current challengers to the final model in Table 4.3, the results showed that governments that face a higher number of ongoing challenges are significantly less likely to offer any kind of accommodation than governments with few ongoing challenges. This suggests

the pattern followed by Yeltsin in the early 1990s. Yeltsin did not care that Georgia, Azerbaijan, Lithuania, Estonia, Latvia, and Belarus had already declared independence by the time he came to power in 1991. Instead, as president of the newly formed state of Russia, his focus was on the remaining Islamic groups in Chechnya, Uzbekistan, Tajikistan, Tatarstan, and Turkmenistan.

A closer look at individual leaders

One implication of the reputation model concerns the motivation of individual leaders. Until now, the models I have tested have assumed that leaders invest equally in reputation building regardless of their tenure in office. In reality, different leaders are likely to have different incentives to invest in reputation building, depending on how long they expect to rule. The longer a leader expects to be in office, the fewer incentives he or she has to accommodate. To test this prediction, a dummy variable that singled out countries with consistently short leadership tenures was added to the basic model in Table 4.3.

The results displayed in the first column of Table 4.4 strongly support this logic. Leaders with shorter time horizons are much more likely to accommodate separatist demands than other leaders. All else equal, leaders in countries with especially short tenures are 55% more likely to offer territorial autonomy or full independence than leaders in other countries. This suggests that those leaders who expect to be in office for longer time periods are particularly concerned with reputation.

The results also indicate that tenure is much more vital for leaders in autocracies. Predicted probabilities derived from Table 4.4 indicate that being an autocrat in a country with long tenures decreased by 64% the probability of offering territorial autonomy or

that governments are trying to build their reputations to reduce the costs of both current and future conflicts.

Table 4.4. *Ordered probit analysis of factors affecting government responses to self-determination demands – discounting and counting the future*[a]

	Level of government accommodation	
	Model 1	Model 2
REPUTATION MODEL		
Number of potential future		
challengers		
Number of ethnic groups	–.162 (.029)**	–.126 (.034)**
Leader time horizon		
Short tenure	1.92 (.756)*	1.55 (.662)*
Short tenure* democracy	–.207 (.096)*	–.197 (.090)*
Value of all land occupied by		
potential challengers		
Combined economic value		.027 (.019)
Combined strategic value		–.156 (.086)^
Combined proportion of population		–.486 (.841)
VALUE OF LAND CURRENTLY UNDER DISPUTE		
Economic value	.095 (.056)^	.065 (.089)
Strategic value	–.017 (.103)	.068 (.143)
Land area	–.196 (.854)	.490 (.978)
RELATIVE CAPABILITIES: CURRENT DISPUTANTS		
Population of group	–2.91 (1.41)*	–2.47 (1.71)
Mountainous terrain	–.009 (.007)	–.008 (.007)
Neighboring ethnic groups	–.076 (.128)	–.092 (.126)
Government instability	–.737 (.345)*	–.598 (.343)^
Relative military capabilities	.289 (.117)*	.328 (.132)*
CONTROLS		
Average level of democracy	.077 (.026)**	.087 (.027)**
Year conflict began	–.015 (.008)^	–.013 (.009)
Violent challenge	.701 (.278)*	.527 (.327)

Table 4.4. *(cont.)*

| | Level of government accommodation | |
	Model 1	Model 2
Constant 1	−30.7 (16.3)	−27.3 (17.1)
Constant 2	−30.2 (16.3)	−26.8 (17.1)
Constant 3	−28.5 (16.2)	−25.2 (16.9)
Pseudo R^2	.196	.222
χ^2	82.3**	86.3**
N	100	95

^ $p < .10$, * $p < .05$, ** $p < .01$

a Heteroskedastic-consistent standard errors clustered by country.

full independence. In other words, autocrats who have the potential to be in office for a long period are particularly loath to offer any kind of concession. One explanation for the importance of tenure for autocracies is that this longevity depends more critically on a leader's toughness than it does for leaders in democratic countries. Rivals to a life-long autocrat may be watching for signs of weakness before attempting a takeover. In that sense, giving in to separatists may be one of the clearest ways a long-serving autocrat can reveal weakness. For democracies, there was almost no difference (a 2% shift) between countries with short leadership tenures and other countries.[37]

---

[37] Yet another possibility is that government concerns about reputation build-ing also depend on the strength of the government. Since stronger govern-ments can defeat most challengers, they may have less incentive to invest in reputation building. If true, only the behavior of weak governments should be affected by the number of remaining challengers. To test this possibility, in alternate tests I added a series of interactions between government strength (and relative government strength) and the number of ethnic groups to the model

The value of deterrence

One final implication of the reputation theory still needs to be tested. Governments should care not only about the number of challenges they could face in the future, but also about the costs and benefits of deterrence. The higher the combined value of land that could come under dispute in the future and the higher the costs of fighting for this land, the more incentives a government has to be tough. The last column of Table 4.4 directly tests this relationship by including a series of variables that measure the combined economic value, the combined strategic value, and the combined population of all future lands.

The results are not dramatic but they do support the reputation model. In line with the theory, the greater the combined strategic value of future lands, the *less* likely a government is to accommodate any given challenge. When the strategic value of all future lands was high, governments were 40% more likely to refuse any form of accommodation than if the combined value was low.

Although the combined economic value of lands was not significant in this model, it is difficult to determine exactly which future costs and benefits governments are most concerned about.[38] All of the different measures of future costs and benefits are significantly and negatively correlated with government accommodation in bivariate analysis, and they are also highly intercorrelated (r = .77 or lower). That means that the results that we see in Table 4.4 are

in Table 4.3. The results provided little support for this account. None of the interactions was significant, suggesting that reputation is important for all kinds of governments.

[38] The insignificant results for combined economic value may not, however, be surprising. One explanation for these null findings may be that economic resources can be divided more easily, making settlements easier to reach. This is the hypothesis offered by Huth (1996b) in his study of interstate territorial conflicts where he also found a positive although insignificant relationship between economic stakes and compromise settlement. It could also be that credible commitments to share economic power over time are easier to make than those promising to share strategic assets.

not particularly robust to different specifications. When combined strategic value is dropped from the value, combined economic value becomes negative and significant. Thus governments could be focused on both economic and strategic value. In short, Table 4.4 tells us that government decision making is closely linked to future land value and future costs but does not clearly reveal which aspects of the future governments care most about.

Robustness checks

So far, we have found that governments are more likely to cooperate with separatists when there are few ethnic groups in a country, when there are few disaffected groups left to challenge, when a leader expects to be in power only a short time, and when valuable land is not likely to come under dispute in the future. Although these results are consistent with the predictions made by the reputation theory two potential problems exist with the analyses that still need to be addressed. First, merging both violent and non-violent challenges in the same analysis could bias the results by combining two disparate phenomena. In order to test for this possibility, I separated the two and repeated the analysis. The smaller number of cases in each part of the analysis reduced significance levels somewhat but the results confirm the central role that reputation plays in both sets of cases. Whether the separatist group engages in a violent conflict or not, accommodation is less likely in countries with a large number of potential challengers.

Finally, I also looked at how long it took the government to accommodate a group rather than how much the government was willing to accommodate. Here, I used the date of the last accommodation and a simple dummy variable indicating whether the government offered territorial accommodation or not. This Weibull hazard model confirmed the role reputation building plays in government decision making. Governments took much longer to accommodate a separatist group in cases where a government could potentially face more challengers and lose more valuable territory. All of these tests increase confidence that the conclusions in Tables 4.1 to 4.4 are robust [analysis not shown].

Does reputation building deter?

One final question needs to be answered. If it is true that government behavior is motivated by a desire to deter additional challenges, then it should also be true that refusing to accommodate one challenger has the desired deterrent effect. If it does not, then investing in reputation would have little merit, and studies questioning the efficacy of reputation building would likely be correct.

A closer look at the data suggests that a government strategy of reputation building in the face of a multi-ethnic population is effective. Governments that refused to accommodate or offered only modest political reforms when they were first challenged faced a subsequent challenge for self-determination only 29% of the time (sixteen of fifty-six cases). By contrast, governments that granted territorial autonomy or independence to their first challenger faced a subsequent challenge 57% of the time (twelve of twenty-one cases). This pattern was evident in the former Yugoslavia in 1991. Soon after Slovenia gained independence, Croatia declared independence as well.

In Table 4.5, I subjected this relationship to a more rigorous test. Here, I attempted to see whether government accommodation still triggered additional challenges even after one controlled for the duration of the conflict, violence, the number of remaining challenges, and the number of years since the first challenge. The results in Table 4.5 confirm the earlier bi-variate relationship.[39]

---

[39] Further analysis indicates that, in net the effects of accommodation, subsequent challenges were not more likely democracies, poorer countries, or nations with more limited military capabilities. These additional independent variables were not included in the final model because they further reduced the already small number of cases in the regression.

Table 4.5. *Logit analysis of factors that lead to a subsequent challenge*

Independent variables	Subsequent challenge
Past accommodation	1.30 (.577)**
Number of ethnic groups	.110 (.094)
Years since accommodation	.036 (.054)
Duration conflict	–.020 (.049)
Violent conflict	.592 (.572)
Constant	–2.36 (.87)**
Pseudo R^2	.10
N	73

* $p < .05$, ** $p < .01$

All else equal, governments that gave in to their first challenge were still significantly more likely to face a subsequent challenge whether or not they had fought long, hard battles before giving in.[40] All else equal, governments that offered territorial autonomy or full independence were 31% more likely to face a subsequent challenge.[41]

If we look not just at whether a government faced any subsequent challenge but rather at the number of subsequent challenges, there is yet more evidence that giving in comes at a price. Countries that offered no territorial autonomy faced, on average,

[40] Note the number of cases in Table 4.5 declines to seventy-three because the analysis focuses on the repercussions of the first challenge in each country. The question is whether accommodating an early challenger affected the behavior of any other group in the future.

[41] There is some evidence that ethnic groups are wise to initiate these subsequent challenges. Countries that accommodated a first demand for autonomy were apt to accommodate subsequent demands. In all but two countries, governments that faced one or more subsequent challengers under these circumstances offered some form of accommodation to at least one of the subsequent challenges.

well under one subsequent challenge (.78 challenges), whereas countries that offered territorial autonomy faced, on average, slightly over one subsequent challenge (1.19 challenges). And countries that gave their first challenger full independence faced, on average, two additional challenges (2.0 challenges). As in the laboratory experiments, early accommodation meant more battles in the future.

These preliminary results support the idea that reputation building is an effective means to deter future challenges. In each country, the actions of the government in response to current conflicts appear to have widespread repercussions for potential future conflicts. This is a critical finding that deserves further attention. In the next chapter I focus on the logic and consequences of reputation building from the perspective of the challengers themselves. If I find a government's effort to build a reputation and deter future challenges has a strong effect on the behavior of ethnic groups using an entirely different dataset and methodology, this will represent particularly strong evidence in favor of the theory.

CONCLUSION

Table 4.6 briefly summarizes the main findings from this chapter.

What this chapter revealed is that governments invest in reputation and that this investment appears to pay off. Looking at all self-determination movements between 1955 and 2002, I found that governments were significantly more likely to accommodate a challenge when the number of future challengers and the combined value of future stakes were high. I also found that governments that refused to accommodate one challenger were significantly less likely to face a challenge from a second or third group down the road. Fighting a war against an early challenger is clearly a strategy governments pursue in order to influence how others play the game.

Despite these strong results, this chapter reveals little about the strategic behavior of challengers. Leaders may consciously

Table 4.6. *The main factors determining the government decision to accommodate*

REPUTATION	
Number of potential challengers	More challengers → Less accommodation
Land value potential future challengers	Higher value → Less accommodation
Leader time horizon	Longer tenure → Less accommodation
Time horizon in autocracies	Autocracy with long tenure → Less accommodation
OTHER	
Average level of democracy	More democratic → More accommodation
Year conflict began	Longer challenge → More accommodation
VALUE OF DISPUTED LAND	
Economic, symbolic, strategic value	Not clearly related to accommodation
RELATIVE CAPABILITIES	
Military, strategic, demographic	Not clearly related to accommodation

invest in reputation, but we still have only limited evidence that these actions significantly affect ethnic group behavior. If the theory is true, potential separatists should wait until after they observe the government granting concessions to another group before they themselves challenge.[42] They should also launch their challenge at those times when a government has fewer incentives to fight. Determining whether separatists behave as the theory predicts is the subject of Chapter 5.

[42] Work by Fearon (1994) gives us insight as to why some ethnic groups might choose to challenge the government before any others. Fearon argued that ex ante observable variables should be taken into account by rational potential challengers in their decision to challenge or not. Since ethnic groups understand that governments have greater incentives to fight early challengers, especially if there are many additional challengers waiting in the wings, only the most resolved challengers will move early.

5   Ethnic groups and the decision to seek self-determination

For reputation building to matter, a government's decision to fight early challengers must have the effect of deterring other ethnic minorities from seeking self-determination. If ethnic minorities are not influenced by a government's past behavior and if they do not consider the strategic incentives governments have to invest in reputation, then investments in reputation will make no sense. This chapter, therefore, is a critical test determining whether reputation building is a rational strategy to pursue even if governments believe it is.

This chapter tests two implications of the reputation theory for ethnic groups. First, ethnic groups should be more inclined to seek self-determination if the government has already granted autonomy or independence to another separatist group.[1] Second, ethnic groups should be less likely to challenge in situations where government leaders have strong incentives to invest in reputation building. These incentives are likely to be shaped by the number of ethnic groups in a country (especially those that are geographically concentrated and have grievances against the state), the number of remaining challengers, a leader's tenure in office, and the value and costs of fighting for future lands. If the theory is correct, these factors should determine how costly self-determination will be to obtain, and should influence decisions to challenge or remain silent.

---

[1] In the last chapter, I presented some preliminary evidence of the efficacy of government actions in deterring future challenges that was based on the country as the unit of analysis. In this chapter I offer a more rigorous test of the effects of government accommodation, that focuses on the decision from the perspective of the individual ethnic group and takes the individual group as the unit of analysis.

DATA AND METHODOLOGY

Case selection

Why do ethnic groups seek self-determination? And is their decision influenced by their government's reputation and its incentives to behave tough? In order to answer these questions, I collected annual data on every ethnic group in every country from 1940 through 2000 as identified by the Minorities at Risk (MAR) data project.[2] These data were then compiled into a cross-sectional time series format with annual observations for each group.[3] Based on this format a dataset of 15,905 group years was created.[4]

As with any selection of cases, this list of ethnic groups taken from MAR is not problem-free. MAR only includes ethnic groups that are discriminated against by the central government or organized in support of group interests, and then only those groups that reside in countries with a population of half a million or more. Including only this sub-set of ethnic actors, therefore, could bias my results in a number of ways. For example, the causal factors that lead a government to discriminate against a group could also be related to that group's decision to secede, potentially biasing estimates of the effects of these causal factors. In addition, excluding ethnic groups that reside in countries with low populations could create a selection bias.

---

[2] These dates were chosen because they coincided with the most recent data available from MAR in 2004.

[3] Not all ethnic groups and all countries exist for the entire time period. If a country became independent after 1940, as Eritrea did in 1991, or Bangladesh in 1971, data were limited to the time frame when the group/country existed. Also MAR did not include four ethnic groups that were listed by the Center for International Development and Conflict Management (CIDCM) as self-determination movements: the Wa in Burma, the Muslims in Sri Lanka, India's Kashmiri Buddhists, and Dayaks of Indonesia. These groups are not included in the dataset because of this.

[4] To help ensure that one country (or a small number of countries) with many potential challengers did not have an undue influence on the results, countries were sequentially deleted from the analysis. Also, standard errors for non-independence within countries were corrected using the cluster option in Stata (a statistical program). In no case did this appreciably affect the substantive findings.

I did not choose the list of MAR cases lightly. Three different comprehensive lists of ethnic groups were considered in addition to the MAR list – the *Encyclopædia Britannica*, the CIA *Factbook*, and Fearon's list in his 2003 dataset on ethnic groups. In the end, however, each of these sources was rejected because it included many ethnic groups for which no group-level data are available. Even basic data such as population size are difficult or impossible to acquire for many of the ethnic groups not listed in MAR. One alternative would have been to test the competing hypotheses using only country-level data, but this option would have made it nearly impossible to assess the group-level decisions that are at the heart of this analysis. Thus, while MAR's list of ethnic groups is not ideal, it allows me to move away from national aggregate data and focus on the individual attributes of ethnic groups that may be driving their behavior. Relying on MAR's list of ethnic groups, however, means that the results cannot be generalized to explain the behavior of all ethnic groups in all countries, only those that are politically active or discriminated against in all countries with populations of a half a million or more.

Measuring the dependent variable

The main dependent variable, *Challenge*, is the initial decision by an ethnic group to demand self-determination from the central government. This variable was coded using the list of self-determination cases provided by the Center for International Development and Conflict Management (CIDCM) and again, it includes both armed and unarmed movements. To be classified as a challenge, the leaders or organization of a movement had to publicly state that they wanted greater political autonomy, association with kin in neighboring states, and/or independence.[5] Cases were coded 1 in the first year the demand was made, and 0 for all previous years. Of

---

[5] For greater elaboration of the coding rules see Marshall and Gurr (2003).

the 339 ethnic groups included in the dataset, 122 (36%) initiated a self-determination movement at some point between 1940 and 2000. And slightly over half of all challenges (66 cases) were coded as violent challenges.[6] Most of these movements occurred in Asia, Africa, or the Middle East, but no single country accounted for more than 10% of the cases.[7]

Measuring the independent variables – the reputation theory
Government accommodation
The reputation theory made three specific predictions about how ethnic groups are likely to behave given government incentives to act tough. To test whether a government's past behavior affected the decision to challenge, I created a dummy variable, *Past accommo-dation*, indicating whether the government had ever granted either political autonomy or independence to another separatist group.[8] Ethnic groups were coded as having observed past government accommodation for the year in which accommodation was granted and every year thereafter. Coding this variable required careful read-ing of each case from the time a challenge was initiated until all activity directed toward self-determination had ceased. Detailed notes were taken on the sequence of demands made by the party seeking self-determination, the dates these demands were made, the means by which this information was communicated to the govern-ment, and how the government responded if it responded at all. In the case of the Ambonese in Indonesia, for example, independence was first declared on April 25, 1950 through a telegram to President

---

[6] To be classified as violent, a movement had to pursue at least a minimum level of violence (defined as isolated acts of terrorism) but could engage in everything up to full-scale civil war. Coding was based on the Rebellion Index used in MAR Phase IV. Violent cases all had a rebellion score of 1 or greater.

[7] Six cases of self-determination were ongoing during the first year of the dataset (1940).

[8] In practice, few governments offered ethnic groups full-scale independence (only 3 groups were granted independence). Instead, most were offered some form of greater territorial autonomy (16 groups).

Sukarno and a public broadcast on Radio Ambon, and violence broke out two months later when the separatists (known as the Republik Maluku Selatan, or RMS) attempted to occupy the town of Namlea. Since neither the Sukarno government nor the military agreed to negotiate a settlement at any point during the conflict, this case was coded as having experienced no accommodation. This can be contrasted to East Timor, where formal negotiations commenced in 1998, a referendum on independence was held in August 1999, and a UN transitional administration was established in September 1999 to ensure that the military would not be able to stand in the way of independence. This case was coded as having experienced government accommodation in 1999, and all other ethnic groups were coded as having observed "past accommodation" from that year forward.[9]

Political autonomy was operationalized to include any instance where the government agreed to constitutional or statutory reforms that created regional governments whose leaders were directly elected and not appointed by the central government. I restricted the coding to political forms of autonomy and to full independence because these were the most frequently stated objectives of groups seeking self-determination. Thus, if a government only granted autonomy over cultural issues such as language policy or religious practices, or only offered autonomy over economic policies such as the right to tax, it was not coded as accommodation. Unless a group had the right to make decisions about how resources would be allocated and rules enforced, it was not considered sufficient autonomy to escape central government control.

---

[9] Note that accommodation was only coded as having occurred if the terms were implemented or attempts were made to implement the terms. If a government offered autonomy or independence but these terms were never put into practice, it was coded as if no accommodation had taken place. This is an important distinction to make because ethnic groups considering secession are not only observing whether a government is willing to grant concessions, but if it is then willing to faithfully implement these terms.

The number of potential future challengers

Hypothesis two predicted that repeated play would affect ethnic group decisions to challenge. Four different proxies were used to test whether the number of potential future separatists had this effect.[10] The main measure was again the *Number of ethnic groups* as identified by the *Encyclopædia Britannica*. As discussed in Chapter 4, the advantage of using this measure is that it ensures that the number of groups is not endogenously determined by government policy or government behavior of any kind. Not all groups, however, are equally likely to seek self-determination. To test for the effect of potentially threatening groups I again substituted two more nuanced measures of future challengers into the analysis. They were the number of *Ethnopolitical groups* and the number of *Concentrated groups* in each of the countries.[11]

A more subtle prediction was drawn from the theory regarding a leader's tenure in office. It is possible that leaders who expect to rule for short periods of time have fewer incentives to signal toughness because they expect to face fewer challenges. In order to measure this, I included several measures of how long a leader might expect to stay in office. The first was a dummy variable indicating whether individual leaders had especially short average tenures in a given country.[12] The second was simply the average leadership tenure in

---

[10] As I indicated in the previous chapter, this hypothesis assumes that both the government and ethnic groups can determine who the future challengers are likely to be. Although no one can know exactly how many groups will seek self-determination in the future, both the government and its ethnic groups are likely to have some knowledge about potential troublemakers since all inhabit the same confined geographical space.

[11] To test for the possibility that the relationship between government concessions and the number of potential challengers is non-linear, various non-linear models and thresholds were tested but all provided a significantly worse or at best similar fit to the linear model presented here. It did not appear that there was a critical threshold beyond which increasing the number of groups no longer affected government actions. Nor did it seem that the impact of the additional potential challengers decreased as the total number increased.

[12] I singled out countries whose leaders had an average tenure of one standard deviation below the average of all countries over a fifty-year period.

the leader's country over the time period of the dataset. The final measure was the leader's age.

The sequence of challengers

Since measuring the absolute number of challengers overlooks the fact that governments may have less incentive to deter groups that have already challenged, I included measures for the *Number of remaining challengers* and the *Number of groups that have already challenged* in a country in Table 5.5. The former was measured by taking the total number of potential challengers (based on the number of disaffected groups listed in MAR) and subtracting the number of self-determination movements that had already been initiated.

The value of deterrence

Finally, the reputation theory predicted that ethnic groups should be more apt to challenge when a government's value for retaining future lands is low, and the costs of fighting for them are high. To test the value hypothesis, the same measures of value were included in this model as in the previous chapter. Specifically, two measures of future value were added to the model. *Future economic value* was a combined score of the number of marketable resources on all land occupied by all potential future challengers. *Future strategic value* was a scale indicating the number of critical strategic resources (sea outlets, shipping lanes, military bases, international borders, attack routes, and mountain ranges) connected to the land occupied by all future challengers.

The costs a government would have to pay to retain these lands were again difficult to measure since strength tends to vary over time, and data on group capabilities are poor. Three admittedly rough proxies were again included: (1) the *Proportion of territory* held by disaffected groups that had not yet challenged, (2) the *Combined size of the population* represented by all these groups, and (3) the number of *Neighboring co-ethnics* who could supply resources, staging areas, and potential escape routes to these groups.[13] Presumably, the greater the number of groups with these features, the more costly it would be for the government to fight these groups and the more attractive it would be to initiate a challenge. The exact measurement and coding of all of these variables, as well as details on data sources, are included in Appendix 3.

Measuring the independent variables – existing explanations
Existing explanations have rightly pointed out that ethnic groups must have both the motive and the opportunity in order to seek self-determination movement. If ethnic groups have no reason to separate and no chance to organize resistance, no formal challenge would ever be launched. In order to account for these important underlying conditions, a host of different measures were also included in the model.

Motives
Five key reasons for seeking self-determination are frequently cited in the literature: 1) political discrimination, 2) economic discrimination, 3) cultural discrimination, 4) deprivation, and 5) loss of rights. *Relative political discrimination* assesses the degree to which an ethnic group has fewer political rights and less power than the dominant group in society. It focuses on access to power, voting rights, and legal protection. *Relative economic discrimination* measures the income, property holdings, educational status, and professional and commercial positions of group members compared to members of the dominant group. *Relative cultural discrimination* calculates a group's ability to use its own language and practice its religion and social customs, and the degree to which it has freedom of residential choice relative to the dominant group in society.[14] The

---

[13] As noted in the previous chapter, these variables can either be seen as measuring the costs a government would incur or as measuring the value of what they could lose. The exact interpretation of any significant results is, therefore, not without questions.

[14] Data on each of these variables were obtained from MAR.

expectation here is that the greater the inequity between a minority group and a country's dominant ethnic group, the more incentives there are to secede.

Since there is some disagreement about whether groups are motivated more by relative inequality or by absolute levels of discrimination, I included three measures of the absolute level of economic, political, and religious discrimination in alternate tests. *Economic discrimination* and *Political discrimination* were both measured using five-point indexes that ranged from no discrimination to almost total exclusion and the absence of basic rights along each dimension. *Religious discrimination* was a four-point scale that measured how concerned group representatives were with religious freedom. Since these three measures are available in less than one-half of the group-years, they are not included in the main model.[15]

Some have argued that the loss of rights is a more important source of grievance than either absolute or relative well being. In fact, in a study of all ethnopolitical groups between 1998 and 2000, Marshall and Gurr found that one of the strongest determinants of self-determination demands was whether a group had lost political autonomy sometime in the past. The Ibo in Nigeria, Karens in Myanmar, Tibetans in China, Palestinians in the West Bank and Gaza, Kashmiri Muslims in India, and South Ossetians and Abkhazians in Georgia, all experienced major losses of political autonomy, and all launched armed self-determination movements.[16] To take this potentially important variable into account, I included a measure of *Lost autonomy*, indicating whether the central

---

[15] A number of different measures of government repression were also included in alternate models to see if different types of oppression affected the outbreak of a challenge. It is possible that the decision to actively seek autonomy tends to occur in those cases where an ethnic group has been systematically targeted, and that in the absence of government force, such actions would rarely be pursued.

[16] Marshall and Gurr (2003: 34).

government had ever taken away fundamental political control from a given ethnic group.[17]

Groups suffering from low living standards or basic deprivations were also hypothesized to be more apt to seek self-determination, and one commonly used measure of income was included in the main model: *GDP per capita* (gross domestic product (GDP) measured in 1985 dollars and lagged one year).[18] In alternate tests I also looked to see if changes in the rate of economic growth and infant mortality affected the likelihood of rebellion.[19]

Opportunity

Theories that focus on underlying grievances are often complemented by those that focus on the ability of ethnic groups to mobilize and sustain an organization over time.[20] A group may have grievances against the state, but unless it is also able to organize and recruit individual soldiers to fight for a particular cause, and then supply these soldiers over time, no viable challenge is likely to be launched.[21] Access to such support was measured using two

[17] While this variable is frequently included in analyses of civil war and ethnic rebellion, a healthy dose of skepticism is warranted as to the direction of causality. Since MAR codes things like "remembered kingdoms" as lost autonomy, it is possible that groups with active separatist movements deliberately reconstruct and emphasize past "independence" as a means to mobilize support. If this is true, then it is the desire for self-determination that is causing groups to define territory as having been "lost" rather than the other way around.

[18] GDP can also be seen as an indicator of government strength. Since statistical analysis cannot determine which of these interpretations is more accurate, a significant relationship can be interpreted as potentially supporting either theory.

[19] Since infant mortality is only available for about half of the group-years, it is not included in the final model. Male secondary school education is sometimes used to measure human development. I did not include it in this analysis because it is highly correlated with infant mortality and is available for a significantly smaller number of group-years.

[20] See Tilly (1978) and Hechter (1992).

[21] Unfortunately, region or group specific data on many ethnic groups are limited. For ethnic groups that have never initiated a territorial challenge and are not characterized as disaffected by MAR/CIDCM, there is generally no

indicators: the *Size of the ethnic group population* – measured as the proportion of the national population identified as members of the ethnic group, and the presence of a *Youth bulge*. Youth bulge was measured as the ratio of the youth population (age 15–24) relative to the adult population of a country.[22]

Ethnic groups must also overcome difficult collective action problems if they hope to organize effective resistance. Two measures were added to the main model to take into account the difficulties groups face assembling individuals, building a common identity, and organizing activities. First, a measure of the *Geographic concentration* of the group was included. This measure indicated whether a group was widely dispersed (0), primarily urban or a minority in one region (1), a majority in one region (2), or concentrated in one region (3). The other measure was a dummy variable, *Autonomy*, indicating whether the group had ever been historically autonomous. In alternate tests, a five-point index of *Group cohesion* that ranged from no significant collective identity to a strong group identity was also tested.[23]

Since the mobilization of these forces usually requires substantial monetary resources, the model also incorporates a measure that attempted to estimate a group's access to finance. *Neighboring countries* indicated the number of neighboring countries where segments of the ethnic groups under observation also resided, and was taken as an indicator of a group's ability to obtain outside aid or sanctuary.[24]

cross-country data on the economic or strategic resources contained within the land area they occupy. Thus, the measures used to predict the activation of ethnic group self-determination movements are necessarily less exact and complete than the measures that were used in the previous chapter to predict government responses to active self-determination movements.

[22] I also used a measure of the ratio of the youth population to the total population of the country in alternate tests. The results were the same.

[23] Cohesion was not included in the final model because it is only available for less than a quarter of the group-years. Data exist only for 1980–95.

[24] As an alternate measure, I also included the proportion of the nation's population that had emigrated to the United States – presumably a rough proxy for monetary support from abroad. This diaspora measure had no effect on

Groups are also thought to be advantaged by how difficult it is for the government to control and police peripheral areas. Presumably, the weaker a government, the less control it has over its territory and the better able ethnic groups are to organize resistance. Self-determination movements emerged, for example, in Yugoslavia, Afghanistan, and Somalia under weak governments with less than full administrative control over their territories. Several proxies were employed to assess government capacity.[25] The first was *Government instability*. In line with Fearon and Laitin's interpretation, governments that had experienced rapid regime change (defined as a three or more change in their Polity IV score in any of the three prior years) were viewed as more susceptible to challenge than those that were more stable.[26] The second measure was *Anocracy*. Regimes that are neither fully democratic nor fully autocratic have also been singled out as being particularly ill-equipped to maintain central authority and deal with internal challenges.[27] Oil was the third proxy used to measure government strength and indicated whether a country obtained at least one-third of its export revenues from oil or natural gas.[28] *Mountainous terrain* was included as a measure of government reach and capacity. The final measure was *Country population*, since larger populations are likely to be more difficult to manage than smaller ones.[29] In alternate tests, I also included a series of measures

the decision to initiate a challenge but since the measure combined all ethnic groups from the same country and had missing data for many countries, few strong conclusions should be drawn.

[25] In alternate tests I also included measures of the number of military personnel and annual military spending (per capita), as well as a measure of the geographic size of a country.

[26] Fearon and Laitin (2003). Note, however, that a three or more point change in a country's polity score may not necessarily imply weakness or instability, simply institutional change. This variable, therefore, may be a better measure of the quality of institutional relationships than government capacity.

[27] Gurr (1993) and Fearon and Laitin (2003).

[28] Alternate tests that used the percentage of exports from fuel and the ratio of primary commodity exports to GDP (which is a common proxy of the abundance of national resources) led to similar results.

[29] A measure of the log of the country population was also included. It led to the same substantive conclusions.

of the government's military capabilities and the relative capabilities of the two sides. Specifically, I assessed the effects of total military expenditures by the government and the total number of military personnel on ethnic group decisions to challenge. I also created an amalgam measure, *Relative military capabilities*, that compared the potential military strength of the ethnic challenger (measured as the total population of the group) with the government's actual military forces (measured as the average number of military personnel during a challenge). Countries with relatively small defense expenditures and relatively small armies were expected to be more attractive targets for potential secessionist movements. Given the potentially endogenous nature of government military spending, these measures were not included in the final model.[30]

Two additional variables were included as controls. The results of the last chapter and a range of other studies have demonstrated that democracies are more likely to accommodate demands for greater self-rule than non-democracies and are less likely to experience violent challenge as a result.[31] A variable, *Democracy*, was therefore included in the final model. Finally, the number of self-determination movements has been increasing since the late 1950s, spiking sharply at the end of the Cold War.[32] In order to control for this effect, the *Year* of each observation was also included.

EMPIRICAL ANALYSIS

Testing conventional accounts
I begin the empirical analysis by isolating the effects that motives and opportunity have on decisions to seek self-determination. I use this baseline model to reveal just how much of ethnic group behavior is explained by underlying conditions as opposed to reputational

---

[30] It is not clear if a government is investing heavily in the military because it is weak and needs to try to overcome a significant challenge, or because it simply wants to demonstrate strength in the face of weak challenge.
[31] See especially Gurr (1993).   [32] See Marshall and Gurr (2003: 29).

dynamics. Table 5.1 shows the results of a rare event logistic regression with *Challenge* as the dependent variable.[33]

Grievances

Table 5.1 reveals that a number of different measures associated with motive and opportunity are linked to the decision to seek self-determination. Three factors in particular appear important. Ethnic groups whose cultural rights were more limited than the dominant group are significantly more likely to challenge. Preventing a group from using its own language and denying a group the ability to practice its religious and social customs, and limiting a group's residential choices, tended to provoke separatist movements.[34] Groups that had once enjoyed political autonomy but had lost it, such as the East Timorese, the Quebecois, and indigenous peoples in Nicaragua, were also more likely to seek self-determination than those with no such history.[35] These results confirm that grievances against the state provide an important impetus for groups to secede.

Table 5.1, however, reveals only a small part of the picture. Since many of the measures of discrimination and repression are available for only a sub-set of the group-years in the dataset, I undertook a series of alternate regressions that added each of these measures one at a time. These tests suggest that any number of different grievances could be encouraging groups to secede. In addition to a group's status relative to other groups, there is some evidence that the absolute level of discrimination a group faces, especially political discrimination, is important. Groups that were denied

[33] Multi-collinearity is not a problem with this model. The only variables that are even moderately highly correlated (.3 to .5) are the three relative status variables. When I re-ran the analysis with each relative status variable separately, the results did not change in any significant way.

[34] Marshall and Gurr (2003) also found that relative status, and in particular cultural rights, were important.

[35] Alternate tests also suggested that changes in economic conditions influenced ethnic group decision making. Ethnic groups in countries facing negative economic growth, as measured by growth in GDP, were more likely to enter into a territorial conflict with the government.

Table 5.1. *The determinants of self-determination: current costs and opportunities (rare event logistic regression)*

	Model 1	Model 2	Model 3
MOTIVES/GRIEVANCES			
Cultural status	.311 (.145)*	.227 (.168)	.257 (.171)
Political status	.022 (.080)	.091 (.095)	.057 (.104)
Economic status	.011 (.110)	.080 (.112)	.136 (.114)
Loss of rights	.739 (.108)**	.676 (.177)**	.701 (.208)**
GDP per capita	.000 (.003)	.000 (.003)	−.007 (.006)
OPPORTUNITY			
Group resources			
Group geographic concentration		.426 (.152)**	.411 (.159)*
Proportion of national population		−.190 (1.01)	−.545 (1.06)
Youth bulge		−.045 (.046)	−.080 (.037)
Neighboring co-ethnics		−.054 (.117)	−.056 (.123)
Government weakness			
Government instability		.559 (.482)	.448 (.444)
Anocracy		.304 (.355)	.123 (.299)
National population		.155 (.138)	.141 (.124)
Mountainous terrain		.000 (.009)	.006 (.008)
Oil reserves		−.245 (.514)	−.317 (.462)
CONTROLS			
Democracy			.021 (.025)
Year			.045 (.012)**
Constant	−6.59 (.403)**	−7.83 (1.94)**	−94.6 (24.1)**
N	9235	9046	9046

Note: Figures are regression coefficients with standard errors in parentheses.
^ p < .10, * p < .05, ** p < .01

access to political power, voting rights, and other aspects of equal legal protection were more likely to initiate demands for territorial autonomy or independence than those that were not.[36] Active government repression also tended to incite violent and non-violent separatist movements. Ethnic groups were more likely to demand self-determination if arrests on their members increased, restrictions on their movement increased, and military campaigns against them grew. Violent demands for independence in Aceh, for example, escalated as the number of military personnel and the extent of military repression in that region increased.[37] These findings suggest that the decision to secede is at least partly dependent on the internal ethnic policies a government chooses to pursue.

Alternate tests also revealed a significant and robust link between declining incomes and the desire for self-determination. Groups in countries that were facing deteriorating economic conditions were especially apt to launch a separatism movement. As a former rebel in Aceh stated in December 2006, "[i]f the economy here is OK and the Indonesian government doesn't play around with us, what do we need separatism for?"[38]

The only measures of grievances that did not affect group behavior had to do with the overall social and economic health of a state. Groups that resided in countries with lower incomes and groups that lived in countries with high infant mortality rates were no more likely to challenge the central government than those that did not. Poor countries such as Benin, Honduras, or Mozambique are no more likely to experience self-determination challenges than rich

---

[36] Interestingly, economic discrimination did not appear to be a factor here. Groups that had lower incomes, less access to education, and were economically disadvantaged compared to other groups in their own country, were not particularly likely to try to secede. Even when all of the other proxies for grievances were dropped from the model, there was no indication that economic status or GDP per capita affected the likelihood of a challenge.

[37] The inclusion of a repression measure had little substantive impact on the other relationships in Table 5.1.

[38] Mydans (2006).

countries such as Canada, Spain, or Sweden. These findings reinforce the belief that groups are less influenced by absolute conditions than by relative conditions, or changes in their overall well being. It is not the status of the country as a whole at a particular point in time that matters, but the status of each individual group over time that seems to influence behavior.

Opportunity

Ethnic groups also appeared to be affected by the opportunity costs of rebellion, initiating challenges more often when organization was easy. Column two of Table 5.1 demonstrates that geographically concentrated groups are significantly more likely to seek self-determination. This confirms findings by Toft (2003) who argued that concentrated groups can mobilize more fighters and resources than dispersed groups and are more likely to have dense networks that make coordination easier.[39]

Other measures of opportunity did not, however, help to predict group behavior. None of the other measures of a group's access to resources seemed to influence the decision to demand self-determination.[40] Larger ethnic groups and groups who could recruit from a population base that had a large proportion of men between 15 and 24 were no more apt to initiate self-determination movements than those with smaller groups or older populations. The Oromo, who make up 40 percent of Ethiopia's population, for example, were as likely to challenge for independence as the Chittagong Hills Tribes, who make up less than 1 percent of Bangladesh's population.

A group's ability to operate outside the reach of the central government also did not appear to factor into the decision to challenge the central government. Ethnic group challenges were not linked to

---

[39] Toft (2003: 22).

[40] Alternate tests indicate that the amount of land occupied by the group also did not affect the likelihood of engaging the government. Moreover, alternate tests indicate that none of these measures of a group's access to resources became significant when included as the sole proxy for opportunity.

the presence of mountainous terrain in the country.[41] In addition, more populous countries, such as China and Brazil, were no more likely to experience self-determination movements than less populated ones, such as Botswana and Australia.[42] And groups with ethnic brethren in neighboring countries – presumably a potential source of resources and an escape route from the government – did not have a higher rate of challenge.

Finally, signs of government weakness – at least as measured using existing proxies – were at best marginally related to group behavior. Ethnic groups were no more likely to challenge governments that were unstable or anocracies than those that were not. And economic resources such as the availability of oil did not appear to play a role in the decision to secede.[43] Moreover, alternate tests that included the *Relative military capabilities* revealed no link between the relative strength of the government and the ethnic group and the decision to initiate a challenge. Only when the total military expenditures of the government were included as the sole proxy for opportunity was there a small sign that government strength mattered. In this one model, government military strength was negative and almost significant – suggesting that ethnic groups might be particularly leery of more militarily powerful central governments.

One conclusion to draw from all of this is that groups respond to structural conditions but only the most basic ones. A loss of autonomy and geographic concentration seem to be critical conditions for groups to seek self-determination – not at all surprising given that the goal is to gain (or regain) control over a particular piece of land. At the same time it is clear that many of the measures that were used in this analysis to assess motives and opportunity

---

[41] This finding could change with the availability of more region-specific data.

[42] Neither total population nor total population logged were significantly correlated with the decision to challenge.

[43] This is true if one considers actual oil reserves as is the case in Table 5.1, and is also true if economic resources are measured by the presence of valuable mineral deposits in the country and by potential oil reserves.

are at best imperfect proxies. It is certainly possible that other more exact measures of grievances and resources might help to account for some of the actions ethnic groups take. As a result, one cannot fully dismiss the relevance of any of the different aspects of motives and opportunities at this point.

Controls

In this initial baseline model, I had expected to find a significant relationship between democracy and self-determination challenges. I did not. Table 5.1 reveals that ethnic groups in democratic countries are no less likely to secede than those in authoritarian countries. This is especially surprising because democracies – as shown in the previous chapter – are more willing to accommodate these challenges. One explanation is that ethnic minorities in democracies have sufficient political outlets to address their demands, making greater autonomy or independence generally unnecessary. A second explanation is that ethnic minorities have fewer grievances with their democratic government, and therefore, fewer reasons to separate.

Table 5.1 does confirm, however, that the number of separatist movements is increasing. All else equal, ethnic groups have been significantly more apt to initiate challenges toward the end of the twenty-first century than in earlier decades.

Testing the reputation theory

The goal of the chapter is not, however, to determine if motives and opportunity are associated with separatist movements. It is to determine whether ethnic groups, given these underlying conditions, behave strategically and use reputation to determine if and when to challenge. Thus, the next step in the empirical analysis is to add measures associated with reputation building to see if they affect behavior. What we see is that reputation building is a central factor driving the decision making of potential separatist movements.

Table 5.2. *Past accommodation and the decision to secede*

| | Challenge | | |
Past accommodation	Yes	No	N
Yes	3.1%	96.9%	11,688
No	0.8%	99.2%	389

Past accommodation by the government
The first goal of this analysis is to see if a government's past behavior significantly affected the decision to demand autonomy or independence. Table 5.2 presents the simple, bi-variate relationship between past accommodation and the decision to call for greater self-rule. The evidence presented in Table 5.2 reveals that groups are more likely to try to secede if they face a government that has already granted concessions to another ethnic group. In any given year, the vast majority of ethnic groups did not initiate a challenge, but if a government had backed down ethnic groups were four times more likely to demand self-determination. Less than 1 percent of all groups in any given year chose to challenge if a government had never granted any concessions. By contrast, over 3 percent of all ethnic groups on average in any given year challenged if the government had.

These results hold up when tested in a larger regression model that includes all measures of group grievances, structural opportunities, and controls included in the earlier models. Table 5.3 again shows that the decision to seek self-determination is strongly related to how a government behaved in the past.[44] This confirms

[44] It is also interesting to note that the frequency with which a government had offered accommodation in the past was not as important as ever having accommodated. When a measure of the number of times a government had offered territorial autonomy or independence in the past was added to the model in Table 4.3, it was insignificant. This supports predictions made by the reputation theory that any concessions should trigger additional challenges

observations made by Donald Horowitz in his influential work on ethnic conflict. According to Horowitz,

> [t]he creation of Pakistan in 1947 gave great impetus to the demand for Sikhistan, a Sikh state in the truncated Indian Punjab. If the Punjab could be divided once, why not twice? The same was true in post-Biafra Nigeria. Once twelve states had been created, a flood of movements sprung up to demand still more ethnically based states.[45]

It also confirms the relationship found in the laboratory experiments. Ethnic groups that observed a government making concessions in one period were more apt to demand their own set of concessions.[46] Backing down clearly has a deleterious effect in terms of additional challengers.

The potential number of future challengers

A government's past behavior, however, is not the only way groups can judge how governments are likely to behave in the future. As I argued in Chapter 2, groups can also assess whether governments will fight or cooperate based on three conditions known to encourage reputation building. The first has to do with the number of potential challengers in a country.

Table 5.3 shows that ethnic groups are increasingly *less* likely to seek self-determination as the number of ethnic groups in a country *increases*.[47] This finding is quite striking because intuitively one

---

because very resolute governments are unlikely to make concessions at all. A single act of accommodation, therefore, is enough to trigger a sharp reaction.

[45] Horowitz (1985: 280).

[46] Since there is some concern related to the coding of some of the MAR variables, I re-ran the analysis dropping all MAR variables. I also re-ran the analysis dropping all of the non-significant variables in Table 5.1. Finally, I tried a range of other specifications of the model with different combinations of variables. The basic results are robust and did not change under these different specifications.

[47] There is little indication that ethnic groups in countries with more groups challenge less because more groups means many weak groups. Ethnic groups in countries with a large number of groups tended to be more concentrated and more regularly had the advantage of mountainous terrain than ethnic groups

Table 5.3. *The determinants of self-determination: the role of strategic information (rare event logistic regression)*

	Model 1	Model 2
STRATEGIC INFORMATION MODEL		
Past government behavior		
Past accommodation	1.07 (.506)*	1.52 (.541)**
Future government incentives		
Number of potential challengers		–.144 (.061)*
MOTIVES/GRIEVANCES		
Cultural status	.231 (.167)	.351 (.182)^
Political status	.039 (.101)	.045 (.103)
Economic status	.015 (.112)	.060 (.113)
Loss of rights	.705 (.214)**	.778 (.191)**
GDP per capita	–.043 (.058)	–.000 (.005)
OPPORTUNITY		
Group resources		
Group geographic concentration	.449 (.170)**	.480 (.165)**
Proportion of national population	–.606 (1.10)	–.417 (1.18)
Youth bulge	–.077 (.033)	–.086 (.029)***
Neighboring co-ethnics	–.055 (.122)	–.081 (.129)
Government weakness		
Government instability	.509 (.451)	.291 (.426)
Anocracy	.174 (.305)	.048 (.302)
National population	.046 (.144)	.291 (.145)*
Mountainous terrain	.004 (.008)	.005 (.009)
Oil reserves	.155 (.488)	–.054 (.427)
CONTROLS		
Democracy	.008 (.023)	.007 (.022)
Year	.038 (.011)**	.033 (.010)**
Constant	–81.6 (21.7)**	–72.5 (20.0)**
N	9046	8968

Note: Figures are regression coefficients with standard errors in parentheses.

^ p < .10, * p < .05, ** p <. 01

would expect countries with many ethnic groups, such as Indonesia, Kenya, Iran, or India, to experience proportionally more violent self-determination movements than those with few ethnic groups. The opposite, however, is true. Some of the most multi-ethnic countries in the world have never experienced a violent separatist challenge, while some of the most homogeneous countries such as the Philippines have experienced many challenges.[48]

The effects of information and reputation building are even more clearly revealed when the significant coefficients from Table 5.3 are converted into relative risks.[49] Table 5.4 shows the relative change in the risk of a self-determination challenge (in a single year) as each independent variable moves from low to high (from the tenth to the ninetieth percentile).[50]

The relative risk figures in Table 5.4 confirm the importance of information in a group's decision to challenge. In any given year, an ethnic group was five times more likely to demand autonomy or independence from a government that had already backed down than from one that had not. The same was true for the one other measure associated with reputation building. Ethnic groups in countries with a large number of ethnic groups (and thus a higher number of future challengers) were roughly one-third as likely to seek self-determination in any given year as groups in countries with few ethnic groups.

Table 5.4 also shows the degree to which ethnic groups are influenced by grievances. Groups that face the most severe restrictions on

---

in countries with few other groups. More groups did, however, mean that each individual group was likely to comprise a smaller portion of the total country population.

[48] Three other factors that had no clear effect on the decision to launch a challenge were the level of democracy, the geographic size of a country, and international contagion. The latter two measures were dropped from the final model because they were available for half or less of the years/cases.

[49] King and Zeng (2001).

[50] For each calculation, all other independent variables are held constant at a hypothetical median case using a simulation procedure developed by King et al. (2000).

Table 5.4. *Relative risk of a self-determination challenge*

Variable	Relative risk of challenge (single year)
Strategic information model	
Past accommodation	
No → Yes	5.3
Number of ethnic groups	
Low (3) → High (18)	–0.35
Motive/grievances	
Relative cultural status	
Little discrimination (0) → High discrimination (4)	2.6
Lost autonomy	
No → Yes	20.5
Opportunity	
Group geographic concentration	
Low (0) → High (3)	4.2
Controls	
Year	
1940 → 2000	6.9

cultural and religious freedom are almost three times more likely to initiate a challenge than groups that face no such restrictions. A loss of political autonomy mattered even more. In any given year, the odds of initiating a challenge were twenty times higher for groups that had lost autonomy than they were for groups that had not. Finally, opportunity costs also clearly factored into group decisions to seek self-determination. More concentrated groups were four times more likely to seek self-determination than groups that were almost evenly distributed around the country.[51]

---

[51] Interestingly, groups in the year 2000 were seven times as likely to initiate a challenge than groups in 1940 – all else equal.

All of this suggests that the decision to launch a territorial challenge is a complex one. Ethnic groups need a motive to seek separation from the central government, and they need the opportunity to build and sustain a movement, but they also carefully collect information about how the government is likely to react and use this information when deciding whether and when to challenge. Including this important strategic variable, therefore, allows us to understand more fully the range of factors ethnic groups consider before deciding to rebel.

Which groups are relevant? We know that ethnic groups contemplating secession care about the number of ethnic groups in the country. Each additional ethnic group acts as an added incentive for the government to fight a separatist challenge and, therefore, as a disincentive for any ethnic group to act. But the number of ethnic groups in a country is at best a rough approximation of the number of potential challengers that actually exist. In order to distinguish between groups that are likely to seek independence and those that are not, I include two more nuanced measures of future challengers: the number of geographically concentrated groups in a country, and the number of disaffected groups.

The first two models of Table 5.5 reveal that ethnic groups are especially concerned with the number of concentrated or disaffected groups in their countries. In each case, the effect of having one additional group in the country is greater than the effect (evident in Table 5.4) when all ethnic groups were included in the calculation.[52] Ethnic groups in countries with a large number of geographically concentrated groups were one-fifth as likely to initiate a challenge as ethnic groups in a country with no concentrated groups. The comparable figure for the effect of the number of disaffected groups was one-quarter. Before launching a potentially

---

[52] Unfortunately, since each of these measures was highly correlated, they could not be included in the same model and it was impossible to definitively determine which of the three most closely shapes ethnic group decision making.

Table 5.5. *The determinants of self-determination: which groups matter? (Rare event logistic regression)*

	Concentrated groups	Disaffected groups	Remaining groups
STRATEGIC INFORMATION MODEL			
Past government behavior			
Past accommodation	1.21 (.520)*	1.36 (.593)*	.907 (.536)^
Future government incentives			
Number of potential challengers			
Concentrated groups	−.182 (.069)**		
Disaffected groups		−.129 (.061)*	
Remaining groups			−.137 (.058)*
Groups that have already challenged			.198 (.096)*
MOTIVES/GRIEVANCES			
Cultural status	.221 (.172)	.276 (.169)	.341 (.162)*
Political status	.024 (.097)	.027 (.102)	.055 (.091)
Economic status	.094 (.095)	.082 (.099)	.024 (.111)
Loss of rights	.749 (.204)**	.680 (.204)**	.776 (.206)**
GDP per capita	−.065 (.048)	−.049 (.049)	−.036 (.051)
OPPORTUNITY			
Group resources			
Group geographic concentration	.561 (.173)**	.507 (.168)**	.563 (.176)**
Oil reserves	.041 (.446)	.047 (.453)	−.329 (.415)
Proportion of national population	−.756 (1.14)	−.835 (1.13)	−.008 (1.14)
Youth bulge	−.092 (.033)**	−.091 (.034)**	−.045 (.035)
Neighboring co-ethnics	−.093 (.126)	−.102 (.122)	−.014 (.136)

Table 5.5. (*cont.*)

	Concentrated groups	Disaffected groups	Remaining groups
Government weakness			
Government instability	.441 (.465)	.396 (.447)	.139 (.388)
Anocracy	.163 (.323)	.179 (.314)	.045 (.301)
National population	.276 (.121)*	.258 (.136)^	.189 (.145)
Mountainous terrain	.004 (.009)	.004 (.008)	.002 (.009)
CONTROLS			
Democracy	−.014 (.021)	−.005 (.021)	−.010 (.024)
Year	.041 (.011)**	.035 (.011)**	.017 (.012)
Constant	−87.9 (22.2)**	−76.8 (21.5)**	−41.1 (22.6)^
N	8883	8968	8968

Note: Figures are regression coefficients with standard errors in parentheses.

^ $p < .10$, * $p < .05$, ** $p < .01$

costly self-determination movement, ethnic groups appear to consider how many motivated potential challengers are out there for a government to try to deter.

The third model of Table 5.5 considers whether ethnic groups are more focused on the number of ongoing challenges or the number of groups who have not yet challenged but could do so in the future. The table reveals that potential separatist groups are particularly concerned with those groups that have not yet challenged. The greater the number of ethnic groups waiting in the wings, the more reluctant any group is to make demands.

Interestingly, the last model of Table 5.5 also reveals that ethnic groups are more willing to initiative their own challenge when the number of ongoing challenges is higher. Exactly why there is a positive relationship is not immediately clear. But one logical possibility is that ethnic groups believe that their challenge is more likely to be successful at a time when a government is expending considerable resources across many active challenges. More detailed analyses of individual cases are required to determine whether this explanation is correct. Nevertheless, the fact that ethnic groups distinguish between the number of active challengers and the number of remaining challengers confirms the complex strategic thinking that takes place before groups decide to act.

A leader's tenure in office

One factor was not related to decisions to seek self-determination. The reputation theory predicted that a leader's tenure in office should affect both government and ethnic group behavior. The longer a leader expected to be in power, the more reason he or she had to be tough, and the less incentive an ethnic group had to challenge this particular leader. The data, however, showed little clear evidence that such a relationship exists. Alternate tests indicate that potential challengers in countries with especially short tenure were no more likely to launch a self-determination movement than challengers in countries where leaders ruled for many years. Average leadership tenure in a country also had no significant effect on the decision to seek self-determination.[53] This is somewhat surprising because the findings in Chapter 4 revealed that leaders with short tenures were more likely to grant concessions. One explanation is that leaders are negotiating with groups that have already fought lengthy wars, as President Habibie did with the East Timorese. Thus, the message being sent to other groups is that leaders with short tenures are more willing to negotiate away long-standing battles, but they are not more likely to negotiate with new challengers. A second explanation is that groups

---

[53] The only measure that was marginally linked to group behavior was the age of the leader in office. All else equal, the older the leader in office, the more likely groups were to initiate a challenge. This offers perhaps some support that tenure in office influences behavior, but not a lot. In other tests, I added an interaction between the leader's tenure and the level of democracy in a country but found that it had no measurable effect here.

understand that a leader is likely to be in power for only a short period of time, and that any promises made by such a leader would not be credible. Case study analysis should help tease out why ethnic groups do not increase demands against short-term leaders.

The expected costs of future challenges

The reputation theory presented in Chapter 2 made one final prediction about ethnic group behavior. Ethnic groups should be less likely to demand autonomy or independence as the value of future lands and the costs of fighting for these lands increases. That's because the more valuable these lands, and the higher the costs of fighting for them, the more beneficial is deterrence. Table 5.6 directly tests this prediction by including measures of the economic and strategic value of future lands, and the size of all lands that could come under dispute in the future.

Table 5.6 shows that ethnic groups are influenced by the value of future lands. The greater the combined economic value of lands under the control of disaffected groups that have not yet challenged, the *less* likely an ethnic group was to initiate its own challenge.[54] These results, however, do not tell the whole story. Readers should be aware that each of the different measures of future value and future costs is intercorrelated, and the overall model is not particularly robust to changes in specification. There is, in fact, some indication that potential challengers base their decision to seek self-determination in part on the strategic value of future lands as well as the costs the government would have to incur to fend off future challenges.[55] These findings raise confidence in the predictive power

---

[54] As one might expect, when the value and costs associated with future land are included in the model, the measures that assess the simple number of challengers become insignificant. This suggests that future value and costs associated with future groups are more influential than simply the number of groups.

[55] When included on their own in the model in Table 5.6, both combined strategic value and the proportion of territory occupied by disaffected groups is negatively and significantly related to the decision to initiate a self-determination

Table 5.6. *The determinants of self-determination: the expected costs of future challenges (rare event logistic regression)*

STRATEGIC INFORMATION MODEL	
Past government behavior	
Past accommodation	1.29 (.680)^
Future government incentives	
Number of potential challengers	−.026 (.060)
Economic value of land at risk	−.055 (.026)*
Strategic value of land at risk	−.008 (.052)
Size of territory at risk	−.262 (.403)
MOTIVES/GRIEVANCES	
Cultural status	.350 (.180)^
Political status	.027 (.104)
Economic status	.020 (.109)
Loss of rights	.721 (.212)**
GDP per capita	−.024 (.037)
OPPORTUNITY	
Group resources	
Group geographic concentration	.573 (.176)**
Oil reserves	.271 (.433)
Proportion of national population	−.250 (1.25)
Youth bulge	−.099 (.034)
Neighboring co-ethnics	−.065 (.129)
Government weakness	
Government instability	.291 (.419)
Anocracy	.283 (.337)
National population	.371 (.156)*
Mountainous terrain	.003 (.008)
CONTROLS	
Democracy	−.036 (.027)
Year	.029 (.010)**
Constant	−65.9 (20.2)**
N	8855

Note: Figures are regression coefficients with standard errors in parentheses.

^ p < .10, * p < .05, ** p < .01

of the reputation model, but remain unclear about what aspects of the future governments and challengers are most focused on. Given these complex empirical issues, more detailed case studies are needed to clarify these relationships.

Violent versus non-violent challenges

One final issue needs to be addressed. The analyses to date have grouped violent and non-violent challenges together, treating them as one. Again, I investigate two problems that may result from aggregating the data in this way. Theoretically, one could argue that violent and non-violent challenges are qualitatively different and would not behave in similar ways. Groups, for example, may choose to use violence when seeking extreme goals such as independence but not when seeking autonomy. It is also possible that ethnic groups that are willing to use violence are impossible to deter, making them indifferent to any informational signals a government is trying to send. Finally, ethnic groups may also view violent and non-violent challenges as distinct from each other, refusing to draw inferences across cases. Collecting data on how governments respond to violent challenges, therefore, may tell us almost nothing about how these responses may influence ethnic groups making non-violent demands.

In order to determine whether the decision to aggregate these two types of challenges was an appropriate one, I isolated each group of cases and repeated the previous analysis. The results indicate that reputation matters in both sets of cases. Ethnic groups were significantly more likely to make both violent and non-violent demands if accommodation had occurred. They were also less likely to initiate either a violent or non-violent challenge when governments faced more ethnic groups and more potential future challenges. This suggests that violent and non-violent ethnic groups view each other as

movement. Presumably, in the latter case, groups that have control over a greater area represent a potent force that would be costly to defeat in war and thus provide an extra incentive to build a tough reputation.

engaged in the same strategic game with the government and do draw inferences from each other.[56]

There is, however, an interesting difference between the two types of challenges. Groups engaged in non-violent challenges were the only ones influenced by the level of democracy. The more democratic a country, the more likely an ethnic group was to make peaceful demands for change. Ethnic groups, however, were equally likely to launch violent challenges in democratic or non-democratic countries.

CONCLUSION

Table 5.7 summarizes the main findings from this chapter.

This chapter demonstrated that ethnic groups are being strategic in their decision to seek self-determination and can be deterred. Ethnic groups were significantly less likely to try to secede if they faced a government that had never granted autonomy or independence to another group. They were also significantly less likely to act if they believed the government had strong incentives to be tough because numerous ethnic groups existed, or because lots of valuable land could come under dispute in the future. These results held even when controlling for ethnic group grievances and opportunities to rebel.

The fact that ethnic groups behaved so closely to the predictions of the reputation model makes it impossible to claim that reputation building doesn't matter. Chapter 4 showed us that leaders clearly invested in reputation building when faced with multiple ethnic minorities. This chapter showed that ethnic groups were strongly influenced by this behavior. This is powerful evidence that, in the appropriate setting, reputation building is a rational strategy to pursue and that it has the desired effects.

Three tasks remain. The first is to determine whether private information is the mechanism causing governments and ethnic

---

[56] In this study I do not attempt to explain why ethnic groups might pursue violence as opposed to non-violence, or why some movements become more violent over time. For an excellent discussion of this phenomenon see Sambanis and Zinn (2004).

Table 5.7. *The main factors determining the separatist decision to challenge*

STRATEGIC INFORMATION	
Past government accommodation	Accommodation → Higher chance of challenge
Number of ethnic groups	More groups → Higher chance of challenge
Land value potential future challengers	Higher value → Higher chance of challenge
GRIEVANCES	
Various types of discrimination	More discrimination → Higher chance of challenge
Loss of political autonomy	Lost autonomy → Higher chance of challenge
OPPORTUNITY	
Geographic concentration	More concentrated → Higher chance of challenge
OTHER	
Year	More recent → Higher chance of challenge

groups to behave the way they do. Are ethnic minorities actively trying to collect information about the government, and is the government actively trying to manipulate this information? In other words, are private information and incentives to bluff the critical link connecting the parts? The second task is to control for potential sources of bias in the empirical analyses that may have created false positives. Can we debunk the theory when we look more closely at individual cases? The third is to determine whether I have inadvertently failed to include potentially important causal variables as a result of data limitations or error. These are issues that will be addressed in the case studies in Chapters 6 and 7.

Part III Case studies

Halfway through this project, I gave a talk at Yale University where I discussed, among other things, the research design of this book. I mentioned that the book would end with two case studies that would trace the details of government and ethnic group disputes over self-determination in Indonesia and the Philippines. A colleague I greatly respect pointed out the fundamental challenge I would face. "The problem with case studies," he said, "is that no one believes them."

Case studies are frequently misused. Sometimes they are employed simply to confirm a relationship that has already been revealed in large-n studies. Other times they are included to add color to otherwise dry and abstract theory. Often they are presented as proof of a particular theory even though the cases were selected in a biased way and were known to be confirmatory. It is no surprise, therefore, that people have become skeptical of this type of analysis.

But just because case studies can be done poorly does not mean that they do not serve a potentially important role in an empirical investigation. When done right, case studies can fill large holes left open by the quantitative analysis and can supply important details about the real impetus behind decisions. I have included case studies in this book for three reasons. First, the large-n studies presented in Chapters 4 and 5 tell us almost nothing about causality. They revealed that governments are more likely to fight ethnic separatists in countries with many ethnic minorities, and that ethnic minorities were more likely to rebel after government accommodation, but they don't tell us why either party behaved this way. The interpretation is that private information and incentives to bluff are driving these relationships, but this interpretation, while logical, has only been inferred from the data. Without case studies we would not know which of the many possible mechanisms really is at play.

The second reason to include case studies is to check whether critical variables were inadvertently omitted from earlier analyses or were poorly measured. We know, for example, that reliable data on the military capabilities of ethnic minorities do not exist, and measures of the psychological or symbolic value of land are poor. The fact that the statistical analysis did not find any significant relationships between these measures and different outcomes does not mean they do not exist. Close analysis of specific cases is necessary to obtain more information about these potentially important variables and determine whether their significance has been systematically underestimated in earlier tests.

The third reason has to do with additional theory building. The model presented in Chapter 2 could not explain a number of seemingly "irrational" behaviors exhibited by certain players in both the laboratory and in the field. The Kurds in Iraq, Iran, and Turkey, for example, chose to challenge their respective governments even though they knew heavy punishment was likely. Other ethnic groups, such as the Hungarians in the former Czechoslovakia, have chosen to stay quiet even after their government appeared willing to concede. Moreover, some governments, such as India, have backed down against ethnic challengers even when they knew many other groups existed. Case studies can help to explain why these outliers behaved this way.

CASE SELECTION

All of the cases included in the large-n studies were considered as possible candidates for closer examination. In the end, however, Indonesia and the Philippines were chosen because they were as similar as possible on all of the key independent variables except the one most closely associated with reputation building: the number of ethnic groups. Both Indonesia and the Philippines emerged out of a history of colonialism, both were led by long-standing autocrats who were then replaced by a series of short-lived, more democratic leaders, and governments in both cases experienced a post-authoritarian restructuring and shock that was relatively similar.

In terms of ethnic groups, minorities in both countries have experienced discrimination and repression at the hands of successive governments. Minorities in both countries have been the victims of transmigration policies, and have sought self-determination, in part, because the government had rescinded autonomy they had enjoyed in the past. The one big factor associated with reputation building that was not the same between the two countries was the number of ethnic groups. Indonesia is one of the world's most ethnically diverse countries, the Philippines is not.[1]

Still, Indonesia and the Philippines are different in a number of respects that make any comparison imperfect. Indonesia, for example, is a predominantly Muslim country, the Philippines predominantly Catholic. In addition, Indonesia's colonial legacy was with the Dutch, while the Philippines' was with the United States. The Philippines was consolidated with less difficulty and violence than Indonesia, and has traditionally had more private control over resources than Indonesia.[2] Still, the fact that the two countries are similar on many of the key factors should offer some insights into government and ethnic group behavior in these two cases.

The case studies that follow do not answer all the questions we have about reputation building or prove that different presidents cared more about reputation than about oil or natural gas or other interests. They also do not prove beyond a doubt that ethnic leaders were deterred because of signals they received about government toughness. But they will reveal additional details about why different players behaved the way they did and add to the cumulative base

---

[1] Indonesia is one of the most ethnically diverse countries in the world with over 360 tribal and ethno-linguistic groups, many of which are geographically concentrated on islands or peripheral regions of the archipelago. The Philippines, dominated by Christian Malays, has only two main minority groups.

[2] See Che Man (1990: 46).

of evidence this study has collected about reputation building and its effects. What we will see is that Indonesia's presidents did engage in costly signaling and that this signaling did deter at least some ethnic groups from seeking self-determination, even in those cases where groups had otherwise strong reasons to rebel.

6   Indonesia: many ethnic groups, few demands

The next two chapters evaluate whether reputation building really is the mechanism causing governments to fight so aggressively against ethnic separatists, and whether it is also causing ethnic groups to remain silent. I start with Indonesia for four reasons. For one, Indonesia is one of the most ethnically diverse countries in the world, with over 360 tribal and ethno-linguistic groups, many of which are geographically concentrated on islands or peripheral regions of the archipelago. If incentives to invest in reputation exist, they should exist here. Second, Indonesia's ethnic groups have behaved quite differently across regions and over time. Some ethnic minorities, such as the East Timorese and the Acehnese, have demanded and fought for independence, while the vast majority of ethnic groups, such as the Balinese and the Minahasa, have not. This intracountry variation allows us to study differences across regions. Third, government leaders have reacted to these challenges in diverse ways. President Suharto, for example, spent thirty-three years aggressively repressing dissent, claiming this was necessary to "safeguard the unity of Indonesia."[1] While his successor, President Habibie, offered independence to East Timor almost immediately after coming to power. This addresses the main puzzle driving this book, namely why some governments negotiate while others fight. Finally, there is also substantial variation across Indonesia's provinces along key economic, political and military variables. Some provinces, such as East Nusa Tenggara, West Kalimantan, and Maluku, have significantly higher rates of poverty than the rest of

---

[1] Schwarz (2000: 210).

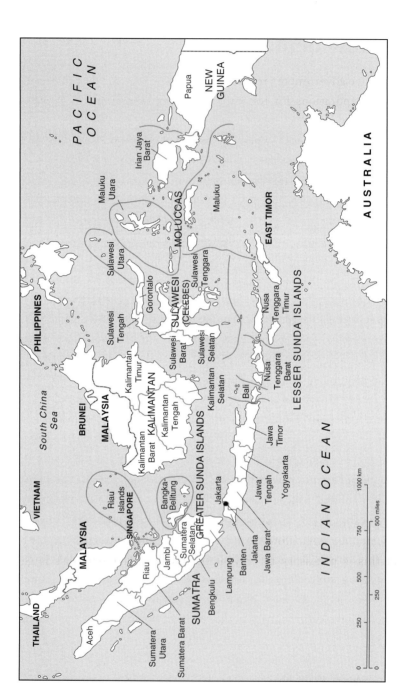

MAP 6.1 Map of Indonesia

the country.[2] While other provinces, such as Aceh and Riau, are rich in natural resources. Observing which ethnic groups choose to challenge the government, when they choose to challenge, and how successive governments responded, will help reveal whether leaders rely on reputations for toughness to deter separatists, or if other factors dominate decisions more.

In what follows, I trace the interplay between the Indonesian government and its ethnic groups from the declaration of independence in 1945 until the end of President Megawati Sukarnoputri's rule in 2004. One of the main goals of this chapter is to determine whether private information and incentives to invest in reputation building influence the decision by ethnic groups to seek self-determination, and the decision by different presidents to negotiate. Did the Dayak of West Kalimantan choose to remain quiet because they witnessed aggressive crack-downs by the Indonesian military in Ambon and East Timor, or did they remain quiet because they had no reason or desire to rebel? Did Presidents Sukarno, Suharto, Wahid, and Sukarnoputri refuse to negotiate with separatists because they feared this would convince other more valuable regions to secede, or did they refuse to negotiate for reasons unrelated to reputation building?

Determining causation, however, is not easy. First, public statements by leaders may be false or misleading. Government leaders may have incentives to *claim* that their behavior is driven by reputational concerns when in fact they are driven by more self-interested motives. Indonesia's military, for example, has always advocated an unyielding stance toward ethnic separatists, arguing that this is necessary to prevent the breakup of Indonesia's large and diverse archipelago. In reality, however, their tough military stance toward separatists has allowed them to maintain lucrative commercial activities in those regions. Public statements in favor

---

[2] The Sasak living in West Nusa Tenggara, for example, have an infant mortality rate almost four times as high as the Javanese living in Yogyakarta.

of reputation building, therefore, do not necessarily signify that leaders care about their reputation or that they believe it will have any deterrent effects.

Second, it is difficult to attribute causation to events that do not occur. If reputation building succeeds in deterring most ethnic groups from challenging the state, then little or no separatist activity should be observed among most of Indonesia's ethnic minorities. How does one prove that the Batak in Sumatra chose not to secede because they anticipated harsh treatment by the government and not because of some other reason? Ethnic group leaders might admit that they were deterred by the fear of government retribution, as Riau's leader did in 1999, but leaders are more likely to deny any desire to challenge even if they did have plans. A dearth of self-determination challenges in multi-ethnic Indonesia, therefore, might offer some support for the reputation theory, but does not irrefutably prove it.

There are two possible, though imperfect, ways to deal with these problems. The first is to supplement statements by leaders with a careful analysis of their actions. If leaders such as Sukarno and Suharto really are driven by reputational concerns, they should engage in very clear signaling behavior regardless of the speeches they choose to give. Leaders, for example, should publicize the costs ethnic minorities will have to pay for defiance, advertising the brutality of any government crack-down. If civilians are massacred in a government raid, this fact should be exposed, not hidden or denied. In this way, observers can begin to distinguish between those governments interested in deterrence and those that are not. A second strategy is to trace the exact timing of ethnic group demands. If reputation influences ethnic group decisions then there should be a clear temporal connection between a government accommodating one group and additional ethnic group activity. This should be especially revealing since many of the underlying political, economic, and social conditions will not change during these times.

The rest of the chapter is divided into four sections that correspond to the tenure of Indonesia's first four presidents. Dividing the data this way allows me to determine if different presidents have distinct preferences for how to deal with ethnic minorities, or if they follow similar patterns of behavior regardless of type. It also allows me to observe how a leader's tenure may affect incentives to be tough. Each section begins with a summary of the basic economic, political, and military conditions at the time, as well as competing predictions about the likelihood of self-determination disputes given these conditions. This is followed by a discussion of ethnic group activity (or inactivity) and the degree to which this activity was predicted by the theories. Each section ends with an analysis of how the government responded and the justification various leaders gave for their actions.

BUILDING THE NEW REPUBLIC, THE RULE OF SUKARNO 1945–67

Underlying conditions

Indonesia did not become an independent country until 1945 when President Sukarno took power after Japan's brutal occupation during World War II.[3] The country was composed of a series of islands, most of which had been under Dutch colonial rule, and most of which voluntarily agreed to become part of the newly independent state. Still, not all provinces stood to benefit from being incorporated into the larger republic. Per capita income was lowest in the eastern and western provinces of Benkulu, West Nusa Tenggara, East Nusa Tenggara, Gorontalo, Maluku, and North Maluku, and highest in Jakarta and East Kalimantan. Aceh, Riau, and East Kalimantan had significant natural resources that would have made them financially self-sufficient, and Ambon enjoyed significant autonomy during Dutch colonial times that it would lose if incorporated.[4] If self-determination were sought, these were the provinces with at least some reason to do so.

---

[3] The Dutch did not officially recognize Indonesia's independence until 1949.

[4] East Timor and West Papua remained under Portuguese and Dutch control respectively at this time and are, therefore, not included in this list.

In terms of opportunity, ethnic groups also faced a government that was weak, poor, and deeply divided by ethnic, regional, class, and religious differences at this time.[5] Until the mid-1950s, Sukarno was essentially a figurehead president and it was not until 1963 that he was able to consolidate political control and put down the many internal power struggles that plagued his government. If grievances and opportunity were sufficient reasons to seek self-determination, numerous demands should have been made between 1945 and 1963 while the government was still quite weak.

Ethnic group activity

Of the over 300 ethnic minorities in Indonesia, only two sought self-determination during Sukarno's fifteen years in office: the Ambonese of Maluku in 1950, and the Papuans of West New Guinea in 1963.[6] This small number of challenges fits the predictions of the reputation theory. Given the large number of potential separatist regions, Sukarno had strong incentives to react aggressively to these early demands.

Almost immediately after Sukarno came to office, the Ambonese of Maluku sent a telegram to the president stating that they were setting up the independent Republic of South Moluccas on the main islands of Amboina, Buru, and Ceram in the Maluku islands.[7] The islands did not contain particularly rich resources, nor were the Ambonese victims of discriminatory or exploitative government policies. The main grievance motivating the Ambonese was the autonomy they would lose by joining the new state. Unlike almost all the other regions in Indonesia, Ambon had enjoyed a privileged relationship with the Dutch. The capital of the Dutch East Indies had been located

---

[5] In 1950 Indonesia ranked 68 out of 75 countries in terms of gross domestic product (GDP). Fifteen years later, it ranked 117 out of 125 countries (Gleditsch, 2002).

[6] West New Guinea is referred to by a number of different names. The Indonesia government's official name for the region was first West Irian and then Irian Jaya. Indigenous inhabitants and human rights non-governmental organizations (NGOs), however, refer to it as West Papua. I defer to its indigenous name throughout the book.

[7] For a more in-depth history on the revolt, see especially Chauvel (1990).

in Ambon, the Ambonese were educated by the Dutch, and the pre-dominantly Christian population was given a key role in the colonial administration and military.[8] By joining Indonesia, Ambon's elites would not only lose their favored political and military positions, but they would also be entering a state dominated by a Muslim majority that was resentful of Ambon's former colonial sympathies.

West Papuans had a similar reason to seek separation. When Indonesia's independence was recognized by the Dutch in 1949, the Netherlands refused to cede West New Guinea to the new Indonesian state and instead sought to grant the region independence. By 1961, the Netherlands had allowed the region to hold elections, form a Papuan council, and raise its own flag next to that of the Dutch.[9] Loss of autonomy, therefore, was the key factor motivating both the Ambonese and West Papuans to seek independence.

Government responses and analysis

The Sukarno government's response to demands by the Ambonese and Papuans is revealing. If Sukarno was driven purely by economic and strategic interests, his government should have fought hard to retain West Papua and it should have let Ambon go. While West Papua is the largest and one of the richest provinces in Indonesia, Ambon is a small island in eastern Indonesia known mainly for its trade in cloves. Sukarno, however, chose to fight equally aggres-sively for both. Sukarno's immediate response to the telegraph from Ambon was brutal repression. Within a month, the Indonesian mili-tary crushed the rebellion, imprisoned the leaders, and sent 12,000 soldiers and their families into exile in the Netherlands. According to one expert,

> The TNI [Indonesian military] launched its attack on the
> Ambonese islands in September 1950, but it was nearly three

---

[8] Frederick and Worden (1993: 47).

[9] The rebels of the Free Papua Organization have never been able to advance against the much better-equipped Indonesian army. But the mountainous terrain means that the military has also never been able to gain complete control.

months later, and after great human and material sacrifice, that it finally occupied the town of Ambon.[10]

At no point during the conflict did Sukarno or the military agree to negotiate.

Sukarno was similarly harsh against the relatively weak Free Papua Movement. In a speech before a crowd of 30,000, Sukarno declared: "If this arouses the world – we don't care, we don't care, we don't care! We want West Irian!"[11] Military efforts were headed by Brigadier General Suharto, Sukarno's eventual successor to the presidency, and his policy included murder, political assassination, imprisonment, torture, and aerial bombings. According to one expert, "[r]esistance to the regime grew and was met with armed brutality. The army behaved in the fashion that was customary in the outer regions: the soldiery with lethal savagery, the officers turning human and other resources to their own enrichment."[12] Within two years, Sukarno had taken the province by force.

Certainly, part of West Papua's appeal for Indonesia was its abundance of natural resources. Once incorporated, Papua would contain 24 percent of Indonesia's total forests, 54 percent of its biodiversity, and enormous mineral deposits and hydrocarbon fields.[13] But its resources do not explain why Sukarno was so public about the costs the Papuans would have to pay to remain independent. It also does not explain why Sukarno fought so hard for the tiny islands in Maluku rather than simply allowing them to leave. It was the decision to fight so publicly and brutally in both places that suggests that a more protracted strategy of deterrence was being pursued.

SUHARTO 1967–98

Underlying conditions

Sukarno's fifteen-year rule ended in 1967 when he was reluctantly replaced by General Suharto following a six-month power struggle.

---

[10] Chauvel (1990: 258–9).   [11] *Keesing's Record of World Events*, June 1962.
[12] Challis (2001: 145–6).   [13] Forbes (1992: 13).

The first fifteen years of Suharto's tenure were economically good ones for the country as a whole, especially between 1970 and 1980 when per capita income doubled and economic growth increased by an average of 7 to 8 percent a year.[14] Still, a number of provinces continued to have economic, political, and/or religious reasons to seek independence.

In terms of economic grievances, two types of groups had incentives to seek independence: those that continued to suffer under deep poverty and those that occupied land with significant natural resource wealth. West Nusa Tenggara, East Nusa Tenggara, Sulawesi Tenggara, Maluku, and West Papua continued to have the highest percentage of their population living below the poverty line.[15] In contrast, Aceh and East Kalimantan were both found to contain large deposits of natural gas in 1971, and gold was discovered in East Kalimantan in 1987. If arguments based on economic grievances were correct, these would be the regions likely to challenge.

In terms of political grievances, Suharto reinstated and greatly expanded the transmigration program initiated by the Dutch in 1905. Between 1969 and 1995, more than 8 million landless people were moved from Java, Bali, and Madura to less populated areas in West Papua, Kalimantan, Sumatra, and Sulawesi. Although popular with settlers who were often given economic inducements to move, the program generated deep hostility from indigenous groups in the targeted regions. Transmigration was highest between 1979 and 1984, and directed most heavily at the provinces of Lampung and South Sumatra.[16] If discriminatory or despised government policies were the only factors in the decision to rebel, then self-determination

---

[14] Vatikiotis (1998: 35).

[15] *Badan Pusat Statistik* (*BPS*, Statistics Indonesia), www.bps.go.id.

[16] Twenty provinces in total received transmigrants, but two provinces in particular received far more than any other: Lampung (received almost four times more than the next closest, and represented more than half of all transmigrants), and South Sumatra (unu.edu website).

movements in both of these regions should have emerged during this time.[17]

Discontent also arose over the government's treatment of Christians within Indonesia. Suharto systematically repressed Christian activity in North Sumatra, East Nusa Tenggara, and North Sulawesi as large numbers of Javanese began converting to Christianity. Thus, even though the 1970s and early 1980s were a period of economic improvement for Indonesia as a whole, the economic downturn between 1982 and 1986, as well as the aggressive transmigration policies, discriminatory religious policies, and expropriation policies pursued by the Suharto governments, created incentives for a number of provinces to seek self-determination.

Ethnic group activity

Events during Suharto's tenure are telling. Suharto faced no self-determination challenges in his first ten years in office. None of the groups experiencing economic, political, or religious discrimination chose to rebel. Lampung, which received four times more transmigrants than any other province, remained quiet. East Kalimantan, with its newly discovered natural gas fields, remained quiet. East Nusa Tenggara, which was both extremely poor and religiously oppressed, did nothing. The only two provinces that chose to challenge Suharto were East Timor in 1975 and Aceh in 1976.

The East Timorese were the first group to confront Suharto and they did so for one reason. In 1975, Portugal abandoned its colony and Suharto invaded, declaring it Indonesia's twenty-seventh province. The East Timorese did not want to become part of Indonesia, had never been part of Indonesia, and were adamant that they should be allowed to determine their fate after the Portuguese left. Suharto, however, gave them no choice. Violent resistance began immediately.

---

[17] Although after years of transmigration the Lampung Pubian represented a very small fraction of the population in Lampung.

The Acehnese were the only other ethnic group to seek self-determination during Suharto's thirty-three-year reign, and the reason was again related to autonomy. On two separate occasions the Indonesian government had promised Aceh a degree of self-rule, and in both cases Jakarta failed to deliver. The first came in 1950, when Sukarno promised to grant Aceh special status as a reward for its help in the war for independence against the Dutch. The second came in 1959 when Sukarno offered Aceh autonomy over religious, cultural, and educational affairs. Neither offer was ever fully implemented and by 1976 a small movement emerged, the Free Aceh Movement, or Gerakan Aceh Merdeka (GAM), led by Hasan Muhammad di Tiro, demanding independence.[18]

Aceh's decision to challenge Suharto is illuminating for at least three reasons. First, the Acehnese were the first ethnic group to seek self-determination from a government they had voluntarily agreed to join. They were, therefore, quite different from the Ambonese and East Timorese who had been incorporated into Indonesia against their will. Why did the Acehnese suddenly decide to separate in 1976 after so many years of silence? Second, the Acehnese were also the first group occupying a resource-rich region to actively seek independence. In fact, unlike most other regions in Indonesia, Aceh produced more wealth for Jakarta than they received in return. To what degree did natural resources play a role in the decision to seek independence and the government's decision to fight? Finally, the Acehnese were the first group to actively seek independence after observing the government's brutality in East Timor. Why were the Acehnese not deterred from seeking self-determination when it was clear how Jakarta was likely to respond?

The timing of Aceh's challenge strongly suggests that economic resources were the catalyst for independence, more so than any unfulfilled promises of autonomy. The Acehnese had lived for decades with the knowledge that special autonomy had not been

---

[18] For an excellent account of GAM during its early years see Ross (2005).

implemented, yet they chose to rebel only after vast natural gas reserves were discovered in 1971 and exploited by the government.

But why were the Acehnese not deterred by the brutality of the government's military campaigns, especially the ongoing one in East Timor? A closer examination of GAM reveals that a majority of Acehnese did not support di Tiro's initial attempt at independence and would have preferred not to challenge Suharto.[19] In 1976, GAM was a small, underfinanced guerrilla movement consisting of at most two hundred members.[20] It was not until 1998 that GAM developed a large popular base, and this only occurred as a result of the military's harsh repression in the preceding eight years. The fact that di Tiro and GAM had such a difficult time building the movement suggests that oil and natural gas may have been sufficient to convince di Tiro and a handful of supporters to fight for independence, but not the majority of Acehnese who were likely to pay the heavy costs of fighting.

Government response and analysis

Suharto's response to self-determination movements in both East Timor and Aceh mirrors what one would expect from a leader wanting to signal toughness. Starting in 1975, Suharto pursued a policy of brutal repression in East Timor. Between November 1975 and April 1976 Indonesia sent an estimated 35,000 Indonesian troops to the island and within four months killed approximately 60,000 Timorese.[21] According to Martinho da Costa Lopes, bishop in the capital city of Dili, "[t]he soldiers who landed started killing everyone they could find. There were many dead bodies in the streets – all we could see were the soldiers killing, killing, killing."[22]

One explanation for the viciousness of the response is that Indonesia had strong material incentives to fight for East Timor

---

[19] See especially Smith (2002: 68–89) and Rabasa and Chalk (2001).

[20] See Ross (2005: 41).

[21] Total deaths would eventually number approximately 250,000 East Timorese out of a total population of about 1 million.

[22] Quoted in Taylor (1991: 68).

since the Sunrise oil field had just been discovered off its coast in 1974. This discovery, however, does not explain why Suharto was willing to continue fighting long after the field was determined to be relatively small, or why Suharto was willing to spend considerably more money to hold on to East Timor than the government could ever expect to extract from these reserves.[23]

A second explanation often given is that Jakarta had strong strategic reasons for gaining control over East Timor. Some have argued that Suharto and his generals fought so hard for East Timor in order to prevent a communist state from being established in the middle of Indonesia.[24] This was echoed by Suharto's close advisors, General Ali Murtopo and Brigadier General Benny Murdani, who claimed that it was important to annex East Timor to prevent a "Cuba on the doorstep."[25] This argument, however, cannot explain why Suharto continued to fight for the region long after the threat of communism had disappeared. If Jakarta had been truly motivated by the fear of a communist foothold, its value for retaining the region should have vanished in 1989 with the demise of the Soviet Union. Suharto, however, continued to fight for East Timor for an additional ten years and never agreed to negotiate at any point during his tenure.

Suharto's government was equally harsh towards both GAM and the Acehnese civilian population. By June 1990, Suharto declared Aceh a Military Operations Area (Daerah Operasi Militer, or DOM), and placed it under martial law. The army was given a "virtual free hand" to crush the rebels using any means possible and counter-insurgency was pursued in a very public manner.[26] According to one account:

> Soldiers keep a high profile, driving in daylight with headlights, advertising the fate of captured insurgents. Arrested GPK [GAM]

---

[23] Indonesia stood to gain only 18 percent of the revenue from the field after it signed a deal with Australia in 1989 ceding the remaining 82 percent to them.

[24] See for example Elson (2001).   [25] Schwarz (2000: 201).

[26] Rand report, 2002, p. 30.

suspects cowered in the back of open trucks with semi-automatic weapons thrust under their noses by soldiers.[27]

Again, the main explanation offered in the literature for this response is that Aceh was too economically and strategically important for Suharto to give up. Aceh is one of Indonesia's richest provinces, with large reserves of oil, natural gas, coal, and mineral deposits.[28] It also borders the strategically important Strait of Malacca. The Suharto administration's behavior toward both Aceh and East Timor, however, suggests that the government had a much longer-range view of the problem. In January 1990, General Murdani gave a fiery speech in Dili where he made clear that:

> There have been bigger rebellions, there have been greater differences of opinion with the government ... We will crush them all! This is not in order to crush East Timorese but to safeguard the unity of Indonesian territory physically and in other ways.[29]

Still, citations, even those taken directly from policymakers, are not indisputable evidence of a leader's real motivation. One would gain additional confidence in the theory if one observed a clear difference in behavior between leaders driven by concerns of present value and leaders driven by concerns over reputation. If Suharto was motivated more by oil or natural gas, or his military prospects against the East Timorese and the Acehnese, he should have been sensitive to the cost calculations for each of these wars. Once it became clear that a war could not be easily won, or won at a reasonable price, attempts to negotiate a settlement should have taken place. If, however, Suharto was driven by the desire to deter, then a different set of calculations would matter. In this case, the costs of fighting the East Timorese and Acehnese would be compared to the costs of fighting potential copy-cat challengers in Riau, East Kalimatan, and South Sulawesi, and Suharto should be willing

---

[27] Pisani (1990: 12).   [28] Lekic (1999: 9).   [29] Schwarz (2000: 210).

to incur much higher costs even if victory was unlikely. The fact that war in East Timor continued for almost fifteen years at a high cost to the government and ended in victory for the East Timorese, and the fact that the war in Aceh continued for decades with little military advancement, suggests that a longer-term strategy was being pursued.

A second way to distinguish between the different mechanisms is to see how the government handled information surrounding these wars. A government motivated by the desire to defeat an opponent rather than signal toughness, would have had incentives to limit media attention and hide any losses. A government motivated by a desire to signal toughness would likely provide as much evidence as possible that it was willing to fight hard under any conditions even if it drew international censure.

A review of headlines in the *Jakarta Post* between 1975 and 1998 reveals that the government did little to limit information about government brutality.[30] During this time, there were 133 newspaper articles that mentioned military repression in East Timor in the headline or lead paragraph. Headlines such as "Army Crackdown gives East Timor Little Hope," "Terror in Timor," "Timorese Nightmare," and "Fear and Repression Still Rule Area Occupied by Indonesia" were common. This attention caused Indonesia to become known as a major violator of human rights by the international community, but did not cause Suharto to change his policy.

Two events, in particular, show that Suharto was not deterred from engaging in public violence even if television cameras were present to capture the event. During Pope John Paul II's first visit to East Timor in October 1989, police violently beat pro-independence demonstrators in front of journalists filming the visit.[31] Two years

---

[30] The *Jakarta Post* is a daily English language newspaper oriented towards local English speakers and the diplomatic community. It is known to have strong ties to the government.

[31] Ricklefs (2001: 390).

later, the military opened fire on a funeral procession when it evolved into an independence demonstration, even though international television cameras were filming.[32] Had Suharto been focused solely on winning the war in East Timor it is likely that he would have avoided this type of publicity rather than seek it out.

A third way to distinguish between mechanisms is to examine the effect government brutality had on the immediate war effort. If Suharto was interested only in eliminating rebellions in East Timor and Aceh, he should have pursued tactics that reduced popular support for the rebels. In Aceh, however, the brutal and public way in which the military repressed the Acehnese turned the local population against the government and created enormous public support for a previously small movement.[33]

All of this suggests that Suharto had real reputational reasons for inflicting heavy costs on East Timor and Aceh. Suharto almost certainly had some interest in East Timor's Sunrise oil field and in Aceh's extensive oil and gas reserves, but he also appeared to be quite anxious about preventing other *more lucrative* oil regions from seeking independence as well. Aceh had abundant oil, but Riau, East Kalimantan, and northwestern Java had much more.[34]

The reputation theory helps to explain why there were so few separatist challenges during Suharto's time in office, and why Suharto responded as violently as he did. It does not, however, explain why Suharto failed to encounter an increasing number of challenges toward the end of his tenure when he should have had stronger incentives to negotiate, or why he did not make concessions to the East Timorese and the Acehnese as his time in office came to an end.[35] Not only did Suharto increase the brutality by

---

[32] Ricklefs (2001: 395).   [33] Ricklefs (2001: 389).

[34] In 2000, Riau alone produced nearly half of Indonesia's total output of oil, worth about $10 billion a year. There have been separatist grumblings in Riau, but no attempt to organize violent resistance.

[35] This is not completely true. Independence movements did become more aggressive in East Timor and West Papua during this time (General Board of Global Ministries (GBGM) news archive).

which he fought the two groups in the 1990s, but he continued to reject any mention of negotiations even in his last months in office.[36]

In some ways, Suharto's behavior toward the end of his tenure is similar to the behavior we observed in our subjects in the laboratory as well as the behavior of autocrats in Chapter 4. Recall that conciliatory defenders in the experiment were willing to invest in reputation building much longer than the theory predicted and that entrants were willing to remain quiet much longer than expected. In Chapter 3 I hypothesized that defenders were behaving this way because they were risk averse; they did not want to appear weak until it was clear that only a few challengers remained. Suharto may have been similarly risk averse, but his behavior suggests a second possible explanation.[37] Suharto appeared to be playing a signaling game not only with various separatist groups around Indonesia, but also with various internal political rivals. As an authoritarian leader in a country with a relatively independent military, concessions would likely have hastened his removal from office by an army with no interest in negotiations. Making concessions in his last months in office would not only signal to ethnic groups that his government was weak but would also signal to Suharto's political rivals that he was vulnerable to overthrow. Reputation building, therefore, does appear to be particularly important for authoritarian leaders whose tenure in office is likely linked to the ability to deter political as well as ethnic competitors.

---

[36] By 1997, it must have been clear to most ethnic groups that Suharto would not be in power much longer; Suharto was seventy years old in a country where the average life expectancy for males was sixty-two (Population Resource Center, Demographic Profile of Indonesia).

[37] It is also possible, however, that Suharto simply believed he would be in office for a much longer period of time, making continued investments in deterrence worthwhile. As late as March 1998, seventy-two days before he was forced to resign, Suharto publicly declared that "God willing, I will be in this same forum five years from now to deliver my accountability speech." His continued investment in reputation, therefore, may have also matched his expectation about future interactions.

THE SURPRISING TENURE OF HABIBIE: 1998

Underlying conditions

Suharto resigned in May 1998 in the wake of a severe economic crisis and was replaced by his vice-president, B. J. Habibie.[38] From the start, Habibie was viewed as nothing more than a transitional leader whose role was to serve out the remainder of Suharto's five-year term and perhaps institute some political and economic reforms. Within weeks of entering office, however, Habibie allowed political parties to organize, removed controls over the media, released political prisoners, and made preparations to hold free and fair elections for both the parliament and the president.[39] His government also radically reversed Suharto's long-standing policy towards East Timor in January 1999. In a move that surprised many, Habibie announced that his government was willing to offer East Timor independence. According to Habibie, East Timor would be able to "decide by themselves" whether they would remain part of Indonesia or become their own independent state.[40] A referendum for August 1999 was scheduled.

Two reasons are frequently given for why Habibie chose to offer the East Timorese independence. First, Indonesia was under increasing international pressure to settle the damaging war, particularly from neighboring Australia, which threatened to support the East Timorese if Habibie resisted.[41] Second, the war in East Timor was draining Indonesia's increasingly limited resources.[42] By 1999, the

---

[38] Schwarz (2000: 408).

[39] See Bertrand (2004: 10). By the time Habibie's successor, Abdurrahman Wahid, came to power in 1999, Indonesia had gained significantly on Polity IV's measure of democracy, moving from a –7 to a +7 in a short period of time. (Polity IV is a dataset on the political characteristics of a state.)

[40] "Indonesia's Habibie wants East Timor problem fixed by 2000," CNN.com, February 11, 1999.

[41] Australia's support was particularly important because it was one of the few countries that officially recognized Indonesia's sovereignty over East Timor. See Keesings, January 1999 (www.keesings.com/keesings_record_of_world_events).

[42] Many scholars have argued that the heavy casualties suffered by the military in East Timor influenced the decision. See especially Schwarz (2000: 421–2).

government had spent hundreds of millions of dollars to prosecute the war and killed approximately one-quarter of East Timor's population, yet was still unable to eliminate resistance.

Ethnic activity

Separatist activity increased during Habibie's seventeen-month tenure, but not as much as the reputation theory would have expected. Recall that the hypothesis $H1_{eg}$ in Chapter 2 predicted that ethnic groups would be significantly more likely to challenge if they had observed the government accommodating another group. This was supported in the laboratory experiments in Chapter 3, which found that defenders who had backed down faced significantly more challenges as a result, by the results in Chapter 4 on subsequent challenges, and by the results in Chapter 5 on ethnic group decisions to seek self-determination.

Habibie's decision to allow the East Timorese to vote on independence *was* followed by a surge in demands, but only from those groups that had already sought self-determination. Within weeks of Habibie's announcement, the Christian Ambonese, unhappy with Jakarta's continuing policy of transmigration and the increasing Islamization of the island, again declared the establishment of the independent Republic of South Maluku after decades of quiet. West Papuans did the same. In February 1999, three weeks after Habibie's concessions to the East Timorese, John Ondawame, international spokesman for the Free Papua Movement, told reporters "we would like to see the Indonesian government's new policy towards East Timor be repeated again in West Papua."[43] And in November 1999, activists in Aceh argued that "[i]f East Timor was granted the right to vote on its future, then there is no reason Aceh should not be next."[44] The rapid outburst of demands led many newspaper headlines to

---

[43] *Courier Mail* (1999: 19).
[44] Quote by Kautsar, an activist in Aceh, from Lekic (1999: 9).

decree that that Indonesia was "falling apart," and western diplomats to worry about "the Balkanisation of Indonesia."[45]

But why did other ethnic groups not rebel? Ethnic groups in Riau, North Sumatra, East Kalimantan, and North Sulawesi had all expressed dissatisfaction with Jakarta, but all remained silent. Part of the answer appears to be that these regions were deterred by the signal Jakarta had already sent about the price of independence. Habibie may have agreed to grant East Timor independence, but it was only after the region had first suffered heavy consequences. Moreover, even after the referendum was held, the military continued to signal that independence would not be easy. According to Ricklefs,

> [I]t seems that ABRI [Indonesia Armed Forces] officers decided that, if a referendum should produce a vote for separation, they would engineer the devastation of East Timor. This was probably meant to be part revenge and part salutary warning to other parts of the nation which might seek greater autonomy.[46]

Between August and September 1999, between 100 and 1,500 East Timorese were killed and approximately another 250,000 fled to West Timor as pro-Indonesian militias supported by the Indonesian military conducted brutal campaigns. Thus, even as Habibie was publicly declaring his intention to allow East Timor to decide on secession, the military was signaling how it was likely to respond.

The information ethnic groups were receiving about Habibie's willingness to negotiate, therefore, must be taken in the context of all the information they were receiving about the price of independence. Despite Habibie's willingness to grant independence to the East Timorese, the signal other ethnic groups were receiving was that it would be very costly. Ethnic groups, thus, continued to be deterred despite these concessions to East Timor. In March 1999, Tabrini Rab, leader of Riau's nascent indigenous movement, canceled plans

---

[45] Estrade (1999: 21).   [46] Ricklefs (2001: 412).

to declare independence, claiming the fear of military retribution. According to Colonel M. Gadillah, the local military commander for the Indonesian army, who spoke with Rab: "[w]e discussed on Wednesday what [they] would gain and lose if Riau were to break away from the republic. [Rab] understood that his idea would only cause, instead of solve, problems as happened in Aceh and Irian."[47]

Habibie's decision to accommodate the East Timorese and the varied reaction to this decision by different ethnic groups suggests an important extension to our theory of reputation building. Recall that the theory made a number of simplifying assumptions, one of which was that governments had only two ways to respond to an ethnic group demanding self-determination: they could either make a concession and thus avoid war, or they could fight.

In reality, governments have a third option: to fight a lengthy battle and then offer a deal. Jakarta was able to fight the East Timorese for almost fifteen years and then make a concession, without losing its reputation for being tough against separatists. Habibie's concession did encourage existing groups to renew their demands for independence, and in this sense he did suffer some reputational loss – but it was relatively small compared to the loss of reputation that would have occurred had concessions been made in the absence of a fight. Habibie's behavior, therefore, suggests that a leader can negotiate with one group without fearing a flood of challenges, as long as those groups know they will have to pay a very high price to gain independence.

Government response and analysis

Although Habibie made concessions to East Timor, he refused to negotiate with separatists in Ambon, Aceh, and West Papua.[48] Beginning in

---

[47] *Tempo News* (1999).

[48] Habibie, however, did initiate a new policy of decentralization and regional autonomy. As early as May 1999, Habibie signed two laws to decentralize political and economic power. The first was Law no. 22/1999 on regional government, which assigned all government functions except for finance, foreign affairs, defense, religion, and state administration down to the district level. The

late 1998, Jakarta renewed military violence against each region, and again, the violence was very public. In May 1999, less than four months after Habibie offered independence to East Timor, the Indonesian military massacred thirty-eight protesters in Aceh. According to a reporter, "[t]he bloodbath was filmed and shown on television across Indonesia, which is unusual and led some to suggest it was broadcast to send a message to separatists across the country."[49]

This desire to deter additional separatists was expressed by numerous government officials during this time. In November 1999, Habibie's adviser, Dewi Fortuna Anwar, told reporters that "one cannot even entertain the idea of Indonesia splitting up because – where does it stop? ... If Aceh goes, the legacy of Indonesia goes. Each province will vote itself out."[50] Indonesia's state minister of regional autonomy, Ryaas Rasyid, argued that Aceh was "the most serious situation we are facing now. If Indonesia should disintegrate, it would start in Aceh and Irian Jaya, that's what I believe."[51] Habibie himself was careful to differentiate East Timor from other regions in Indonesia. He made clear that East Timor was distinct from Aceh, Riau, and other provinces in three key respects: East Timor had not chosen to voluntarily join the republic in 1945, East Timor had never been part of the original Dutch colony, and there had been significant international support, especially from the United Nations, for independence for East Timor. The same support did not exist for other provinces in Indonesia. According to the foreign minister, Ali Alatas, "[t]he other provinces have different bonds than East Timor, which only became part of Indonesia in 1976, including the fact that East Timor was never colonized by the Dutch. So it is not necessary and not relevant to compare the other provinces with East Timor."[52]

---

second, Law 25/1999, allowed local governments to keep a greater share of revenue generated from natural resources from the area, as well as personal income tax. Full implementation was promised by 2001, but few believed this would occur. For more details see Lloyd (2000: 3) and Ahmad and Mansoor (2000).

[49] Thoenes (1999: 3).   [50] Gunalan (1999: 48).   [51] Chew (1999).

[52] *Republika*, Jakarta. In Indonesian, January 29, 1999.

Events surrounding Habibie's concessions to East Timor reveal that reputations cannot be as easily lost as the theory would have expected. Leaders can make concessions and not appear weak if their governments have already signaled that concessions will not be granted easily. Habibie did offer independence to East Timor, but this independence was the result of a path that few groups would want to follow. Moreover, Habibie was able to quickly convince other groups that East Timor was unique within Indonesia and the same arrangement would not be made with any other regions. According to Habibie, "[w]hile independence of East Timor may not be enough to break up the republic, the secession of Aceh would be interpreted very differently." Thus, governments need not fight to the bitter end, but only long enough to deter other less resolute groups.

THE FACTIOUS YEARS OF ABDURRAHMAN WAHID: 1999–2001

Underlying conditions

The tenure of B. J. Habibie ended in October 1999 after Indonesia's first free elections were held. Habibie was replaced by Abdurrahman Wahid (also known as Gus Dur), a popular Muslim scholar and moderate political leader who was in poor health and known to be unpredictable. Wahid gained power not because he won the popular vote (Megawati Sukarnoputri obtained significantly more votes than Wahid), but because the National Assembly appointed him believing he would be a more pliable leader. During his tenure, it was the army and Suharto's Golkar party that continued to hold all the key security ministries and that dominated decision making.

Ethnic activity

No new ethnic groups chose to challenge Wahid in the twenty-one months before he was impeached. On the one hand this is surprising. Wahid was not expected to have a long tenure in office due to his poor health, and appeared quite sympathetic to the concerns of different minorities. Almost immediately after entering office, Wahid made clear that he would continue to pursue Indonesia's new policy of decentralization, and made the surprising announcement that a referendum for Aceh was possible. Wahid also pursued more conciliatory policies towards the Papuans, allowing them to raise their own flag, and permitting the use of "West Papua" as the name of the province rather than Irian Jaya.

The fact that no province – including Riau and East Kalimantan – chose to challenge the government at this time, therefore, is puzzling from the perspective of the reputation theory. Ethnic groups facing a leader who appeared conciliatory and whose tenure was likely to be short should have taken this opportunity to seek self-determination. The fact that none did suggests that Riau and East Kalimantan either had no desire for independence, or were deterred despite these signals of weakness.

A closer look at Wahid's presidency and his relationship to both the legislature and the military, however, reveals how little influence Wahid had over policy, a fact that was probably known to most ethnic leaders. When Wahid first indicated that he would consider a referendum for Aceh similar to East Timor's, his generals reacted angrily, saying that the president was expressing his personal views, not the views of the government. Wahid's defense minister, Juwono Sudarsono, stated that there would be "no independence option."[53] An Army spokesman, Major General Sudrajat, responded that independence for Aceh was out of the question. The fact that no major political party supported the referendum and the military was totally opposed to it should have caused ethnic groups throughout Indonesia to heavily discount whatever Wahid said.[54]

The fact that different centers of power existed within the Indonesian government, and different actors dictated policy,

---

[53] Symonds (2000). [54] Aspinall and Crouch (2003: 6).

suggests another way the theory may be extended. Recall that the model in Chapter 2 assumed that both "the government" and the "ethnic group" were unitary actors. This simplification captured the realities of Indonesian government under the centralized and authoritarian regimes of Sukarno and Suharto, but it does not capture the more complex interplay of preferences that emerged as Indonesia slowly and fitfully attempted to democratize. Wahid may have been willing to offer concessions, but ethnic groups continued to draw inferences from what the Golkar party and the military said and did.

Government response

Not surprisingly, Wahid soon adjusted his policy to match these more powerful groups. In January 2000 Wahid warned the Papuans that he would not tolerate any move towards independence, and by November Wahid gave the go-ahead for military suppression. According to Wahid, "there should be no effort to proclaim [independence], secede from the Unitary State of the Republic of Indonesia, be that in Irian Jaya, or Papua, or in Aceh."[55]

The military had two motives for wanting to repress separatist movements in Aceh and West Papua and for not seeking a peaceful settlement. Economically, Aceh and West Papua's wealth was easy to exploit and served as the army's main source of income. Losing these two provinces to independence would mean a significant loss of income for them.[56] According to Aspinall and Crouch:

> Military and police personnel also take advantage of disturbed conditions to involve themselves in illegal logging and the marijuana trade while ordinary soldiers, and especially police, regularly impose illegal tolls on traffic along the highway

[55] Symonds (2000).

[56] Indonesia's army received only about 30 percent of its annual budget from the central government, forcing it to find the other 70 percent elsewhere.

between Banda Aceh and Medan in north Sumatra. The security forces therefore have an interest in keeping the conflict going at a level high enough to make enterprises feel vulnerable and in need of the protection that the military and police can offer.[57]

Immediate economic interests, therefore, did play a role in the Army's desire to deny secession to Aceh and West Papua. But deterrence mattered as well. It appeared that the generals were also quite worried that additional separatist movements would emerge, stretching their already limited capabilities. The military did not have the ability to suppress additional movements and still protect their economic interests in West Papua and Aceh.

Wahid's tenure reveals the limitations of the unitary actor assumption. If one observed only Wahid's behavior, the inference to draw would be that Jakarta was willing to negotiate. But if one took a deeper view of who dictated policy at this time, the reputation of the government remained intact. Wahid may have had few incentives to be tough given his poor health and short tenure, but the military had good reason to defend the status quo. Their tenure was likely to be much longer.

UNITARY GOVERNMENT ONCE MORE: MEGAWATI
SUKARNOPUTRI: 2001–4

Underlying conditions

Megawati Sukarnoputri was installed as president of Indonesia in July 2001 by a legislature that unanimously voted to remove Wahid on charges of corruption and incompetence.[58] Megawati, the daughter of President Sukarno, was aloof but popular, and was expected to serve out the remainder of Wahid's term. Although the economy remained fragile, Indonesia did experience somewhat higher economic growth

---

[57] Aspinall and Crouch (2003: 44).
[58] Sukarnoputri means "daughter of Sukarno" and is not the family's surname. Since Javanese do not have surnames she is simply referred to as Megawati.

during her first two years in office, and greater political stability. Things continued to improve through 2004.[59]

Ethnic activity and government response

No new self-determination movements emerged during Megawati's tenure, although challenges continued in Aceh and West Papua, with sporadic violence in Ambon. This limited separatist activity was not surprising given Megawati's tough early stance toward separatists. In June 2001, shortly before taking office, Megawati commented on what she called "the intention of some citizens to separate from Indonesia," by saying that "there is no country in the world that would tolerate disintegration."[60] In her first state-of-the-nation address, Megawati announced that she was willing to start a new relationship with the provinces, but that "one thing remains clear. Everything must remain within the context of safeguarding the territorial integrity of the unitary state of the Republic of Indonesia."[61] And as late as May 2004, five months before leaving office, Megawati flew to Ambon and declared that "[a]ll forms of separatism should be wiped out because they threaten the Unitary Republic of Indonesia."[62]

Megawati and her government supported these statements with action. Within two years, Megawati doubled the number of soldiers and police in Aceh from around 30,000 to almost 60,000.[63] "Our main objective of sending troops to Aceh," announced Megawati, "is to salvage the country which has been built by a series of generations of this nation with blood, sweat, and tears."[64] Moreover, the Indonesian coordinating minister for politics and security, Soesilo Bambang Yudhoyono, informed the Acehnese that they would suffer a beating, and proudly announced that he expected the number of

[59] *BPS.*

[60] "Megawati pledges to uphold national unity," *The Jakarta Post,* June 2, 2001.

[61] The Dawn Group of Newspapers, Friday August 17, 2001.

[62] Roberts (2004).   [63] Ross (2005: 50).

[64] Jakarta TVRI 1 Television. In Indonesian, October 5, 2003.

internally displaced persons in Aceh to exceed 100,000 as a result of the military campaign.[65]

Ethnic leaders in other regions were aware of what Megawati's policy towards separatists was likely to be. West Papua's Ondawame predicted that the new president's strong nationalist policies and close ties to the Indonesian military were likely to result in a severe crack-down on their independence movement.[66] In an interview in August 2000, Ondawame remarked that "Megawati is a new face but … she is even more nationalistic and more intolerant than Wahid."[67] Ondawami's assessment was correct. That month, Megawati ordered a large buildup of troops in West Papua as well.

Megawati also refused to implement the special autonomy law promised to West Papua by her predecessor. According to Negro Alpius Kogoyo and Hans Gebze, two leaders supporting separatism in West Papua, her refusal was no surprise: "the Megawati government fears that the genuine implementation of the special autonomy law will open up more space for the movement for self-determination."[68]

Megawati's leadership corresponds exactly to the predictions of the reputation theory. Fearing disintegration, the president took an early and consistent stance against negotiations with any group. She supported this stance with both public speeches against conciliation as well as harsh repression in the regions. Both the president and the military were now consistently following an unyielding stance toward separatists.

Between 2002 and 2004 GAM was the target of a series of government offensives in which the organization lost approximately half of its members, including its commander, Abdullah Syafei'l Dimatang. The situation improved in December 2004, but only as a result of a devastating tsunami, which killed more than 150,000 Acehnese, including many members of GAM. Within four days of

---

[65] From text of statement by Dr. John Otto Ondawame and Andy Ayamiseba, entitled "The West Papuan People's Representative Office in Vanuatu condemns the attack on Aceh," carried in English by Kabar Irian news web site, May 21, 2003.

[66] Woods (2000).   [67] Quoted in Woods (2000).   [68] Lane (2003).

the tsunami, GAM declared a cease-fire to allow aid to be delivered, and the Indonesian government temporarily removed restrictions to allow rescue efforts in that area. By February 2005, negotiations were taking place between GAM and the government, and a peace deal was officially signed six months later. Details of the peace agreement as well as its implementation, however, reveal that few concessions were made by the government and the terms better reflect capitulation by a severely weakened GAM than any compromise by the government. In May 2008, implementation of the agreement was stalled, although the cease-fire continued to hold.

CONCLUSION

The preceding case study served three purposes. First, it helped solve the puzzle of why so many leaders would refuse to negotiate with ethnic groups seeking self-determination, even if the territory under dispute is not particularly valuable. Starting in 1950, successive Indonesian presidents were willing to fight hard to retain provinces that were both resource rich and resource poor. In fact, the Indonesian government's most costly battle was against the East Timorese, who occupied a small, poor, and relatively barren part of the archipelago. Sukarno and Suharto's behavior toward this province suggests that they fought so hard not because East Timor would make the government rich, but because letting it go could convince other more valuable regions to leave.

Second, the analysis also helped solve the puzzle of why so many ethnic groups in Indonesia chose *not* to rebel, and why the few that did rebel did so despite its heavy cost. The fact that so few ethnic groups chose to seek self-determination in Indonesia is consistent with the idea that deterrence worked. This is especially telling since at least two additional provinces, Riau and East Kalimantan, had both the motive and the resources to secede.

In addition, the Ambonese, East Timorese, Acehnese, and Papuans challenged the government even though it was clear that they would be severely punished as a result. The case revealed that these early movers were unique in one important way. Of the four regions that voiced demands for independence (Ambon, West Papua, East Timor, and Aceh), three were incorporated into Indonesia against their will, and one (Aceh) had been promised significant autonomy that was then not delivered. No other province in Indonesia experienced such losses. Lost autonomy, therefore, more than any other factor, appeared to be a major motivator in the decision to challenge.

Finally, the case also highlights one other important causal variable. The details of the Indonesia case reveal that the value of different pieces of land does influence behavior in ways not captured in the previous chapters. While strategic and psychological value did not appear to play a major role in government or ethnic group decisions, the economic value of land played three roles worth emphasizing. First, Aceh and West Papua's economic assets clearly influenced the preferences of the military to continue fighting and to resist negotiations. Second, oil and natural gas in Riau and East Kalimantan also appeared to factor into government calculations of the importance of deterrence. Both the present and future economic value of land in Indonesia, therefore, appeared to influence Jakarta's decisions to fight. Finally, economic value did not appear to play as heavy a role in ethnic group decisions as one may have predicted. Of the four regions that did choose to seek self-determination, only Aceh and West Papua were likely to benefit economically from independence; the resource poor regions of East Timor and Ambon were not. Moreover, a number of rich regions within Indonesia, namely Riau and East Kalimantan, chose not to secede. A loss of revenue or economic exploitation, therefore, did not appear to be sufficient to convince wealthy provinces to secede.

In short, a careful look at government and ethnic group decision making in Indonesia between 1945 and 2004 reveals that reputation building is a more complex process than what is captured in the model. Most leaders invest in reputation building, and most ethnic groups are deterred by this behavior, but this basic dynamic does not capture the ways in which reputations can be manipulated, and the ways in which reputation may be ignored. Governments can signal toughness with very public displays of force, yet under certain conditions they can also be quite conciliatory without triggering a host of additional challenges. It is the full range of information ethnic groups receive about the government and its history that shapes their beliefs rather than any single isolated act at any one time.

7 The Philippines: few ethnic groups, many demands

This chapter continues to investigate reputation building by focusing on the Philippines – a country similar in many ways to Indonesia but with notably fewer minority groups. While Indonesia has one of the highest numbers of ethnic minorities in the world, the Philippines has one of the lowest. The main ethnic divide in the Philippines is between Christian Malays who represent 92 percent of the population, and two minority groups – Muslim Malays, on the southern island of Mindanao, and the indigenous Igorot in the mountains of central Luzon in the north.[1] Both ethnic groups are geographically concentrated, both have experienced high levels of poverty relative to the rest of the Philippines, and both have significant natural resources that have been exploited by the central government. Unlike Indonesia, however, all of the minority ethnic groups in the Philippines have sought self-determination, and all of them have been offered sizeable concessions as a result.

Again, the main goal of this chapter is to explore the behavior and motivations of both government and ethnic group leaders in a country where few incentives exist to invest in reputation building, at least against ethnic separatists. Unlike the government of Indonesia, the government of the Philippines was willing to grant considerable autonomy to the two groups seeking self-determination. When confronted with demands from the Moros in Mindanao and the Igorot in the Cordillera region of Luzon, almost all presidents in

---

[1] Demographics of the Philippines, http://experts.about.com/e/p/ph/Philippines.htm

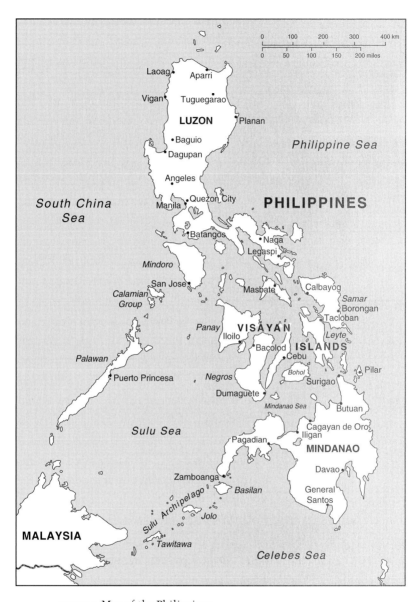

MAP 7.1 Map of the Philippines

the Philippines quickly and publicly made concessions.[2] This case study, therefore, will help disclose why the Moros and Igorot were willing to challenge and why to the government seemed so amenable to accommodation.

Determining the influence of reputation building in this particular case, however, will not be easy since reputational dynamics are not expected to materialize. Unlike Indonesia, respective administrations in Manila should not mention any concerns with "disintegration," "reputation," or the possibility of a "domino effect." They should simply be more willing to negotiate. Showing a higher incidence of accommodation will be in line with the reputation theory, but will not prove that reputation building (or its absence) is causing behavior.

Still, the case offers an opportunity to explore other factors influencing behavior, as well as to address any disconfirming evidence. Two patterns that we will see in this case, in particular, seem to contradict what the reputation theory would predict. The first has to do with the timing of the self-determination movements in both Mindanao and the Cordillera. It took many decades for both the Moros and the Igorot to formally demand self-determination despite an environment seemingly conducive to conciliation. The reputation theory would have expected both groups to demand self-determination as early as 1946 when the Philippines first became independent, especially given their low living standards and exploitation at the hands of the government. The Moros, however, did not actively seek independence until 1972, and the Igorot not until 1984. Why did both groups take so long to make demands when it should have been clear that the government was likely to have strong incentives to compromise?

The second puzzle has to do with the decision by Muslims in Mindanao to continue fighting even after fairly deep concessions

---

[2] The Cordillera was a term given to the chain of mountains in northern Luzon which contains ten principal cultural groups. The name Igorot, the Tagalog (Philippine language) word for mountaineer, was often used to refer to all groups. For more information see Library of Congress Study: Philippines, Upland Tribal Groups. http://lcweb2.loc.gov/cgi-bin/query/r?frd/cstdy:@ field(DOCID+ph0060).

were granted by the government. According to the reputation theory, concessions should have been offered and accepted by the Moros soon after a violent campaign began in 1972. Early resolution occurred with the Igorot, but not with the Moros. Why has an agreement with the Moros been so much more difficult to reach, and what factors continue to stand in the way of settlement? This chapter, therefore, not only explains why government leaders have conformed to predictions of the reputation theory by consistently negotiating with separatists, but also why separatists have not.

CONFLICT RISK IN THE PHILIPPINES: THE RULE OF PRESIDENT MANUEL ROXAS, 1946–8

Underlying conditions and predictions

According to the reputation theory, both the Moros and the Igorot should have demanded independence in 1946 when the United States handed power over to the majority Christian Malays. Not only were the Moros religiously distinct from the rest of the population, but they had long resisted absorption into the larger Christian population. Moreover, joining the larger state would mean that Mindanao would continue to face Manila's unpopular transmigration policy. Starting as early as 1903 and escalating in the mid-1930s, Manila actively encouraged large numbers of Christians to migrate from heavily populated areas of the central and northern Philippines to Muslim regions in the south.[3] This transmigration policy was quite similar to the one pursued in Indonesia, which targeted outlying regions in West Papua, Kalimantan, Sumatra, and Sulawesi. Demanding self-determination at this time would have prevented Christian domination over the region either due to absorption into the larger republic or through continuing in-migration of Christians from

---

[3] Between 1903 and 1960 the Muslim proportion of the Mindanao population declined from 31 percent to less than 20 percent, despite a high Muslim birthrate. See Wenstedt and Simkins (1965).

the north. The puzzle in 1946, therefore, was why the Moros chose to peacefully incorporate themselves into the new state rather than demand independence as the Ambonese, Timorese, and West Papuans had done in Indonesia.[4]

There appear to be at least two reasons why the Moros did not seek self-determination at this time. First, the traditional leaders of the Moros – the datu – were offered lucrative political appointments at the provincial and municipal level by Manila if they agreed to join the state.[5] The datu had a history of aligning themselves with the central government (they had done so during the American colonial period) as a way to access income which they would then distribute to the local population as a way to sustain support.[6]

Second, the standard of living for most Muslims living in Mindanao improved after the war.[7] Muslims benefited from war-damage payments and reconstruction aid coming from the United States, as well as large amounts of government spending on roads and infrastructure. Life in Mindanao also improved as a result of loans and resources accompanying Christian migrants as they moved south.[8] It was not until the early 1970s when President Marcos began expropriating Muslim land and redistributing it to Christian migrants and other regime supporters that economic disparities between Muslims and Christians escalated and grievances increased.

The Igorot living in the mountains of Luzon also did not seek self-determination at this time but for different reasons. The Igorot

[4] This is especially puzzling since Muslim Malays were relatively well armed at this time as a result of firearms being abandoned by Japanese and American soldiers at the end of World War II.

[5] McKenna (1998: 87).

[6] The symbiotic relationship between traditional Muslim elites and the state would not be broken until a new generation of young, university-educated Muslim leaders emerged in the 1960s.

[7] This was true of most administrative regions in the Philippines after the war.

[8] McKenna (1998: 121–2).

were neither the poorest people in the Philippines nor particularly badly treated by the government. In fact, the main goal of the Igorot was to shed their stereotype for being backward and isolated, and instead assimilate more tightly into the larger Filipino population. Assimilation had a number of advantages. For one, the Igorot entered the new republic with relatively high educational credentials and a command of English gained as a result of an elementary education system established for them by the Americans in the early 1900s.[9] These skills were likely to give them an advantage in competing for jobs in the larger Filipino community. Second, the Igorot were more antagonistic toward each other than they were toward Malays. Composed of seven major sub-groups, the Igorot were not a cohesive ethnic group with a strong "Igorot" identity or a desire to work together. In fact, inter-Igorot relations had a long history of in-fighting which included headhunting.[10] It was not until the Marcos regime threatened the region with environmentally destructive damming and logging projects in the early 1970s that the group began to coalesce.[11]

Thus, neither the Moro nor the Igorot communities had a strong motive or desire to rebel in the two years that Manuel Roxas ruled. Manila's transmigration policy in Mindanao had not altered demographics sufficiently to create major grievances in the south, and the destructive development projects of the Marcos era had not yet been initiated in the north. Moreover, even if sizeable grievances had been present, neither the Muslims nor the Igorot were sufficiently well organized to launch a challenge. Muslim datu had chosen to align themselves with the state, while the Igorot preferred to cooperate with Manila rather than work with each other. Large portions of both groups, therefore, favored greater integration rather than greater self-rule.

---

[9] For a more detailed description of American programs in the Cordillera see Finin (2005: 72–5, 185–6).
[10] See Fallon.   [11] See especially Finin (2005).

CONFLICT RISK IN THE PHILIPPINES: THE RULE OF PRESIDENT ELPIDIO QUIRINO, 1949–53

Underlying conditions and predictions

Manuel Roxas was replaced in April 1948 by his vice president, Elpidio Quirino, after Roxas died of a heart attack. No demand for self-determination was made by either the Moros or the Igorot during his tenure, and neither group is mentioned in any of the literature on Quirino, including his memoirs. The main internal security problem facing the government was the Communist revolt of the Hukbalahap (the Huk) which emerged in central Luzon in 1946 as a result of oppressive land policies. But this movement was unconnected to the Igorot and any desire for self-determination until the late 1970s.

Underlying conditions, however, were changing in Mindanao. In an attempt to undercut the Huk insurgency, Quirino's secretary of national defense, Ramon Magsaysay, began to offer free land in Mindanao to insurgents willing to lay down their arms. The program was extremely successful in reducing support for the insurgency, but created deep resentment among Muslims who watched Christian settlers being given land and loans not available to them.[12]

In contrast to the increasing dissatisfaction within the Muslim community, the mountain people of the Cordillera focused instead on continued assimilation. By the early 1950s, educated Igorot had done quite well, and a new generation was acquiring college degrees with the goal of assimilating even further. The problem, as will be discussed in greater detail below, was that later generations found it increasingly difficult to gain jobs commensurate with their educational qualifications, and it was this road-block that helped re-direct their energies into the future Cordillera separatist movement.[13] In the meantime, however, the Igorot were quite content to blend deeper into the state.

---

[12] See McKenna (1998: 117).   [13] Finin (2005: 177–8).

CONFLICT RISK IN THE PHILIPPINES: THE RULE OF RAMON MAGSAYSAY, 1953–7

Underlying conditions and predictions

Elpidio Quirino's tenure ended in 1953 when he lost re-election to Ramon Magsaysay. Magsaysay was able to finally put down the Huk rebellion in 1954, but at the expense of increasing Christian–Muslim violence in the south.[14] According to McKenna,

> outlaw activity commonly referred to as "banditry" was widespread in Cotabato and throughout the Muslim south in the 1950s. Much of it involved rather straightforward criminal activity, especially highway robbery and cattle rustling. Other incidents, however, have the appearance of social banditry, and a few ... approached the level of genuine armed insurgency against the state.[15]

The government responded to this violence by appointing a special committee to investigate the source of the discontent. Although the Magsaysay administration was aware of the increasing economic disparity between Christians and Muslims in Mindanao, the report blamed this disparity on Muslim culture rather than on any policies being pursed by the state.[16] According to the report, '[i]n their ignorance and in their trend toward religious fanaticism, the Muslims are sadly wanting in the advantages of normal health and social factors and functions.'[17] Manila was not yet ready to acknowledge that transmigration and its negative effects might be responsible for the poor conditions experienced by Muslims in the south, or the rising sectarian violence that resulted.[18]

---

[14] Steinberg (2000: 114).   [15] McKenna (1998: 319).   [16] McKenna (1998: 139).

[17] Quoted in McKenna (1998: 139) from the Congress of the Philippines, House of Representatives, 1955.

[18] The violence that did occur during this time was sectarian violence between Christians and Muslims. It occurred in areas of mixed populations especially in Cotabato where the increase in the non-Muslim population was most significant. See McKenna (1998: 137) and Gutierrez and Borras (2004: 15).

Government policies toward the Igorot were somewhat more supportive, with Magsaysay taking small but symbolically important steps to incorporate the Cordillera further into the state. Magsaysay, for example, agreed to allow the province to elect its own governor, a move that delighted those living there. According to one expert, "[w]ith the...popular election of the governor of Mountain Province, the Igorot inhabitants can no longer be classified as wild, Non-Christian Tribes. They are Filipinos."[19] Thus, while the Moros were becoming increasingly dissatisfied with policies emanating from Manila, the Igorot gladly accepted the policies they were offered.

CONFLICT RISK IN THE PHILIPPINES: THE RULE OF CARLOS GARCIA, 1957–61

Underlying conditions and predictions

Ramon Magsaysay's tenure ended when he died in a plane crash in March 1957. Almost immediately, his vice president, Carlos Garcia, set up the Commission on National Integration (CNI), whose goal was to improve the economic, social, and political conditions of non-Christian Filipinos.[20] This was viewed by many as the first serious attempt by the government to address Moro grievances.

Although the CNI was authorized to institute a wide variety of development programs including irrigation projects and road building, the only part of the program to receive more than token funding was a college scholarship program designed to allow Muslims and Igorot to attend universities in Manila. These scholarships were the first opportunity many Muslims and Igorot had to leave their respective regions for a higher education and this opportunity turned out to be critical for creating a new set of leaders with both the motive and the ability to organize resistance.[21] One of the founders of the Moro

---

[19] Finin (2005: 186).   [20] McKenna (1998: 139–40).
[21] Although many of the scholarships went to children of the datu, the program enabled a relatively large number of non-elite Muslims to attend university for the first time. See McKenna (1998: 140–2).

National Liberation Front (MNLF), Nur Misuari, for example, came from this group of young Muslim intellectuals and represented a new generation of Muslim elites with no ties to the traditional datu.

The scholarship program also gave rise to growing Igorot nationalism as well as increased consciousness about the value of greater self-rule. Initially, the Igorot welcomed the opportunity to leave the mountainous Cordillera and move into the larger cities, seeing this as an avenue for greater assimilation. As one Igorot teacher and journalist wrote, "[i]t will not be long before we hear of an Igorot secretary of national defense or ambassador or President of the Philippines."[22] Greater exposure to the larger Christian community, however, brought greater competition for jobs and a higher incidence of discrimination. Educated Igorot found it difficult to fully assimilate once they left their mountain villages, and with this discrimination came a deeper sense of their own ethnicity.[23] It was education and urbanization, therefore, that helped to create a stronger sense of group identity and revealed the limitations of continued integration.

CONFLICT RISK IN THE PHILIPPINES: THE RULE OF PRESIDENT DIOSDAN MACAPAGAL, 1961–5

Underlying conditions and predictions

Carlos Garcia left office in 1961 after losing an election to his vice president, Diosdan Macapagal. President Macapagal was known as "the incorruptible" and was one of the great, respected, and loved presidents of the Philippines. During his four years in office he decentralized the economy, fought graft and corruption, and encouraged commerce and industry in the provinces. He also pushed for greater political decentralization by transferring power toward provincial and local governments.

Macapagal's time in office was good for Mindanao. Between 1961 and 1966 economic growth increased in Mindanao relative to

---

[22] Finin (2005: 195).   [23] Finin (2005: 193).

the country as a whole, as a result of increasing logging and agriculture, and the continuing influx of Christian settlers who brought money to the region.[24] Still, it was during Macapagal's tenure that the first demand for independence was made.

In December 1961, Ombra Amilbangsa, a member of the Philippine legislature and a proclaimed descendant of the original sultans of Sulu in Mindanao, introduced a bill in Congress calling for the "reestablishment" of Sulu as an independent country.[25] This demand was not taken seriously by either the government or by most Muslims, and the demand is not mentioned in most histories of the Philippines. Still, this seemingly inconsequential act exposes an important feature of the reputation theory. According to the reputation theory, governments only have incentives to offer concessions to an ethnic group if it can credibly threaten to inflict costs on the government. This, however, was not the case with Amilbangasa and his Sulu "movement." What this act reveals is that governments do not have incentives to make concessions to all challengers all the time, even if the government is predisposed to be conciliatory. Challengers must have at least some ability to inflict costs to warrant such concessions. Under these conditions, concessions made no sense.

President Macapagal continued to reach out to the Igorot by appointing Gabriel Dunuan, an Igorot, commissioner of the CNI in November 1961. This was the first time an Igorot had been appointed to a Philippine cabinet post and the response within the community was enthusiastic.[26] Dissatisfaction may have been increasing among Igorot college students, but the vast majority of the Igorot population still had no interest in secession.

---

[24] Sicat (1972: 354).

[25] This challenge was not included in the datasets used in Chapters 4 and 5 because it was too insignificant to meet Center for International Development and Conflict Management (CIDCM) requirements for a self-determination movement. Still, the demand launched by Amilbangsa offers the opportunity to determine whether government behavior differs toward these weak groups in any noteworthy ways.

[26] Finin (2005: 208).

CONFLICT RISK IN THE PHILIPPINES: THE RULE OF FERDINAND MARCOS: 1965–86

All of this changed soon after Ferdinand Marcos was elected president in 1965. In less than three years, the Moro National Liberation Front (MNLF) was founded demanding independence for Muslim areas in Mindanao, Sulu, and Palwan. Three factors accounted for the timing of the Moro movement: the increasing economic and political imbalances created by the continued large influx of Christian settlers into the region, the emergence of a new group of non-datu Muslim leaders educated in Manila, and the increasing military brutality against Muslims in response to growing Christian–Muslim violence.

Increasing economic and political imbalances. Although transmigration policies had been pursued for decades, it was during the Marcos administration that these policies became particularly costly to the Muslim population. In the early 1970s, the Marcos administration passed a series of laws allowing the government to legally expropriate Muslim-owned lands and redirect these lands to Christian settlers and foreign owned plantations. Marcos' motivation was simple. Mindanao's rich resources (which included large forests, fertile soil, and mineral resources such as gold, nickel, zinc, and manganese), combined with its politically weak population, created the opportunity for him to exploit the region for the benefit of friends and supporters.[27] Although Muslims represented 61 percent of Mindanao's population at the time, they represented only 4.3 percent of the total population of the Philippines.[28] It was Mindanao's easily exploitable land that attracted Marcos' attention and caused him to institute policies that created deep dissatisfaction among its electorally weak Muslim population.[29]

---

[27] Steinberg (2000: 124).
[28] Gutierrez and Borras (2004: 14).
[29] Ganguly and Macduff (2003: 201).

The emergence of an educated, politically active Muslim elite.
The expropriation of land and the continued in-migration of settlers,
however, was not the only reason the MNLF was formed. Mindanao
had suffered under government sponsored in-migration for decades
and it was only in the late 1960s that organized resistance emerged.
A second contributing factor was a new group of educated leaders
capable of challenging the dominance of the datu and mobilizing
support against the status quo. The first organized resistance occurred
in March 1968 when word got out that Christian army officers had
massacred as many as 200 Muslim military recruits in Manila Bay.[30]
The Jabidah killings, as the massacre was called, motivated Muslim
students in Manila to form a number of political organizations dedicated to the right to self-determination. These movements, although
relatively peaceful, led to the creation of the MNLF by Nur Misuari
in the early 1970s.

*Increased military repression and the imposition of martial
law.* Muslim separatist activity escalated when Marcos imposed
martial law in September 1972 and demanded that Muslims in the
south surrender their arms.[31] Marcos argued that martial law was
necessary to end the chaos and violence in Mindanao, but the new
policy as well as a growing military presence within the region only
increased violence and enhanced support for the MNLF.[32] According
to Yegar, "[t]he movement, with its goal of self-determination, now
became the foremost Muslim separatist organization and a spear-
head of the antigovernment struggle. Muslim response to the state
of emergency was rapid and spontaneous. New people joined the
revolt."[33]

The official transition from non-violent to violent organization
occurred on October 24, 1972 when several hundred Muslim men
seized the Mindanao State University campus.[34] This was followed

---

[30] McKenna (1998: 140–2).
[31] Marcos abolished congress and ruled by presidential decree from September
1972 until 1978 (Steinberg, 2000: 126).
[32] Yegar (2002: 258).   [33] Yegar (2002: 259).   [34] McAmis (1974: 52–3).

by a series of attacks that continued through 1974, eventually leaving the MNLF in control of large areas in Basilan, Sulu, Lanao, Zamboanga, and Cotabato.[35]

The timing of these attacks helps expose why Mindanao's Muslims switched to a violent strategy after four years of relatively peaceful protests and demonstrations. Contrary to theories that focus on government weakness, the MNLF did not initiate attacks because the government had become weak and vulnerable to challenge. Instead, a violent military campaign emerged only *after* martial law was declared and government control over the region had become stronger. It was restrictions on freedom as well as military repression that helped the MNLF pull together as a movement and confront an increasingly abusive regime.[36]

A similar pattern occurred with the Igorot. Although the indigenous population of the Cordillera did not seek self-determination until June 1984 – more than a decade after the Moros – it was the aggressive policies of the Marcos regime as well as the emergence of a newly educated and urban elite that convinced the Igorot to pursue self-determination. The catalysts for action were two development projects initiated by Marcos at the end of 1972. The first was a logging and pulp production enterprise based in Abra province in the northwestern part of the Cordillera scheduled to begin by 1977. The Cellophil project, as it was called, gave outsiders control over vast forest lands which they intended to exploit. The second was the construction of four hydroelectric dams along the Chico River which threatened to inundate hundreds of traditional villages.[37]

As with Mindanao, Marcos was attracted to the region because of its vast natural resources. The Cordillera is one of the richest territories in terms of agricultural production and mineral resources. In addition to timber and water, 60 percent of the country's vegetables

---

[35] Yegar (2002: 275).   [36] Noble (1981: 65).

[37] These dams, however, were expected to provide as much as over half of the total electrical needs of the Philippines.

were produced in the region, eight big mining companies operated in the area, and approximately 80 percent of the country's gold came from the Cordillera. It was the economic value of Igorot land and the ways in which Marcos could exploit it that brought the state into conflict with the group.

Still, an organized movement for self-determination took years to develop. At first, resistance came in the form of membership in the New People's Army (NPA), the military wing of the Philippine Communist Party engaged in a rebellion against the state since 1969. But by the early 1980s, Igorot members began to defect from the NPA in favor of creating their own organization dedicated exclusively to gaining autonomy. The official demand for self-determination came in June 1984 when a group of educated Igorot organized the Cordillera People's Congress, calling for the establishment of an autonomous region.[38]

The Igorot decision to seek autonomy was a radical departure from their previous desire to assimilate, and reveals the opportunity the government squandered to encourage assimilation rather than secession. Had the government embraced attempts by the Igorot to assimilate and had they resisted the temptation to exploit the Cordillera's natural resources, no demand for self-determination would likely have been made. This is especially true given the enmity between the different Igorot sub-groups and the difficulties they faced creating a unified movement. It was government policies that actively turned the group against the state and led to the desire for secession.

GOVERNMENT RESPONSES

According to the reputation theory, Marcos should have granted concessions to both groups as soon as it was clear that resistance would be costly.[39] Yet, Marcos' immediate response to the attacks by the Moros in 1972 was just the opposite. Marcos responded by

---

[38] Finin (2005: 260).

[39] One of the areas that remain unclear regarding the reputation theory is the point at which concessions are likely to be made. As discussed in Chapter 2, even conciliatory governments are unlikely to make concessions to every

deploying large numbers of combat forces against the Moros, killing an estimated 50,000 people.[40] Marcos' policy, however, did not last long. By November 1974 Marcos declared a two-month unilateral cease-fire during which he offered to negotiate with the rebels. This about-face was quite different from Suharto's response to the Aceh crisis. Suharto had also instituted martial law in Aceh in 1990, but whereas Suharto consistently cracked down on ethnic separatists throughout his thirty-three-year reign, Marcos switched to a more conciliatory policy fairly early in the conflict.

Negotiations aimed at reaching a settlement began in January 1975 and ended almost two years later with the signing of a comprehensive peace settlement on December 23, 1976.[41] The Tripoli agreement, as it was called, was seen as a radical break-through and became the basis for negotiations over the next twenty years. It established an autonomous region for Mindanao that included thirteen provinces and nine cities. Within the region, Muslims would have a high degree of autonomy over their own judicial system, education, administration, economic and financial system, special regional security forces, a legislative assembly, and an executive council. Shari'a law would also be allowed.

The biggest sticking point of the agreement, however, had to do with implementation. According to the treaty, the agreement would only be implemented if a majority of the citizens living in the thirteen provinces voted in favor of the terms.[42] The MNLF, how-ever, rejected any attempt to tie implementation to a plebiscite since all but three of the provinces were by now majority Christian. A plebiscite, therefore, was a clever way for Marcos to placate Muslims living in the most heavily Muslim areas of Mindanao (they would

---

group that asks for them, instead offering deals only to those groups that could otherwise inflict costs on the government.

[40] Library of Congress Country Study, "Phillippines: The Moros."

[41] Santos (2005: 3).

[42] This was in accordance with the Philippine constitution which required a plebiscite to be held whenever a new political unit was created.

likely approve the agreement for their provinces), without alienating the large group of Christians living in other provinces as well.

Neither Marcos nor the MNLF was willing to yield on this issue, and Marcos reacted to the impasse by implementing his own version of the agreement. Two special "autonomous regions," one for Central Mindanao and the other for Sulu, were created with significantly less political autonomy than promised in the agreement.[43] Marcos' behavior is simultaneously revealing and puzzling in terms of the reputation theory. On the one hand, Marcos behaved exactly as the reputation theory would predict: when faced with violent opposition from an organized separatist group, Marcos offered deep concessions in terms of political, economic, and cultural autonomy. Yet, reputationally, Marcos also got his worst possible outcome: he revealed himself to be conciliatory but did not gain peace. Why would Marcos not make the Moros sufficiently happy to end the fighting?

The reputation theory does not address the reasons why a leader might not offer sufficient concessions to buy peace. It simply assumes that governments and ethnic groups are unitary actors who will rationally converge on the terms that will allow them to end their dispute. What is missing from the theory, and what is revealed by this case study, is the role domestic politics plays in setting policy. Marcos may have had few reputational incentives to withhold greater autonomy for the Moros, but he had substantial domestic political incentives to do so. Marcos' main constituents were not Muslims in Mindanao, but Christian Malays who did not favor granting significant autonomy to the south. The compromise Marcos pursued was to offer large public concessions to the MNLF, but then subject these concessions to approval by those Christians whose support Marcos needed to remain in power. In a perfect world, leaders always offer just the right concessions to end a conflict, but in the real world of competing domestic interest groups and competing preferences, a more complicated set of calculations (and compromises) often takes place.

[43] See Bacani (2005) and McKenna (1998: 168).

Still, the decision to grant autonomy was significantly different from what was occurring in Indonesia at this time, and the concessions did reduce the fighting. According to McKenna, "[a]fter the signing of the agreement, the rate of defections from the MNLF accelerated, its support from foreign sources was reduced ..."[44] Yet, while violence from the MNLF decreased, a new more radical organization formed in its wake. In 1978, a group of individuals defected from the MNLF and founded the Moro Islamic Liberation Front (MILF) under the leadership of Hashim Salamat, one of the original founders of the MNLF. Accusing the MNLF of being too secular and moderate, the MILF declared jihad against the central government and demanded nothing less than a separate Islamic state with full independence.[45] Thus, while Marcos' concessions were able to placate some of the more moderate Muslim separatists in Mindanao, they did not prevent a more radical movement from forming.

Almost no information exists about Marcos' dealings with the Igorot during his tenure. Violent protests by the Igorot were successful in convincing the World Bank to withdraw funding for the Chico River Dam Project in 1980, which in turn caused Marcos to freeze the project in 1981. But by the time the Igorot formally demanded self-determination in 1984 the Marcos regime was already in decline and nearing its end. Marcos was willing to stop construction of the hated dams, but formal negotiations on autonomy were not offered.

Marcos' tenure in office reveals the influence of three key variables in the outbreak of self-determination movements. The first is the importance of natural resources in bringing the government and ethnic minorities into conflict. Had Mindanao and the Cordillera contained territory with little or no value, disputes with the government would likely not have occurred. The value of the land, however, was not sufficient to convince each of the groups to rebel. Despite continuing exploitation by the government, self-determination

---

[44] McKenna (1998: 168).   [45] Yegar (2002: 342).

movements did not emerge until a new set of leaders was created within both groups, and these leaders were able to mobilize popular support for self-determination as a result of hated government policies. In Mindanao, the imposition of martial law and the fear this instilled in the eyes of Muslims convinced them that independence was necessary to safeguard their political, economic, and cultural interests. In the Cordillera, the threat of flooding finally made clear to the majority of Igorot that further incorporation into the state would also not serve their interests. It was the combination of economic grievances, elite organization, and government oppression that convinced so many individuals within each group to rebel.

CONFLICT RISK IN THE PHILIPPINES: THE RULE OF CORAZON AQUINO: 1986–92

Underlying conditions and predictions

Both the MNLF and the Cordillera People's Alliance continued to push for self-determination after Ferdinand Marcos was replaced by Corazon Aquino in February 1986. In line with predictions of the reputation theory, Aquino made it clear that one of her top priorities was to ensure that the 1976 Tripoli agreement with the Moros was fully implemented, and that autonomy be extended to the Cordillera.[46] As early as her election campaign Aquino pledged "to respect and substantiate" Muslim aspirations for autonomy.[47] Unlike her counterpart in Indonesia at this time (Suharto), Aquino appeared eager to negotiate a deal.

Aquino attempted to break the impasse that existed over the implementation of the Tripoli agreement by restarting negotiations, this time inviting not only the MNLF to participate, but the MILF as well. Although the MILF declined her invitation, a series of negotiations were held between Nur Misuari and the Aquino government from September 1986 to August 1989. By August 1989 Aquino had agreed to create the Autonomous Region of Muslim

---

[46] Keesings (1999), sp 22.   [47] Keesings (1999), 41.

Mindanao (ARMM), but subject once again to approval by plebiscite. Despite protestations by the MNLF and their call for a boycott, the referendum was held on November 19, 1989. Four of thirteen districts – Lanao del Sur, Maguindanao, Sulu, and Tawi-Tawi – voted for the proposal and it was these four districts that formed the basis of the ARMM that still exists today.

Although autonomy was implemented in each of the districts, violence continued to be pursued predominantly by the MILF and a new radical Islamic organization called Abu-Sayyaf.[48] The fact that violence persisted, however, did not mean that Aquino did not behave in ways predicted by the theory. Aquino had been keen to negotiate with the Moros from the start of her presidency and was willing to create the ARMM – something no president in Indonesia had been willing to do for Aceh, West Papua, or Ambon. But Aquino refused to go as far as transferring control of majority Christian regions to the Muslim minority, or to grant full independence to the more radical MILF and Abu-Sayyaf movements.

The fact that the ARMM was created but violence continued brings us back to one of the main puzzles of the Philippines case. Aquino refused to grant full independence to Mindanao not because she feared this would trigger additional independence movements throughout the Philippines – the Igorot had already made their demands and no other minority group existed to demand independence. Aquino refused to grant independence because this was deeply unpopular with the majority of Christians who represented her main support base. The Manila government, therefore, continued to walk the fine line between placating the demands of Muslim separatists while also mollifying the larger Christian population.

Aquino was also conciliatory toward the rebels in the Cordillera region. Two months after taking office, Aquino agreed to meet with Conrado Balweg, leader of the Cordillera People's

---

[48] Abu-Sayyaf's stated goal was to create an independent Islamic state in western Mindanao and Sulu.

Liberation Army, in what became known as the Mount Data summit. Within a year, Aquino signed Executive Order 220 creating the Cordillera Administrative Region (CAR) comprised of Abra, Benguet, Mountain, Kalinga-Apayao, and Ifugao provinces. This concession was followed in October 1989 with Republic Act No. 6766, which mandated the transfer of significant political power to CAR. CAR would now be ruled by its own autonomous government, headed by an Igorot governor, an Igorot assembly and an Igorot judiciary, with the power to raise taxes. The only features the new government would not have control over were defense, foreign affairs, and currency.

Once again, however, the Aquino government insisted on a plebiscite to gauge the support of citizens living in the five affected provinces, yet unlike the Moros the Igorot agreed.[49] What happened next surprised most outside observers. When the plebiscite was held in January 1990 the majority of voters, most of whom were Igorot, rejected the move toward autonomy. Only Ifugao province agreed to the terms.[50]

A number of hypotheses have been offered as to why autonomy was rejected by the Igorot. Many residents did not appear to understand the difference between an administrative region and an autonomous region or, if they did, did not believe it would be a significant change.[51] This allowed various parties, such as mining companies, to convince the Igorot population that autonomy would be detrimental to them.[52] According to Finin:

---

[49] This was in keeping with Section 18, Article X of the 1987 Philippine Constitution which stated that the creation of autonomous regions in Mindanao and the Cordillera must be approved through such a plebiscite. See Finin (2005: 268).

[50] The supreme court subsequently ruled that a single province (Ifugao) could not make up the Cordillera Autonomous Region on its own, and that the original administrative region established in Executive Order 220 would remain in effect. See Finin (2005: 269).

[51] Library of Congress Country Studies, "Philippines: Regional Autonomy."

[52] Finin (2005: 268–9).

> [M]any Cordillera residents in rural villages, highlander
> activists who had originated the calls for autonomy, and
> traditional politicians were all skeptical about what real good
> autonomy would bring. Ironically, these groups, each for very
> different reasons, all opposed the form of Cordillera regional
> autonomy that was placed on the ballot ... [53]

It appeared that Cordillera residents were either unsure of what was
being offered and how it would impact their life, or they saw the new
autonomous regional government as one that would simply allow
existing politicians to advance their own personal interests.[54]

Little is written about the Cordillera movement after autonomy
was rejected in the January 1990 plebiscite.[55] By most accounts, it
appears that the movement soon faded away. According to Finin,
"[i]n the end, usurpation of the regional autonomy movement by
traditional politicians and confusion about its meaning undermined
public support for such a promising experiment."[56] Today, CAR,
which was originally intended to be autonomous, houses the Abra,
Benguet, Ifugao, Kalinga, Mountain, and Apayao provinces, and is
one of seventeen regions comprising the Philippines.

CONFLICT RISK IN THE PHILIPPINES: THE RULE OF
FIDEL RAMOS, 1992–8

Underlying conditions and predictions
President Aquino was succeeded by Fidel Ramos in the 1992
elections and, like Aquino, Ramos initiated negotiations with the
Moros almost immediately. According to the new president, "My

---

[53] Finin (2005: 269).

[54] This was due, in part, to the fact that the administrative region had already
been co-opted by traditional politicians who gave rural village leaders little
voice in the political process. There was little reason to believe that they would
gain any larger voice from more autonomy.

[55] There is very little written about the history of the Cordillera movement or the
referendum process. For the most detailed account see Finin (2005: 270–2).

[56] Finin (2005: 272).

first concern upon assuming the Presidency in 1992 was to deal with endemic instability."[57] Ramos convinced the MNLF to re-open peace talks in October 1992 by offering to discuss autonomy for all thirteen provinces included in the Tripoli agreement. He also promised to negotiate with the MILF once these negotiations were complete.[58]

Peace negotiations continued through September 2, 1996 when the two sides signed the Jakarta Accord.[59] The agreement included two new provisions designed to increase the size and power of the autonomous region and directly address Moro dissatisfaction with previous deals. First, a plebiscite would be postponed for three years in order to mobilize greater support for its approval. Second, Ramos promised to redraw provincial boundaries in order to create a greater number of provinces with a Muslim majority. In return for these concessions, Nur Misuari agreed to run for election as governor of the existing ARMM under the banner of President Ramos' party.[60]

The Jakarta Accord was viewed as a breakthrough and was enthusiastically received by the MNLF as well as its main supporter, the Organisation of Islamic Conference (OIC). Yet, less than a month after the Accord was signed, the deal stumbled. Christian settlers in the areas affected by the agreement and local government leaders pressed the Christian-dominated legislature in Manila to dilute the Accord.[61] According to one well-known specialist on the Moros, the new structures were given "very limited funding, no police powers, no control over national projects and programmes that were supposed to be within their remit, and no jurisdiction over significant sections of the bureaucracy in the region." The result was a deal that had little real meaning for the MNLF and violence continued as a result.

Ramos, however, followed through with his promise to initiate similar peace talks with the MILF. A month after the Jakarta Accord

[57] Ramos (1999). [58] Santos (2005: 3). [59] Santos (2005: 3).
[60] Gutierrez (1999: 1–2). [61] Bacani (2005).

was signed, the MILF sat down for the first time to negotiate with the government. What followed was two years of negotiations during which the MILF refused to accept anything less than independence. This hard bargaining stance reflected the MILF's strong military position at the time. By October 1996, the MILF had built itself into a formidable force, with more than 12,000 armed fighters and significant support from Muslims in central Mindanao.[62] Intermittent negotiations were held between the government and the MILF between 1996 and 2000, during which almost seventy documents were signed including joint communiqués, resolutions, agreements on cease-fires, procedural issues, and various verifications. No agreement, however, was ever reached on the social, cultural, economic, and political autonomy the MILF was seeking.[63]

Although Ramos did not succeed in resolving the war in Mindanao, he behaved in the conciliatory way the reputation theory would have expected. Ramos strongly supported deep concessions to the MNLF and pressed the legislature to support the Jakarta Accord. He also willingly initiated negotiations with the more radical MILF. Ramos also attempted to resuscitate the CAR by pressing for a new plebiscite after the first was rejected, even campaigning for its passage. Ramos, therefore, seemed sincere in his desire to grant significant autonomy to the three main factions seeking self-determination.[64] Domestic politics, however, again hampered the implementation of any deals that were offered. Majorities in both regions were not willing to vote for the degree of autonomy that the separatist groups sought and congress was able to block additional concessions that would have made the transfer of power more likely.

---

[62] Bacani (2005: 5).   [63] Bacani (2005: 5).

[64] No administration agreed to negotiate with Abu-Sayyaf, which was engaged primarily in bombings, assassinations, kidnappings, and extortion, and is labeled a terrorist organization by the United States Department of State, the Philippines government, and the European Union.

CONFLICT RISK IN THE PHILIPPINES: THE RULE OF
JOSEPH ESTRADA, 1998–2001

Underlying conditions and predictions

Estrada, a popular film actor, won the 1998 election by presenting himself as a political outsider and someone who would advocate for the large portion of the Philippine electorate that was poor. From the start, Estrada pursued a strategy completely at odds with the reputation theory. While other presidents (especially Aquino and Ramos) had been conciliatory from the beginning of their terms, Estrada was militant. His inaugural address set the tone for the policies that would follow: "Huwag ninyo akong subukan (Don't test me)," he claimed.[65] Within a year Estrada suspended all negotiations with the MILF, refused to set dates for the resumption of talks, and insisted that he would not meet with MILF leaders as long as they demanded full independence. Estrada's hardline stance developed into a military campaign in early 2000 when the president gave the go-ahead for the army to attack the MILF's main headquarters and military camps. The president did not resume negotiations with the MILF during the remainder of what turned out to be a highly corrupt and unpopular administration.

Estrada's behavior cannot be explained by the reputation theory. With no additional ethnic minorities interested in secession, Estrada should have been eager to negotiate, yet instead he escalated the violence. It is not clear why Estrada pursued this particular strategy and little justification is offered in the literature or his speeches for this policy. One explanation may be that Estrada needed to wear down the MILF to the point where they were willing to accept something less than full independence. If the government had any real chance of convincing the MILF to accept a compromise short of independence (the only compromise that might be acceptable to the majority of Filipino citizens) it would have to convince

---

[65] This has since become the most famous line of Estrada's inaugural speech.

the MILF that victory on the battlefield was impossible. A second explanation is simply incompetence. Estrada did not appear to focus heavily on events in Mindanao or elsewhere, preferring to spend his time gambling and drinking. Critics accused him of running the Philippines "like a gangland boss" using his position to buy loyalty and plunder the country's coffers. It is possible, therefore, that Estrada represents a leader immune to rational calculations, even if these calculations were necessary to keep him in office. Three years after entering office, Estrada became the first Philippine president to be impeached.

CONFLICT RISK IN THE PHILIPPINES: THE RULE OF GLORIA MACAPAGAL-ARROYO 2001–

Underlying conditions and predictions

President Gloria Macapagal-Arroyo entered office in January 2001 after Estrada was removed from power and she immediately reverted to more conciliatory policies toward the Moros. Within two months of entering office, Arroyo declared a unilateral cease-fire, dropped criminal charges against top MILF leaders, and prepared to release more than twenty suspected MILF supporters. She also signaled that she was serious about negotiating a settlement by putting together new negotiating teams comprised of lawyers, academics, and non-govermental organization (NGO) leaders rather than the military officials used by Estrada.

Arroyo had good reasons to re-start negotiations. In a speech in February 2001, Arroyo announced, "that building peace would be less expensive than supporting an all-out war."[66] According to the premier expert on MILF negotiations,

> there [was] a growing realization in the Philippines that fighting it out on the battlefield simply does not work. The major wars ...

---

[66] Statement by President Gloria Macapagal-Arroyo at a press conference, Malacanang, February 20, 2001.

did not bring Manila or the MILF any tactical advantage. In fact, the offensives were not only costly in terms of human casualties and civilian dislocations, but also led the MILF to wage guerilla warfare that proved more difficult for the government to contain.[67]

By the end of 2001, Arroyo also feared the growth of Islamic extremism in Southeast Asia and saw settlement as a way to contain it.

Negotiations between the government and the MILF were initiated in July 24, 2001 and were described as "fast-paced."[68] The MILF rescinded its demand for full independence and agreed to a cease-fire in return for economic development for Mindanao. But the sticking point in these negotiations continued to be the holding of a plebiscite. President Arroyo insisted that a plebiscite be conducted to determine if other provinces and cities in the south wished to widen the scope of the ARMM. Voters in the four provinces already in the ARMM would be asked if they were in favor of the expansion of the autonomous region, while voters of the non-ARMM provinces and cities would be asked if they were in favor of including their province or city in the ARMM.[69]

Both the MNLF and the MILF announced that they would boycott the plebiscite scheduled to be held on August 14, 2001. Nur Misuari, ARMM governor and chairman of the MNLF, opposed it claiming it violated the 1996 Jakarta Accord which called for the automatic expansion of the coverage of the ARMM after a transition period. The MILF rejected the offer, arguing that the ARMM had done nothing to improve the plight of Muslim Filipinos and was, therefore, not the basis on which they wished to negotiate. The result was that only one additional province (Basilan) and one additional city (Marawi) voted to join the ARMM.[70]

Additional negotiations were held intermittently from the end of 2001 until February 2003 when attacks between the

---

[67] Bacani (2005: 7).   [68] See Cagoco-Guiam (2002: 3).
[69] Cagoco-Guiam (2002: 5).   [70] Cagoco-Guiam (2002: 5).

Philippine army and the MILF caused Arroyo to suspend peace talks. Negotiations resumed between 2003 and 2005, stalling several times amid fighting on the ground and allegations of terror links. Almost ten years after the first concessions were offered in the Tripoli agreement, violence continues.

CONCLUSION

The Philippines case reveals the strengths as well as some of the limitations of the reputation theory. On the one hand, the reputation theory helped clarify why so many presidents in the Philippines (including Marcos) were willing to negotiate with separatist groups, while their counterparts in Indonesia were not. Marcos, Aquino, Ramos, Estrada, and Arroyo never mentioned the fear of disintegration or any triggering effect conciliation might have, and every president except Estrada actively negotiated. On the other hand, it cannot explain why violence lasted so long despite incentives to settle.

What the case shows is the way in which competing interests can stand in the way of settlement even when few incentives exist to be tough. According to Philippine scholar Benedicto Bacini, an expert on the peace process, "there seems to be no question about the resolve of the government ... The greatest concern of many is ... whether the Filipino nation can embrace it as its common roadmap for peace and prosperity in Mindanao."[71] The case, therefore, helps illuminate why Manila was not able to offer sufficiently attractive terms to buy peace. Successive presidents were willing to transfer political power to the Moros and the Igorot, but they were not willing to do so in the absence of majority support from the larger Christian population, and Christians, especially those living in Mindanao, did not want to transfer significant political control to the Muslim minority.

The case, however, also reveals that offers of autonomy, such as the offers Ramos made to the MNLF and the MILF, often do not end

[71] Bacini (2005: 11–12).

the violence because their implementation is simply not credible. Ramos may have been sincere in his desire to grant significant concessions to the Moros, but as long as implementation would be tied to support granted by the Philippine congress, its fulfillment would be dubious.

Thus, the Philippine government found itself caught between its desire to end a costly armed separatist challenge and the significant pressures placed upon it by various interest groups, especially Mindanao Christians, not to make any substantive concessions to Muslim separatists. This has resulted in the creation of a succession of autonomous entities in Mindanao that are limited in size and power, and have not been sufficient to obtain peace.[72] Even governments with few incentives to be tough, therefore, may still find it politically difficult to make the concessions that will allow them to avoid war.

[72] McKenna (2004: 1–2).

Part IV **Conclusions**

8   Reputation building and deterrence in civil wars

This book was about separatist conflicts and why they so often turn violent. The puzzle was simple but important. Disputes that arise between ethnic minorities and their governments over self-determination are the most frequent source of violent conflict in the world today.[1] They are also the most intractable.[2] Between 1940 and 2000, 122 ethnic groups demanded greater territorial autonomy or independence from the central state.[3] In the vast majority of these cases the government responded by refusing to compromise on any issue related to territory, even if they faced armed rebellion as a result.

The answer to the puzzle has to do with a particular bargaining problem that emerges in these types of strategic situations. Whenever a single defender faces a series of smaller opponents seeking a share of a fixed pie, incentives exist to invest in reputation building. It is because there are so many ethnic groups, occupying so much valuable land, in so many countries, that governments in these countries feel compelled to be tough.

Self-determination disputes, therefore, represent a set of cases where war is a rational strategy for governments to pursue (at least against early challengers) because it provides credible information about future intent. War is not being pursued because land is always valuable, because ethnic minorities are so easy to defeat, or because compromises short of fighting can't be found. Many wars have been fought over land that is relatively useless, against ethnic groups that

---

[1] Since 1980, almost half of all armed conflicts have been fought between governments and ethnic minority groups seeking self-determination.
[2] See Walter (2002).   [3] See Gledisch *et al.* (2002).

are formidable, and in the face of autonomy agreements that would make both sides happy. Instead, governments are using war to signal that secession will be costly.

THE THEORY

The argument in this book builds on theories of reputation building and deterrence from economics, especially those related to the chain store paradox. When applied to self-determination disputes, this fairly simple theoretical framework tells a rich story about government and ethnic group behavior. At the most basic level it tells us that governments make decision about whether to negotiate with separatists based in part on the information they believe this will provide to other groups considering secession. Governments – even governments that have little interest in retaining a particular piece of land – have strong incentives to fight if it convinces other more valuable regions to remain silent. Conversely, not all governments need to invest in reputation building. Countries with relatively few concentrated ethnic minorities (such as Canada or Czechoslovakia) gain little from developing reputations for toughness and have the luxury to seek compromise settlements without first fighting a war.

The theory, however, tells us much more about behavior, especially the ways in which different strategic contexts influence decisions to fight or compromise, challenge or stay quiet. Governments, especially conciliatory ones, have declining incentives to be tough as the number of remaining challengers, the value of future lands, and the costs of fighting for these lands decrease. Governments, therefore, should be attentive to the number of remaining challengers as well as their relative value and capabilities when deciding how to act. It is only when future lands represent significant value to the government that costly signaling becomes important.

Ethnic groups are quite aware of the strategic incentives governments have to be tough. They understand that if a government chooses to accommodate, this is strong evidence that a government is likely to be conciliatory in the future. They also understand that a government's incentives to fight (at least governments inclined to compromise) will change over time. Just because a government has never compromised, as was the case with Suharto in the 1970s, 1980s, and 1990s, does not mean that incentives will always favor continued war. As the number of remaining challengers decreases, and the expected utility of fighting decreases, the incentives to negotiate will improve. Thus, ethnic groups will not only look at the government's past behavior to determine how it is likely to behave in the future, but also at the full range of conditions encouraging deterrence over time.

Reputation building is not, however, a perfect tool for preventing war. As discussed in Chapter 2, separatist groups do not always correctly estimate when governments will make a deal. Some move too early, before governments are ready to reveal a willingness to compromise. Others want independence so badly that they challenge even if they know this will initiate war. The fact that reputation building does not prevent all wars, however, does not detract from its ability to prevent a higher number of wars from breaking out over time. In the absence of at least one war with one separatist group, governments would likely be facing many more.

FINDINGS

This book provided a significant amount of evidence in favor of reputation building and deterrence in self-determination disputes. In fact, evidence from three different sources – lab experiments on undergraduates, statistical analyses of data on self-determination movements and ethnic groups, and qualitative analyses of recent history in Indonesia and the Philippines – suggests that the findings are no accident.

Chapter 3 focused on the predictions of the chain store model, and not on the implications of this model for self-determination disputes. The laboratory experiments confirmed important parts of the reputation theory, but also revealed where human beings were likely to deviate from existing expectations about rational behavior.

Most individuals, when placed in a strategic situation analogous to a chain store game, figured out how reputation building could be used to their advantage. Most defenders chose to fight entrants even if they were assigned a "weak" type, and were willing to continue fighting until almost the last challenger. Similarly, most entrants jumped at the chance to challenge after observing a defender backing down. Thus, strong inferences were being taken from the past behavior of the defender.

But the experiments revealed that a sub-set of individuals did not respond to incentives in the way the model predicted. Some individuals were more altruistic, risk averse, or honest than the model took into account, and their behavior affected the results. These findings caused me to modify some of my expectations of what we should observe in the field. In particular, I expected that governments would engage in reputation building even when faced with relatively few groups and that they would focus more heavily on the number of remaining challengers than on the absolute number of challengers. I also expected a small percentage of government leaders to be unexpectedly conciliatory toward early challengers and that this tendency would encourage more ethnic groups to challenge. Results from both the large-n studies and the case studies confirmed the first two predictions. Governments did engage in reputation building even when only a handful of potential ethnic separatists existed. And they did focus heavily on the number of remaining challengers. Additional case analysis, however, would be needed to confirm that some leaders are, in fact, more altruistic, risk averse, or honest and that ethnic groups take advantage of this.

Chapters 4 and 5 are the first studies to demonstrate that reputation building not only predicts when governments will accommodate different ethnic groups, but also when ethnic groups will challenge the government. These chapters are particularly convincing because they provide evidence (using two different datasets) that both government responses *and* group challenges are affected by reputational concerns. As predicted, governments were significantly more likely to accommodate ethnic minorities seeking self-determination if there were few additional ethnic groups in a country. They were even more likely to accommodate if there were few remaining ethnic groups that were geographically concentrated or had grievances against the state. Governments also adjusted their behavior based on the larger strategic context in which they operated. Governments were significantly more likely to make concessions to an ethnic group seeking self-determination if other ethnic groups in that country occupied less valuable land, and were relatively weak.

The quantitative tests also confirmed that ethnic groups change their behavior based on a government's past behavior and the incentives the government has to invest in reputation building. Ethnic groups were significantly more likely to challenge if a government had backed down to another group and if future lands were not very valuable. This pattern was also confirmed in Chapter 4 where governments that had accommodated one group experienced significantly more subsequent challenges than those that had not.

The quantitative evidence, however, did not tell us everything. It revealed that the number of ethnic minorities in a country and the value of the land were statistically related to whether a government accommodated a demand for self-determination. It also told us that statistically significant relationships existed between a government's past behavior and decisions by ethnic groups to try for independence, and between the number of ethnic groups in a country and the likelihood that any one of them would challenge. These results, however, told us nothing about whether reputation building played any role in these decisions.

A closer look at events in Indonesia and the Philippines over the last half-century helped evaluate causality. This more micro-level data confirmed the importance of reputation building, especially in the decisions by successive Indonesian presidents to fight aggressively against separatists in Ambon, East Timor, Aceh, and West Papua, and the decisions by successive Philippine presidents to make concessions in Mindanao and the Cordillera. Presidents Suharto, Habibie, Wahid, and Sukarnoputri were not only concerned about triggering separatist demands from the many ethnic minorities within Indonesia, but they appeared especially concerned about triggering separatist demands in the oil-rich regions of Riau and East Kalimantan. Marcos on the other hand did not appear particularly concerned about encouraging separatist demands within the Cordillera. We also saw how certain nascent separatist groups such as the one in Riau were deterred from activating demands after observing heavy-handed government crackdowns in Aceh. A strategic game centered around reputation was clearly being played by presidents and ethnic minorities in Indonesia and not in the Philippines, just as the theory would predict.

The empirical chapters, however, also revealed the range of factors that influenced governments and ethnic groups in these disputes. Reputation was important, but other factors influenced ethnic groups to seek self-determination and governments to grant concessions. Chapter 4 revealed that governments care deeply about the economic value of the land that is currently under dispute, in addition to the economic value of future lands. The importance of natural resources, especially oil and natural gas, was clear in the case studies on Indonesia and the Philippines. Had Aceh, West Papua, Mindanao, and the Cordillera not been resource rich, there would have been little reason for government intervention in those regions, and self-determination movements would likely not have emerged. Thus, one cannot separate reputation arguments from arguments that focus on present interests or capabilities since the value of reputation building and deterrence depends on the expected value of fighting to hold on to future stakes compared to the expected value of fighting to hold on to current ones.[4] It is this present–future tradeoff that determines whether reputation building is necessary.

---

[4] Not surprisingly, Michael Tomz argued and found this same pattern in his book on reputations in international lending.

EXPLAINING THE OUTLIERS

The reputation theory as presented in Chapter 2 could not explain behavior in all self-determination disputes or even some unusual behaviors observed in cases that generally fit the predictions of the model. Four types of outliers stand out. First, some ethnic groups chose to be the first in their country to seek self-determination when it was clear that the government was likely to fight. The Ambonese and the East Timorese, for example, chose to challenge Jakarta even though they knew this would almost certainly bring them pain. Second, some governments, such as those led by Habibie, chose to accommodate these early groups when it appeared as if this was likely to trigger additional challenges. Third, governments did not always lose a reputation for being tough simply by making one concession to one group. Habibie was able to offer East Timor full independence without convincing new movements to emerge. Reputations, therefore, did not have the grim reaper quality (where a single act of accommodation caused a government to be labeled weak forever) that the theory predicted. Finally, governments sometimes failed to offer sufficient concessions to buy peace even if they showed a willingness to negotiate. The Philippine government had little reason to build a reputation for toughness in a country with only two potential separatist groups, yet the war in Mindanao continues today.

Both the lab experiments and the case studies helped answer these questions and in the process improved the theory. We learned from the experiments that certain defenders did not respond to material incentives to build reputations for toughness, and would not bluff even if they could obtain more payoffs as a result. These subjects gave a variety of reasons for this off-the-equilibrium path behavior, but one common explanation had to do with bluffing. If reputation building was based on lying to an opponent, some individuals simply would not do it. This may explain at least some of the cases where leaders are willing to concede even if this makes life more difficult.

The case study on Indonesia, however, offered a second explanation for why a leader might back down to an early opponent. Habibie was able to make deep concessions to an early challenger (the East Timorese) because that challenger had already paid heavy costs to obtain these concessions. Thus, governments can grant concessions to early challengers and avoid being labeled weak if the price for accommodation has already been shown to be high.

Habibie's behavior also offered two insights into how reputations could be salvaged when concessions are made. For one, Habibie and his government were able to make a credible case that East Timor was quite different from the rest of Indonesia due to its history as a former Portuguese colony, its forcible incorporation into Indonesia, and the significant support it had from the international community. Second, Habibie could draw on the reputation his predecessors had built regarding the price of independence. By 1999 the Indonesian government had already signaled that any attempt at independence, even a successful attempt, would come at a very high price. Backing down to an early opponent, therefore, may not always be as deleterious to one's reputation as the model had predicted.

The case of Indonesia also revealed that early movers tend to be quite different from other separatist groups. All of the early movers in Indonesia had either once been independent or had enjoyed a significant amount of autonomy which was then rescinded by the government they were opposing. Ambon, East Timor, West Papua, and to a lesser degree Aceh, all initiated challenges as a result of Jakarta's unwillingness to allow them to maintain a degree of separateness. The desire to hold onto independence or regain it once it had been lost appeared to be a stronger motivator than any other grievance, and helped distinguish these more committed "early movers" from the rest of the pack. Ethnic groups whose grievances stemmed from economic exploitation or various forms of discrimination either challenged much later when incentives for the government to fight were lower, or did not challenge at all.

Finally, the Philippine case helped answer why government concessions did not always buy peace. The reputation model presented in Chapter 2 did not take into account the fact that governments might not always have the political flexibility to offer ethnic groups as much autonomy as a particular leader would like. This was apparent in all of the negotiations between Manila and the Moro National Liberation Front (MNLF) and Moro Islamic Liberation Front (MILF) where successive presidents, although eager to resolve the conflict, were restrained by Christian majorities and congress. Having no incentives to invest in reputation building, therefore, does not mean that a compromise settlement will always result. Conciliatory governments must still navigate a difficult set of domestic negotiations about the terms of settlement they are allowed to offer.

CONTRIBUTIONS TO THE LITERATURE

This book began as an attempt to explain why governments chose to fight so many ethnic separatists despite the high costs of war. In the process, it has engaged two different sets of literature, making contributions to each. The first and most central contribution is the one related to the outbreak of civil wars, especially secessionist wars. To date, most research on civil wars has focused almost exclusively on the underlying structural conditions that increase a country's risk of war and largely ignored the bargaining problems that may stand in the way of settlement.[5] Potential rebel groups are assumed to act reflexively to the conditions in which they find themselves; if they are poor or discriminated against, they should rebel. Governments, in turn, are assumed to have little influence over the outbreak of war. Yet we know that governments have the ability to prevent or avoid separatist wars by granting various degrees of autonomy or even independence. The contribution this study makes to the study of civil wars is to move beyond these structural arguments and show

---

[5] See for example Collier and Hoeffler (2001), Fearon and Laitin (2003), Esty *et al.* (1995, 1998) and Hegre *et al.* (2001).

how a particular type of bargaining problem (private information), in a particular type of strategic situation (a repeated game), can create real incentives to go to war. The need to build a reputation for toughness in the face of many future challengers is a neglected explanation for civil war.

The second contribution relates to the international relations literature on reputation. The reputation theory presented in Chapters 1 and 2 took pains to identify where reputation building was likely to emerge, and revealed which strategic situations lent themselves to this type of signaling behavior. Reputation building is not likely to be a rational strategy to pursue in all conflict situations all of the time. But it is likely to be rational in situations like self-determination disputes, where a single large defender is interacting with a series of similar opponents seeking similar concessions over time. By looking at the right strategic environment, therefore, this study joins recent efforts by Tomz and Sartori in finding significant empirical evidence for the power of reputation. Reputation building in international relations does matter, but only in the right context.

POLICY IMPLICATIONS

The main motivation to write this book was to understand why disputes over self-determination were so intractable. If additional separatist wars can be prevented, and existing separatist wars resolved, then one of the main types of violent conflict in the world today could potentially disappear. At first glance, the main conclusion policymakers might draw from this study is a pessimistic one: encourage governments to fight brutal wars against any ethnic minority that has the audacity to challenge for greater self-rule. This will reduce the number of additional self-determination challenges that are made and prevent additional wars from being fought.

But there are at least three additional ways to reduce the number of violent separatist wars without first having to fight one. Two are directed at governments. Governments can significantly lower the likelihood of fighting a war against a separatist group by simply resisting the urge to confiscate the autonomy that ethnic groups already enjoy, especially if that ethnic group is geographically concentrated. One of the important lessons we have learned from this study is that lengthy and costly civil wars tend to occur against early movers who are motivated to regain autonomy that they have lost. Indonesia, for example, could have avoided the costly war with East Timor if it had not invaded when Portugal left. It could also have avoided the war in West Papua if it had allowed the region to continue on its path toward independence as the Dutch originally intended. Similarly, the Philippine government could have prevented self-determination movements from emerging in Mindanao if it had allowed it to retain autonomy when the Americans left, and resisted the urge to settle the land with Christians from the north. Governments, therefore, should think very carefully about rescinding autonomy and independence from groups that already enjoy it, for it is these groups that are most likely to fight.

A second lesson for governments is that they need not fight "to the death" in order to deter other ethnic groups from seeking independence. They need only show that gaining independence will be costly. Habibie, for example, was able to grant independence to East Timor and still deter Riau and East Kalimantan by making it clear that independence would only be gained after much bloodshed. This does not mean that governments will be able to avoid war entirely and still deter additional groups. But it does mean that longstanding disputes in places like Sri Lanka and Chechnya need not continue simply because of reputational concerns. Governments in both countries have the ability to negotiate with separatists without triggering additional movements since the signal they have already sent is quite clear.

The final way to reduce costly separatist wars lies in the hands of ethnic minorities considering self-determination. We learned in Chapter 1 that reputation building only made sense if a game is likely to be repeated. The greater the number of potential challengers, the more likely a government is to fight. Ethnic groups, however, have the ability to change a repeated game into a single-shot game, and in so doing eliminate any incentives an otherwise conciliatory government has to be tough. Rather than challenge the government in a haphazard way or sequentially, separatists can coordinate their challenges and launch them simultaneously. In this way, the government faces only a single challenge and has far greater incentives to negotiate. Governments may not offer independence as a result of this coordinated move, but they are far more likely to offer some degree of political autonomy as a result. The emergence of a coordinated movement among indigenous groups in Central and South America in recent years suggests that potential challengers are aware of this strategy.

Finally, one pattern deserves comment. The number of armed conflicts over self-determination steadily increased between 1956 and 1991 and has been declining ever since.[6] This decline in separatist conflicts is the result of two phenomena. First, fewer ethnic groups are demanding self-determination, so the number of new challenges is declining. Second, existing challenges are being resolved at a higher rate. I believe the reputation theory may help explain both of these trends. If it is true that governments are more likely to fight early movers, then the 1960s, 1970s, and 1980s may have been the decades during which governments were building their reputations for toughness. The drop in new challenges that we've seen since 1991, therefore, may be the result of additional ethnic groups being successfully deterred by these earlier wars. The increase in negotiated settlements may be the result of governments negotiating their way out of wars after a sufficient amount of costs have been inflicted. The costly wars that have already been fought, therefore, may have allowed governments to settle now.

---

[6] Center for International Development and Conflict Management (CIDCM) data on self-determination movements.

The findings from this study, therefore, do not paint an inexorably dark picture about self-determination and the prospects for peace. By revealing the incentives governments have to invest in reputation building and tracing the effects they have on behavior, we are able to see how additional violence may be prevented and resolved. Self-determination disputes aren't the most conflict-prone type of dispute because land is so valuable or ethnicity so explosive. They are violent because of the difficult strategic situation governments and ethnic groups find themselves in, and the incentives this creates to fight.

Appendix 1: Instructional materials for subjects

During the instruction period we read the following script and provided subjects with two worksheets.

EXPERIMENT INSTRUCTIONS
Thank you for agreeing to participate in this research experiment on group decision making. During the experiment we require your complete, undistracted attention. You may not chat with other students, or engage in other distracting activities, such as using your phone or headphones, reading books, etc. Please turn all cell phones to silent.

For your participation, you will be paid in cash, at the end of the experiment. Different participants may earn different amounts. You will be paid privately, and are under no obligation to tell others how much you earned. What you earn depends on your decisions and the decisions of others. It is very important that you follow the instructions closely. All participants in this experiment receive the exact same set of the following instructions.

The entire experiment will take place through computer terminals, and all interaction between each of you will take place through the computers. It is important that you do not talk or in any way try to communicate with other subjects during the experiments. If you disobey the rules, you will be asked to leave the experiment.

We will start with a brief instruction period. If you have any questions during this period, raise your hand and your question will be answered so that everyone can hear. If any difficulties arise after the experiment has begun, raise your hand, and an experimenter will come and assist you.

Instructions

Subjects will be split into two groups, a 'first-mover' group and a 'second-mover' group. Your assignment will be the same for the whole session. Whether you are a first-mover or a second-mover is determined randomly and shown on your computer screen once the experiment starts.

The decision situation

The experiment is divided into eight periods. In every experiment round each of the second-movers is paired with eight different first-movers. An experiment round ends when the second-mover has been paired with each of these first-movers once. No one will play the same person twice in an experiment round.

The experiment begins with first-movers choosing between one of two alternatives. The decision situation is projected at the front of the room. These alternatives are labeled A1 and A2 respectively. Choosing 'A1' produces an amount of points that depends on how second-mover subjects respond. Note that if A2 is chosen, the second-mover's choice does not affect the outcome. The second-mover they are paired with then chooses 'if A1 was chosen, I will choose B1' or 'if A1 was chosen, I will choose B2' on a similar screen.

This process repeats until everyone has been paired with everyone *once*. Thus, each second-mover will encounter a sequence of eight different first-movers in a round. Each first-mover will play each second-mover, but each time at a later period in the round.

To illustrate how you will be paired with other subjects and to show you how to read information provided on your screen, we will take you through an example round of the experiment. Please follow our directions exactly. Please click on the icon titled zLeaf on your desktop. On the first screen you are told whether you are a first-mover or second-mover. If you are a second-mover you are also told whether you are type 1 or type 2. We will explain the difference in a moment. Please click OK. On the next screen you are able to make a decision. If you are a first-mover you are paired with a single second-mover, and vice versa. The left hand side of the screen will report information about the second-mover in the pairing. This information will be the choice of previous first-movers they are paired with, and the choice of the second-mover if A1 is chosen.

This screen does not yet have any information. An example of what a first-mover will see in the first period is projected at the front of the room. Now, we are projecting what a second-mover will see in the first period.

If you are in the first row of seats, choose A1 if you are a first-mover and B1 if you are a second-mover. If you are in the second row, choose A2 if you are a first-mover and B2 if you are a second-mover. Please remember to hit OK after your decision. If you are in the third row of seats choose A1 if you are a first-mover and B1 if you are a second-mover. The next screen you see is slightly different than the previous screen. If you are a first-mover, you are now paired with a different second-mover. The information you see on the left side of the screen is information about what this second-mover faced in the first period. Unlike the decision made in the first period, all subjects have a record of what the second-mover faced in the previous period. If the first-mover they were paired with chose A1, you will see how the second-mover responded. If the first-mover they were paired with chose A2, you will not see the decision of the second-mover. If you are a second-mover, you see exactly the same information that the person you are currently paired with sees. This information is your own history: what the first-mover you faced in the first period did, and what your response was if they chose A1.

The screen at the front of the room shows what a first-mover might see in the second period. In this case, they are paired with a second-mover whose choice in the first period did not matter, because the first-mover they were paired with chose A2. The next screen shows what a second-mover might face in the second round. This shows that the first-mover they were paired with chose A2, and thus their choice is not recorded. Are there any questions?

If you are in the first row, choose A2 if you are a first-mover and B2 if you are a second-mover. If you are in the second row, choose A1 if you are a first-mover and B1 if you are a second-mover. If you are in the third row, choose A1 if you are a first-mover and B1 if you are a second-mover. Please hit OK. If you are a first-mover, you are now paired with a different second-mover. The information you see on the left side of the screen is information about what this second-mover faced in the first period and second period. If you are a second-mover, you see exactly the same information that the person you are currently paired with sees. This information is your own history: what the first-mover you faced in the first period did, what a different first-mover did in the second period, and what your responses were if they chose A1. The screen at the front of the room shows what a first-mover might see in the third period. In this case, they are paired with a second-mover whose first period choice was B2 in response to a first-mover that chose A1. In the second period, this same second-mover faced a first-mover that chose A2, and so the second-mover choice was not recorded.

If you are in the first row, choose A1 if you are a first-mover and B2 if you are a second-mover. If you are in the second row, choose A2 if you are a first-mover and B1 if you are a second-mover. If you are in the third row, choose A2 if you are a first-mover and B2 if you are a second-mover. Please hit 'OK'. You now see the screen for the fourth period. The screen projected at the front of the room shows the information a second-mover might see. In the first period, their first-mover chose A2, and thus their response is not recorded. In the second period their first-mover (a different person) chose A1 and they responded B1. In the third period their first-mover chose A2 and thus the second-mover choice is not recorded. Please take a moment to review the information on the left side of your screen. Remember, all of the information reflects what we told everyone to do. In the experiment, everyone will be able to make his or her own choices.

If you are in the first row, choose A2 if you are a first-mover and B1 if you are a second-mover. If you are in the second row, choose A1 if you are a first-mover and B2 if you are a second-mover. If you are in the third row, choose A1 if you are a first-mover and B1 if you are a second-mover. Please hit OK.

This process would continue for eight periods, until all first-movers and second-movers have been paired once. At the end of the eighth period you will see the points you earned in the round.

Instructions for points

You have been provided with a diagram that lists how points are earned by subjects. Please turn to the side that says 'first-mover subjects.'

If you are assigned a first-mover role, you should use this side. Please focus your attention on the screen at the front of the room. First-movers can choose A1 or A2. If the first-mover chooses A2, the FM gets 95 pts and the second-mover gets 300 pts. If the first-mover chooses A1, then the points they earn will depend on what the second-mover does. If the second-mover chooses B1, the first-mover earns 150 pts. If the second-mover chooses B2, the first-mover earns 80 pts.

Now let's talk about the second-mover. The second-mover gets the most points if the first-mover chooses A2 – 300 pts. But if the first-mover chooses A1, then the second-mover's points depend on whether the second-mover is a type 1 or type 2. Approximately two-thirds of second-movers will be type 1, and approximately one-third will be type 2. Type 1 second-movers get more points for choosing B1 (160 pts) than choosing B2 (70 pts). This scenario is listed at the top of the page and is projected on the screen at the front of the room. Type 2 second-movers get more points from choosing B2 (160) than B1 (70). This scenario is listed at the bottom of the page and is now projected on the screen at the front of the room.

Are there any questions?

Please turn to the side that says 'second-mover subjects.' If you are a second-mover, you should use this side. The situation is the same as we just described, but is presented from the perspective of the second-mover. If you are a type 1 second-mover and A1 has been chosen, you receive more points from choosing B1 than B2. If you are a type 2 second-mover and A1 has been chosen, you receive more points from choosing B2 than B1. All second-movers earn the most amount of points by the first-mover choosing A2. All first-movers earn the most amount of points by choosing A1 and the second-mover choosing B1. The next highest amount of points comes from choosing A2. First-movers receive the least amount of points from choosing A1 and the second-mover choosing B2.

Are there any questions?

The experiment may, or may not, be repeated several times. If the experiment is repeated, you will keep the same first-mover/second-mover assignment, and second-movers will keep their same type.

In this experiment, you will be playing for real money. All earnings are expressed in terms of points. Points will be converted into dollars at the rate of $2 per 1,000 points. If the experiment is repeated, this conversion rate will be adjusted. For example, if the experiment is repeated twice, you will earn $2 per 2,000 points. In addition, all subjects are paid a $10 show-up fee. Your earnings do not depend on the earnings of other subjects in your sub-group. For example, if you are a first-mover, your earnings do not depend on the earnings of other first-movers.

At the end of the experiment you will fill out a brief feedback form. When you have completed the feedback form please wait. We will notify you when we are ready for you to exit the room.

We have provided a sheet of paper with the basic information you need to know. On the opposite side of the paper we have listed several questions with answers. Please take a moment to read through this material.

Are there any questions before we begin the experiment?

We will now begin. If you are assigned a second-mover role, please record whether you are of type 1 or type 2 at the top of your worksheet.

BASIC FEATURES OF THE EXPERIMENT

- You will be divided into *two groups*: (1) first-movers and (2) second-movers.

- Second-movers come in *two types*:
  - Two-thirds are type 1 (get more points for choosing B1 than B2);
  - One-third are type 2 (get more points for choosing B2 than B1).
- The experiment will consist of eight periods. We may or may not repeat the experiment.
  - *A single period* = one second-mover paired with one first-mover.
  - *An experiment round* = one second-mover paired with eight different first-movers.
- *Information* will be available on the history of decisions within a round: first-movers see the choices previous first-movers made, and what the second-mover did if A1 was chosen, for the second-mover they are currently paired with. Second-movers see their 'own' history, which is their own decisions and the decisions made by each first-mover they were paired with.
- Points: will be determined by the choice you make and the choice your partner makes. Points are converted into cash.

Review questions

1) What does it mean when you see a blank information screen?
   Answer: You are in the first period and do not have any information about how second-movers decided in previous periods.
2) If you are a first-mover, does the amount of points you earn depend on the amount of points earned by other first-movers?
   Answer: No. The points you earn as a first-mover only depends on your own choices, and the choice made by second-movers you are paired with in a given period.
3) In the experiment there will be eight first-movers and eight second-movers. Of the eight second-movers, *approximately* how many of them will be a type 2 second-mover?
   Answer: One-third, or approximately two or three. This assignment of 'type' is determined by the computer randomly. On average in this experiment, four out of the twelve second-movers will be a type 2 second-mover, who gets more points for choosing B2 than B1.
4) If you are a first-mover, what does the information on the left side of the screen mean?

Answer: This information is what the second-mover you are currently paired with faced in earlier periods in the current round. It lists the first-mover's decision, and the second-mover's response if A1 was chosen.

5) If you are a second-mover, will the first-mover you are paired with in the third period be able to see what you did in the first period? *Answer*: Yes. As long as the first-mover chose A1 in the first period, all following first-movers (seven in a round) you are paired with will see your choice from the first period.

USE THIS SIDE IF YOU ARE A SECOND-MOVER

I am a type ___ second-mover.

If you are a type 1 second-mover:

- If the first-mover chooses A2 you get 300 pts and they get 95 pts.
- If the first-mover chooses A1 and you choose B1 you get 160 pts and they get 150 pts.
- If the first-mover chooses A1 and you choose B2 you get 70 pts and they get 80 pts.
- Type 1 second-movers get more points from B1 than B2 *if* A1 is chosen.

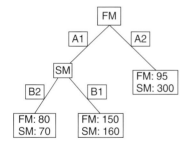

If you are a type 2 second-mover:

- If the first-mover chooses A2 you get 300 pts and they get 95 pts.
- If the first-mover chooses A1 and you choose B1 you get 70 pts and they get 150 pts.

- If the first-mover chooses A1 and you choose B2 you get 160 pts and they get 80 pts.
- Type 2 second-movers get more points from B2 than B1 *if* A1 is chosen.

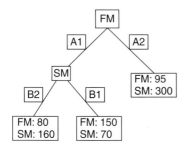

USE THIS SIDE IF YOU ARE A FIRST-MOVER

If you face a type 1 second-mover (probability = two-thirds):

- If you choose A2 you get 95 pts and they get 300 pts.
- If you choose A1 and they choose B1 you get 150 pts and they get 160 pts.
- If you choose A1 and they choose B2 you get 80 pts and they get 70 pts.
- Type 1 second-movers get more points from B1 than B2 *if* A1 is chosen.

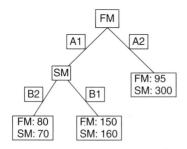

If you face a type 2 second-mover (probability = one-third):

- If you choose A2 you get 95 pts and they 300 pts.
- If you choose A1 and they choose B1 you get 150 pts and they get 70 pts.

- If you choose A1 and they choose B2 you get 80 pts and they get 160 pts.
- Type 2 second-movers get more points from B2 than B1 *if* A1 is chosen.

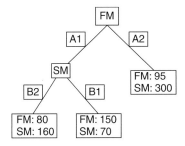

DETAILS OF THE EXPERIMENT DESIGN

Below we describe in more detail the two experiment designs by listing the critical features of each design.

Eight entrants, eight states (sixteen subjects)

(1) Sixteen players assigned to one of two roles, entrant (E) or state (S). We have $E_a1 : E_a8$ and $S_a1 : S_a8$.

(2) For each state there is a probability p that they are a 'strong' type, and probability 1-p that they are weak. This 'type' only changes the state's payoffs.

(3) For the first period each entrant within a group is matched with a single state. E.g., E_a1 is matched with S_a3 in the first period.

(4) The entrant decides if they will 'enter' or 'stay out'; the state is asked whether they will fight *if* the entrant enters.

(5) Payoffs for both players are calculated, but only observed at the end of the round.[1]

(6) After the first period, each entrant is then matched with a different state. E.g., E_a1 is matched with S_a5 for period 5.

(7) Steps 4–6 are repeated, but both the entrant and state see the entire history of play (*not payoffs*) up to the current period involving the

---

[1] Providing this information during the round would needlessly distract subjects away from using information about reputations.

particular state being faced. So, if E_a1 is matched with S_a5 in period 2, they see the decision E_an made against S_a5, and S_a5's response, in period 1. The state sees this same information on the screen asking them whether or not they will fight (if the entrant had chosen to enter). The entrant sees this information on the screen where they choose 'enter' or 'stay-out'. If the entrant does not enter, the state's decision is not recorded in the subject's observed history of play.

(8) This process is repeated until all entrants have played against all states within their group *once*. All players then observe their strategy choices, the strategy choice of the other player (if 'Enter' was chosen), and both per period and total payoffs at the end of the round.

(9) An exchange rate is used to change payoffs into dollars.

(10) In a questionnaire at the end of the experiment, subjects are asked to give advice to future players in the experiment.

Four entrants, four states (twenty-four subjects)

Laboratory logistics required a slightly different experimental procedure when there were only four entrants for each state. The 4 vs. 4 and 8 vs. 8 designs are identical in substance, but the 4 vs. 4 setup extracts much more information about play in this setting than would be possible if an identical procedure to the 8 vs. 8 were used. Subjects face exactly the same set of incentives – other than the different number of entrants each state faces – as in the 8 vs. 8.

(1) Divide subjects into three initial groups of eighty (group A, B, C). Within each group assign four entrant roles and four state roles. Thus, each subject has an ID such that S_{a3} is the third state player in group A.

(2) For each state there is a probability p that they are a 'strong' type, and probability 1-p that they are weak. This 'type' only changes the state's payoffs.

(3) Within each group, subjects play each other *once* (as in the eight-player case).

(4) After finishing playing with a group, subjects do not see their per period or summed payoffs. Instead, the state subjects of group A are assigned to play the entrant subjects of group B, group B states face group C entrants, and group C states face group A entrants.

(5) Players play within their new groups as above.

(6) Groups are rematched one more time (A states face C entrants, B states face A entrants, C states face B entrants).

(7) Entrants see their per period payoffs for each round and their total payoff.

(8) An exchange rate is used to change total payoffs into dollars. All other features are identical to eight-entrant design.

Appendix 2: Coding rules and sources for Chapter 4

DEPENDENT VARIABLE

Accommodation. Coded (0) no accommodation, (1) reform not over territory, (2) some form of territorial autonomy, (3) independence. A dispute was coded as having ended in "no accommodation" if the government was unwilling to make any concessions. If the government was willing to offer some concessions such as greater participation in government, or greater cultural autonomy in response to a challenge, the case was coded as "reform." A dispute was coded as having ended in "territorial autonomy" if the government was willing to grant the challenger greater political autonomy over their own region. Finally, a dispute was coded as having ended in "independence" if the government granted full independence to the challenging party. If a government experienced multiple negotiations with the same challenger over the course of a dispute, the case was coded based on the highest level of accommodation offered. (Source: Keesing's Contemporary Archives, group profiles provided by the Minorities at Risk (MAR) data project (see www.bsos.umd.edu/cidcm/mar/list.html), and individual case histories.)

INDEPENDENT VARIABLES

Hypotheses derived from the reputation theory

Number of ethnic groups. The total number of ethnic groups in a country, as listed in the "People" profile in the *Encyclopædia Britannica* Country Essays from Encyclopædia Britannica Online. Each number comes from the "People and ethnicity" section of the country description. (See website: http://search.eb.com/eb/article?eu=117943.)

   Number of concentrated groups. The total number of ethnopolitical groups that were either a majority in one region, or concentrated in one region. Based on the MAR coding of group spatial concentration. (Source: MAR dataset, version IV, variable GROUPCON.)

Number of ethnopolitical groups. A variable indicating the total number of ethnopolitical groups in a given country. Each group had to meet one of two criteria. A group had to be disadvantaged in comparison to other groups in their society, usually because of discriminatory practices, or a group had to be politically organized to promote or defend their collective interests. (Source: MAR dataset, version IV.)

Combined economic value, Combined strategic value, Combined autonomy. Composite measures that add up the economic and strategic value of all territories occupied by all ethnopolitical groups in the country, as well as the number of ethnopolitical groups that had been historically autonomous from the central government at any point in time. Coding for each individual measure from which these composite measures are created and its source is noted below.

Combined population proportion. A variable indicating the proportion of the total national population represented by all ethnopolitical groups in a country. The measure was the average population for the years 1990, 1995, and 1998, the only years for which MAR data were available, divided by the average total population in those years. (MAR IV, variable GPRO; data on total population were obtained from the World Bank *World Development Indicators* (WDI) and Penn World Tables.)

Hypotheses derived from theories based on present interests
Economic value. A thirty-one point scale indicating how many marketable resources were known to exist on a given piece of land. These resources included oil/petroleum, natural gas, coal, iron ore, steel, aluminum, titanium, bauxite, salt, sulfur, tin, nickel, chromium, cobalt, tungsten, phosphate, gold, silver, copper, zinc, lead, magnesium, uranium, diamonds, water, wheat, timber, fishing, tourism, commercial nuclear plants, or important manufacturing plants.

(Source: US Geological Survey maps, the CIA Factbook and related CIA maps, and group profiles provided by the MAR data project.)

Population proportion. The proportion of the total national population represented by the group launching the challenge under observation. The measure was the average population for the group in the year 1990, 1995, and 1998, the only years for which MAR data were available divided by the average national population in those years. (MAR IV, variable GPRO; data on total population were obtained from the World Bank (WDI) and Penn World Tables.)

Proportion of territory. The percent of the total land mass (in square kilometers, 1995) that an ethnopolitical group occupied. (Source: for identification of the region occupied by a group: Fearon and Laitin dataset, and MAR group profile. For size of region occupied by the group: The Columbia Gazetteer, and the Food and Agriculture Organization of the United Nations. When I could not identify a case with either of these sources, I searched for alternate sources through the Perry–Castaneda Library Map Collection, University of Texas. For total land mass of a given country: World Bank Indicators.)

Strategic value. Scale indicating whether territory included (1) a sea outlet, (2) a shipping lane, (3) a military base, (4) an international border, (5) an attack route, and/or (6) a mountain range. (Source: US Geological Survey maps, the CIA Factbook and related maps, and group profiles provided by MAR.)

Length of residence. Coded 1 if immigration occurred since 1945, 2 = in the nineteenth or early twentieth century, or 3 = pre-1800. (Source: MAR VI dataset, variable TRADITN2.)

Autonomy. A dummy variable coded 1 = the group was historically autonomous at some point in time, 0 = the group was never historically autonomous. (Source: MAR IV dataset, variable AUTON.)

Balance of capabilities: government side

Military personnel/population. Average annual number of military personnel during the duration of the self-determination movement under observation as a percent of the total population, divided by the average total population for a country during the duration of the movement. (Source: J. David Singer and Melvin Small's "Material Capabilities, 1816–1995" dataset, which collected its information from *The Military Balance*, which is published annually by the International Institute for Strategic Studies. Information for 1992–1998 was added using International Institute for Strategic Studies (IISS). Data on total population were obtained from the World Bank (WDI) and Penn World Tables.)

Military expenditures/Average gross domestic product (GDP). Average annual military expenditures in thousands of 1996 US dollars during the self-determination movement under observation as a proportion of average GDP during that same time period. (Source: same as military personnel, see above.)

Government instability. A dummy variable indicating whether the country in question had experienced a 3 or more change in its Polity IV combined democracy/autocracy score in any year during the course of the self-determination movement under observation. (Source: Polity IV, variable POLITY.)

GDP ***per capita***. Measures the average per capita GDP of a country over the duration of a challenge. (Source: Penn World Data.)

Balance of capabilities: formal challenger

Neighboring ethnic groups. The total number of adjoining countries where segments of the ethnopolitical group involved in the dispute also resided. (Source: MAR dataset, variable: NUMSEGX.)

Group concentration. The geographical concentration of a group ranging from widely dispersed to concentrated in one region. (Source: MAR dataset, variable GROUPCON.)

Mountainous terrain. The proportion of the country that is "mountainous" according to the codings of geographer A. J. Gerard. (Source: Fearon and Laitin, 2003; dataset on civil wars.)

Diaspora community in the US. Relative size of the group's population among the US foreign-born population. (Source: US Bureau of the Census (www.census.gov/population/); World Bank.)

Controls

Democracy. A democracy–autocracy measure derived from a government's autocratic features and its democratic features. The incumbent government's autocracy score was subtracted from its democracy score to produce a net democracy number that ranges in value from very autocratic (–10) to very democratic (+10). Based on the average democracy score for a country for the duration of a challenge. (Source: Polity IV dataset, Marshall and Jaggers, 2003, variable: POLITY.)

> **Proportional representation (PR).** A dummy variable coded 1 if a political system was based on proportional representation, 0 if not. Based on the highest level of PR during the duration of the dispute. (Source: World Bank (Keefer Dataset) for years 1975–98; *Stateman's Yearbook* for years 1955–70.)

> **Degree of centralization/federalism.** From the Polity III dataset that indicates the degree to which political authority is centralized (variable: CENT). Coded 1 for unitary states (centralized) where only moderate decision making authority is vested in local or regional governments; 2 for an intermediate category; 3 for a federal state (decentralized) where local and/or regional governments have substantial decision making authority. This variable was coded based on the lowest centralization score during the duration of the dispute. (Source: Jaggers and Gurr, 1996.)

> **Anocracy.** A dummy variable indicating whether a government scored between –5 and +5 on Polity IV's democracy/autocracy measure at any point during a challenge. (Source: Polity IV, Marshall and Jaggers, 2003, variable POLITY.)

> **Duration/years.** Number of years from the year a challenge was initiated to the year it officially ended. (Source: Center for International Development and Conflict Management (CIDCM); and group profiles provided by MAR.)

> **Violence.** A dummy variable coded 1 if a given group scored a 4, 5, 6, or 7 on MAR's "REBEL" scale. Coded 0 if it scored < 4. (Source: MAR dataset, variable: REBEL45X – REBEL98X.)

Descriptive statistics

Variables	Mean	Std. deviation	Minimum	Maximum
Level of accommodation	.64	.921	0	3
Number of ethnic groups	8.01	8.22	1	28
Number of concentrated groups	3.82	2.96	0	10
Number of disaffected groups	5.34	3.69	1	13
Number of remaining groups	3.08	2.73	0	12
Combined economic value	11.1	14.8	0	104
Combined strategic value	3.45	3.62	0	17
Combined proportion of the population	.298	.285	.01	104.19
Short tenure	.080	.272	0	1
Economic value	3.66	2.81	0	18
Strategic value	1.43	1.15	0	6
Land area	.095	.144	0	.769
Population of group	.082	.097	.001	.43
Mountainous terrain	22.3	20.9	0	.94.3
Neighboring ethnic group	1.18	1.17	0	4
Government instability	.500	.502	0	1
Average level of democracy	1.39	6.56	-9	10
Proportional representation	.537	.500	0	1
Centralization	1.5	.806	1	3
Anocracy	.545	.499	0	1
Year conflict began	1975	17.4	1945	2002

Appendix 3: Coding rules and sources for Chapter 5

DEPENDENT VARIABLES:

Challenge: A binary variable coded 1 in the first year a demand was made to obtain greater political autonomy, association with kin in neighboring states, and/or independence, and 0 for all other years. (Source: Center for International Development and Conflict Management's (CIDCM) list of self-determination movements, University of Maryland, 2003.)

INDEPENDENT VARIABLES:

Past Accommodation: A dummy variable coded 1 if the government in question had previously granted either political autonomy or independence to another armed separatist group, and 0 if the government had not (either because it had never faced a previous challenge or because it was unyielding in the face of such a challenge). Concessions that were obtained because of military conquest, such as Eritrea's attainment of independence, were not coded as accommodation. (Source: Keesing's Contemporary Archives, *Encyclopædia Britannica*, Lexis/Nexus, *New York Times*, *The Economist*, Agence France Presse, CNN, BBC, group profiles provided by the Minorities at Risk (MAR) data project (see //www. bsos.umd.edu/cidcm/mar/list.html), and individual case histories.

   Number of previous accommodations: The number of times a government had granted a previous challenger either political autonomy or independence. (Source: see *"Past Accommodation"* variable above.)

   Proportion of previous challenges accommodated: The number of previous accommodations divided by the number of groups that had challenged the government between 1940 and the year under observation. (Source: see *Past accommodation* variable above.)

Number of ethnic groups. The total number of ethnic groups in a country as listed by *Encyclopædia Britannica.*

Number of ethnopolitical groups. A variable indicating the total number of ethnopolitical groups in a given country. To be coded as an ethnopolitical group, a group had to meet one of two criteria. It had to be disadvantaged in comparison to other groups in its society, usually because of discriminatory practices, or it had to be politically organized to promote or defend their collective interests. (Source: MAR dataset, version IV.)

Number of concentrated groups. The total number of ethnopolitical groups that were either a majority in one region, or concentrated in one region. Based on the MAR coding of group spatial concentration. (Source: MAR dataset, version IV, variable GROUPCON.)

Relative political status: A seven-point scale indicating the differentials in political status between the group in question and the dominant group(s) in the country. The scale ranges from –2 (the group is advantaged compared to other groups in society) to 4 where there are extreme differences in political status and positions between the groups and the dominant group. Differentials are objective differences between groups as best as MAR can judge. They are not necessarily the result of deliberate discrimination. Note that these variables are coded for the period immediately preceding the inclusion of the group in the MAR database, and were not updated by MAR thereafter. (Source: MAR IV, variable POLDIFXX 1940–2000.)

Relative cultural status: A five-point scale ranging from 0 (no differences) to 4 (extreme differences) that indicates the differentials in cultural status or traits between the ethnic group in question and the dominant group(s) in the country. Once again, differentials are objective differences between groups as best as MAR can judge them. They are not necessarily the result of deliberate discrimination. Note that these variables are coded for the period immediately preceding the inclusion of the group in the MAR database, and are not updated. (Source: MAR IV, variable CULDIFXX 1940–2000.)

Relative economic status: A seven-category scale of intergroup differentials in economic status and positions. This scale ranges from –2 (the group is advantaged) to 4 (there are socially significant differences in five or six of the following qualities: income, land/property, higher education, presence in commerce, presence in professions, and presence in official positions. Differentials are objective differences between groups as best as MAR can judge them. They are not necessarily the result of deliberate discrimination. Note that these variables are coded for the period immediately preceding the inclusion of the group in the MAR database, and are not updated. (Source: MAR IV, variable ECDIFXX 1940–2000.)

Political discrimination: A five-point index of political discrimination that ranged from no discrimination to a measure of public policies that substantially restricted the group's political participation by comparison with other groups. (Source: MAR variable POLDIS 1980–2000.)

Economic discrimination: A five-point index of economic discrimination that ranged from no discrimination to a measure of formal exclusion and/or recurring repression that substantially restricts the group's economic opportunities compared to other groups. (Source: MAR IV, variable ECDIS 1980–2000.)

Religious discrimination: A three-point scale indicating the degree to which group representatives aired grievances about freedom of religion. (Source: MAR IV, variable CULGR1 1985–1995.)

Lost autonomy: A composite index for groups who have lost autonomy or undergone a transfer of control from one country to another. Values range from 0 (no historical autonomy) to 6 (loss of long-term autonomy after 1980). This indicator gives greatest weight to more recent and substantial political changes in group status. (Source: MAR IV dataset, variable AUTLOST.)

Autonomy. A dummy variable coded 1 = the group was historically autonomous at some point in time, and 0 if it was never historically autonomous. (Source: MAR IV dataset, variable AUTON.)

Per capita income: Real gross domestic product (GDP) per capita in 1996 US dollars and lagged one year. (Source: Penn World Table Version 6, with missing values imputed. For details on how this was done see Gleditsch, 2002.)

Infant mortality rate: Measured in deaths of infants reported per 1,000 live births in each country in each year, and lagged one year. (Source: World Bank, International Economics Department, Socio-Economic Data Division.)

Economic Growth: To measure the rate of economic growth I used yearly change in the real GDP. (Source: World Bank.)

Geographic concentration: A four-point index indicating the degree to which groups are spatially distributed within a country. The index ranges from 0 (widely dispersed), to 3 (concentrated in one region). (Source: MAR IV dataset, variable GROUPCON.)

Group cohesion: A five-point index that measures the extent to which group members have an active, self-conscious sense of group identity based on their defining traits (common history, ethnicity, culture, language, religion, territory, etc.). This index ranges from no evidence of significant collective identity among those who share the defining traits (1) to a situation where most members share highly important values and objectives (5). (Source: MAR IV dataset, variable COHESX 1980–1995.)

Size of ethnic group population: The best estimate of the population of the group in 1990, in thousands. (Source: MAR IV dataset, variable GPOP.)

Proportion of national population: Group proportion of country population in 1998. (Source: MAR IV dataset, variable GPRO. Readers should be aware of the following concerns noted by MAR in their codebook: "Few countries provide census data that distinguishes people according to mutually exclusive group identities. Even when this is attempted, the resulting figures remain somewhat speculative as identity boundaries remain "fuzzy" and, therefore, somewhat fluid." Estimates are used from 1998 because these are considered the most reliable.)

Youth bulge: Measured as the ratio of the youth population (age 15–24) relative to the adult population of a country, and lagged by one year. (Source: Urdal, 2004, www.prio.no/cwp/datasets.asp.)

Primary commodity exports/GDP: The ratio of primary commodity exports to GDP proxies the abundance of natural resources. The data on primary commodity exports and GDP were obtained from the World Bank. Export and GDP data are measured in current US dollars.

Oil and natural gas: A dummy variable coded 1 if a country derived at least one-third of its export revenues from oil or natural gas, 0 otherwise. (Source: Fearon and Laitin, 2003, dataset on civil wars. Data can be accessed at www.stanford.edu/group/ethnic/publicdata/publicdata.html.)

Fuel exports: (Source: World Bank, *World Development Indicators*.)

Government instability. A dummy variable indicating whether the country in question had experienced a three or more change in its Polity IV combined democracy/autocracy score in any of the three years prior to the group-year in question. (Source: Polity IV dataset, Marshall and Jaggers, 2003.)

Anocracy: A dummy variable indicating whether a government scored between –5 or +5 on Polity IV's democracy/autocracy measure, and lagged by one year. (Source: Polity IV dataset.)

Mountainous terrain. The proportion of the country that is "mountainous" according to the codings of geographer, A. J. Gerard. (Source: Fearon and Laitin, 2003. Data can be accessed at www.stanford.edu/group/ethnic/publicdata/publicdata.html.)

Country population: (*Source:* Kristian Gleditsch, 2002. "Expanded Trade and GDP Data," *Journal of Conflict Resolution* 46: 712–24.)

Neighboring ethnic groups. The total number of adjoining countries where segments of the ethnopolitical group also resided. (Source: MAR IV dataset, variable: NUMSEGX.)

Democracy. A measure derived from a government's autocratic features and its democratic features. The incumbent government's autocracy score was subtracted from its democracy score to produce a net democracy number that ranges in value from very autocratic (–10) to very democratic (+10), and is lagged by one year. (Source: Polity IV dataset, Marshall and Jaggers, 2003, variable: POLITY.)

International contagion: An index that reflects the contagion of rebellion by kindred groups across borders and the diffusion of rebellion through a region. (Source: MAR IV dataset, variable ICONREB, 1970–95.)

Government repression: Nine separate measures were used. They included indexes indicating the presence of the following behavior: ethnic leaders were arrested, disappeared, or detained; systematic killings by paramilitaries occurred; restrictions on movement; saturation of police or military; limited use of force against protestors; unrestrained force against protesters; military campaigns against armed rebels; military targets and rebel areas destroyed. (Source: MAR IV dataset, variables REP03; REP09; REP11; REP17; REP18; REP19; REP20; REP21; and REP22. MAR includes data for the years 1996–2000 only.)

Descriptive statistics

Variables	Mean	Std. Deviation	Min	Max
Challenge	.007	.08	0	1
Past accommodation	.051	.22	0	1
Number of ethnic groups	6.61	3.97	0	22
Relative political status	1.62	1.62	–2	4
Relative cultural status	2.67	1.13	0	4
Relative economic status	1.84	1.94	–2	4
Per capita income ($)	4,419	4,777	276	32,307
Lost autonomy	.98	.97	0	4
Group geographic concentration	2.10	1.11	0	3
Government instability	.17	.37	0	1
Anocracy	.27	.44	0	1
Mountainous terrain	21.8	20.4	0	94.3
Size of country population	9.91	1.58	5.40	14.02
Neighboring co-ethnics	1.19	1.19	0	4
Ethnic group proportion of population	.11	.15	.00	.87
Youth bulge	29.9	6.14	12.9	42.9
Oil	.15	.35	0	1
Democracy	–1.09	7.02	–10	10
Accommodation proportion	.025	.13	0	1
Accommodation group size	.001	.017	0	.29
Number of groups already challenged	.67	1.51	0	8
Number of groups yet to challenge	5.94	3.85	0	22

References

Abdulkadiroglu, A., and T. Sonmez, 1998. Random Serial Dictatorship and the Core from Random Endowments in House Allocation Problems. *Econometrica* **66**: 689–701.

Ahmad, Ehtisham, and Ali Mansoor, 2000. *Indonesia: Managing Decentralization.* Indonesia: Fiscal Affairs Department.

Alt, James E., Randall L. Calvert, and Brian Humes, 1988. Reputation and Hegemonic Stability: A Game-Theoretic Analysis. *American Political Science Review* **82** (2): 445–66.

Anderson, Jon Lee, 2001. Home Fires: The Basque Separatists Intensify Their War. *The New Yorker.* Feb 12, 40–7.

Aspinall, Edward, and Harold Crouch, 2003. *The Aceh Peace Process: Why it Failed.* Washington DC: East–West Center.

Azar, Edward, and John Burton (eds.), 1986. *International Conflict Resolution: Theory and Practice.* Boulder, CO: Lynne Rienner Publishers.

Bacini, Benedicto R., 2005. *The Mindanao Peace Talks: Another Opportunity to Resolve the Moro Conflict in the Philippines.* Washington, DC: US Institute of Peace.

Balisacan, Arsenio M., and Hal Hill (eds.), 2003. *The Philippine Economy: Development, Policies, and Challenges.* London: Oxford University Press.

Bartkus, Viva Ona, 1999. *The Dynamic of Secession.* Cambridge: Cambridge University Press.

Bertrand, Jacques, 2004. *Nationalism and Ethnic Conflict in Indonesia.* Cambridge: Cambridge University Press.

Bolton, G. E., and A. Ockenfels, 2005. The Influence of Information Externalities on the Value of Reputation Building – An Experiment. University of Cologne Working Paper Series, Economics **17**.

Bolton, G. E., and A. Ockenfels, 2007. Information Externalities, Matching and Reputation Building – A Comment on Theory and an Experiment. University of Cologne Working Papers Series, Economics **17**. (http://ockenfels.uni-koeln.de/download/papers/bolton_ockenfels_information_externalities.pdf.)

Bolton, Patrick, Gerard Roland, and Enrico Spolaore, 1996. Economic Theories of the Break-Up and Integration of Nations. *European Economic Review* **40** (April): 697–705.

Bowman, Isaiah, 1946. The Strategy of Territorial Decisions. *Foreign Affairs* **24** (2): 177–94.

Brandts, J., and G. Charness, 2000. Hot vs. Cold: Sequential Responses and Preference Stability in Experimental Games. *Experimental Economics* **2**: 227–38.

Brandts, J., and N. Figueras, 2003. An Exploration of Reputation Formation in Experimental Games. *Journal of Economic Behavior and Organization* **50**: 89–115.

Bueno de Mesquita, Bruce, 2002. Domestic Politics and International Relations. *International Studies Quarterly* **46**: 1–9.

Cagoco-Guiam, Rufa, 2002. Negotiations and Detours: The Rocky Road to Peace in Mindanao. *Accord* (August). (www.c-r.org/our-work/accord/philippines-mindanao/negotiations-detours.php, p. 5.)

Camerer, C.F., T.-H. Ho, and J.-K. Chong, 2004. A Cognitive Hierarchy Model of Games. *Quarterly Journal of Economics* **119** (3): 861–98.

Camerer, Colin, and Keith Weigelt, 1988. Experimental Tests of a Sequential Equilibrium Reputation Model. *Econometrica* **56** (1): 1–36.

Cetinyan, Rupen, 2002. Ethnic Bargaining in the Shadow of Third-Party Intervention. *International Organization* **56** (3): 645–79.

Challis, Roland, 2001. *Shadow of a Revolution: Indonesia and the Generals.* Stroud: Sutton.

Chauvel, Richard, 1990. *Nationalists, Soldiers and Separatists. The Ambonese Islands from Colonialism to Revolt, 1880–1950.* Leiden: KITLV Press.

Che Man, W.K., 1990. *Muslim Separatism: The Moros of Southern Philippines and the Malays of Southern Thailand.* New York: Oxford University Press.

Chew, Amy, 1999. Interview – Jakarta Sees High Risk of Aceh Breakaway. *Reuters News*, November 7.

Choucri, Nazli, 1974. *Population Dynamics and International Violence: Propositions, Insights and Evidence.* Lexington, MA: Lexington.

Coakley, John (ed.), 1993. *The Territorial Management of Ethnic Conflict.* London: Frank Cass.

Collier, Paul, and Anke Hoeffler, 2001. Greed and Grievance in Civil War. Research Working Paper 2355, World Bank, Washington, DC.

Crouch, Harold A., 1978. *The Army and Politics in Indonesia.* Ithaca, NY: Cornell University Press.

Daughety, Andrew F., and Robert Forsythe, 1987a. Regulatory-induced Industrial Organization: A Laboratory Investigation. *Journal of Law, Economics, and Organization* **56** (1): 1–36.

Daughety, Andrew F., and Robert Forsythe, 1987b. Regulation and the Formation of Reputations: A Laboratory Analysis, in E. Bailey (ed.), *Public Regulation: New Perspectives on Institutions and Policies.* Cambridge, MA: MIT Press.

DeJong, Douglas V., Robert Forsythe, and Russell J. Lundholm, 1985. Ripoffs, Lemons, and Reputation Formation in Agency Relationships: A Laboratory Market Study. *The Journal of Finance* **40** (3): 809–20.

Diehl, Paul F., 1996. Territorial Dimensions of International Conflict: An Introduction. *Conflict Management and Peace Science* **15** (1): 1–10.

Diehl, Paul F. (ed.), 1999. *A Road Map to War: Territorial Dimensions of International Conflict*. Nashville, TN: Vanderbilt University Press.

Diehl, Paul, and Gary Goertz, 1991a. Entering International Society: Military Conflict and National Independence, 1816–1980. *Comparative Political Studies* **23** (4): 497–518.

Diehl, Paul, and Gary Goertz, 1991b. Interstate Conflict over Exchanges of Homeland Territory, 1816–1980. *Political Geography Quarterly* **10** (1): 342–55.

Di Giovanni, Janine, 2000. Army Loses Faith in Chechen Cause. *The Times* (London), February 17.

Dixit, Avinash, 1982. Recent Developments in Oligopoly Theory. *American Economic Review* **72** (May): 12–17.

Downs, George W., and Michael A. Jones, 2002. Reputation, Compliance, and International Law. *The Journal of Legal Studies* **31**: 95–114.

Doyle, Michael, 1986a. *Empires*. Ithaca, NY: Cornell University Press.

Doyle, M. W., 1986b. Liberalism and World Politics. *American Political Science Review* **80** (4): 1151–69.

Drake, Christine, 1989. *National Integration in Indonesia: Patterns and Policies*. Honolulu: University of Hawaii Press.

Elson, R. E., 2001. *Suharto: A Political Biography*. Cambridge: Cambridge University Press.

Estrade, Bernard, 1999. The Truth Dawns, Indonesia is Falling Apart. *Daily Telegraph*, March 2.

Esty, Daniel C., J. A. Goldstone, T. R. Gurr, P. T. Surko, and A. N. Unger, 1995. *Working Papers: State Failure Task Force Report*. CIA Directorate of Intelligence (November 30).

Esty, Daniel C., J. A. Goldstone, B. Harf, M. Levy, G. D. Dabelko, P. T. Surko, and A. N. Unger, 1998. *State Failure Task Force Report: Phase II Findings*. CIA Directorate of Intelligence (July 31).

Evron, Y., 1987. *War and Intervention in Lebanon*. Baltimore, MD: Johns Hopkins University Press.

Fallon, Joseph E., *Igorot and Moro National Re-emergence: The Fabricated Philippine State*. www.cwis.org/fwj/21/imnr.html.

Fearon, James D., 1994. Signaling Versus the Balance of Power and Interests: An Empirical Test of a Crisis Bargaining Model. *Journal of Conflict Resolution* **38** (2): 236–69.

Fearon, James D., 1995. Rationalist Explanations for War. *International Organization* **49** (summer): 379–414.

Fearon, James D., 2003. Ethnic and Cultural Diversity by Country. *Journal of Economic Growth* **8** (June): 195–222.

Fearon, James D., and David D. Laitin, 2003. Ethnicity, Insurgency, and Civil War. *American Political Science Review* **97** (1): 75–90.

Filson, Darren, and Suzanne Werner, 2002. A Bargaining Model of War and Peace: Anticipating the Onset, Duration, and Outcome of War. *American Journal of Political Science* **46** (4): 819–37.

Finin, Gerard A., 2005. *The Making of the Igorot: Contours of Cordillera Consciousness.* Manila: Ateneo de Manila Univerity Press.

Fischbacher, Urs, 1999. Z-Tree – Zurich Toolbox for Readymade Economic Experiments – Experimenter's Manual. Working Paper No. 21. Institute for Empirical Research in Economics, University of Zurich.

Forbes, Cameron, 1992. Irian Jaya, The Forgotten East Timor. *The Age* (Melbourne). Feb 22, 13.

Frederick, William H., and Robert L. Worden, 1993. *Indonesia: A Country Study.* Washington, DC: Library of Congress.

Friend, Theodore, 2003. *Indonesian Destinies.* Cambridge, MA: Harvard University Press.

Fudenberg, D., and D. K. Levine, 1998. *The Theory of Learning in Games.* Cambridge, MA: MIT Press.

Ganguly, Rajat, and Ian Macduff (eds.), 2003. *Ethnic Conflict and Secessionism in South and Southeast Asia: Causes, Dynamics, Solutions.* London: Sage Publications.

Garcia, Cathy Rose A., 1999. Suspension of Peace Talks with Communist and Secessionist Groups: Hard Lessons in Fortifying a Fragile Peace Condition. *Business World.* Mar 10, 8.

George, T. J. S., 1980. *Revolt in Mindanao: The Rise of Islam in Philippine Politics.* Oxford: Oxford University Press.

Gilpin, Robert, 1981. *War and Change in World Politics.* New York: Cambridge University Press.

Gleditsch, Kristian S., 2002. Expanded Trade and GDP Data. *Journal of Conflict Resolution* **46** (October): 712–24.

Gleditsch, Nils Petter, Peter Wallensteen, Mikael Eriksson, Margareta Sollenberg, and Havard Strand, 2002. Armed Conflict 1946–2001: A New Dataset. *Journal of Peace Research* **39** (September): 615–37.

Goemans, Henk Erich, 2000. *Domestic Politics and the Causes of War Termination: The Fate of Leaders and the First World War.* Princeton: Princeton University Press.

Goertz, Gary, and Paul Diehl, 1992. *Territorial Changes and International Conflict.* London: Routledge.

Grieco, Joseph, 1988. Anarchy and the Limits of Cooperation. *International Organization* **42** (3): 485–507.

Gunalan, N., 1999. If Aceh Secedes, Nation will Break Up. *The Straits Times*, November 12, 48.

Gurr, Ted Robert, 1970. *Why Men Rebel.* Princeton: Princeton University Press.

Gurr, Ted Robert, 1993a. Why Minorities Rebel: A Global Analysis of Communal Mobilization and Conflict since 1945. *International Political Science Review* **14** (April): 161–201.

Gurr, Ted Robert, 1993b. Minorities at Risk: A Global View of Ethnopolitical Conflicts. Washington, DC: United States Institute of Peace.

Gurr, Ted Robert, 2000. *Peoples Versus States: Minorities at Risk in the New Century.* Washington, DC: United States Institute of Peace.

Gurr, Ted Robert, and Will H. Moore, 1997. Ethnopolitical Rebellion: A Cross-Sectional Analysis of the 1980s with Risk Assessments for the 1990s. *American Journal of Political Science* **41** (4): 1079–103.

Gutierrez, Eric, 1999. The politics of transition. *Accord: An International Review of Peace Initiatives.* (www.c-r.org/acc_min/gutier.htm.)

Gutierrez, Eric, and Saturnino Borras, Jr., 2004. *The Moro Conflict: Landlessness and Misdirected State Policies.* Washington, DC: East–West Center.

Hechter, Michael, 1992. The Dynamics of Secession. *Acta Sociologica* **35** (December): 267–83.

Hegre, Havard, Tanja Ellingsen, Scott Gates, and Nils Petter Gleditsch, 2001. Toward a Democratic Civil Peace? Democracy, Political Change and Civil War, 1916–1992. *American Political Science Review* **95** (March): 33–48.

Hensel, Paul, 1996. Charting a Course to Conflict: Territorial Issues and Interstate Conflict, 1916–1992. *Conflict Management and Peace Science* **15** (1): 43–73.

Holmes, Charles W., 1999. The Little War with Big Stakes: Russia's Conflict in Dagestan has Major Implications for its Own Stability. *The Montreal Gazette*, August 22, 3.

Holsti, Kalevi J., 1991. *Peace and War: Armed Conflicts and International Order, 1648–1989.* New York: Cambridge University Press.

Hopf, Ted, 1994. *Peripheral Visions: Deterrence Theory and American Foreign Policy in the Third World, 1965–1990.* Ann Arbor, MI: University of Michigan Press.

Horowitz, Donald, 1985. *Ethnic Groups in Conflict.* Berkeley: University of California Press.

Huntington, Samuel, 1993. The Clash of Civilizations. *Foreign Affairs* **72** (summer): 22–49.

Huth, Paul K., 1988a. *Extended Deterrence and the Prevention of War.* New Haven: Yale University Press.

Huth, Paul K., 1988b. Extended Deterrence and the Outbreak of War. *American Political Science Review* **82** (2): 423–443.

Huth, Paul K., 1996a. Enduring Rivalries and Territorial Disputes, 1950–1990. *Conflict Management and Peace Science* **15** (1): 7–42.

Huth, Paul K., 1996b. *Standing Your Ground: Territorial Disputes, 1950–1990.* Ann Arbor, MI: University of Michigan Press.

Huth, Paul K., 1997. Reputations and Deterrence: A Theoretical and Empirical Assessment. *Security Studies* **7** (1): 72–99.

Huth, Paul K. and Bruce Russett, 1984. What Makes Deterrence Work? *World Politics* **35** (4): 496–526.

Huth, Paul K. and Bruce Russett, 1988. Deterrence Failure and Crisis Escalation. *International Studies Quarterly,* **32** (1) (March): 29–45.

Huth, Paul K., D. Scott Bennett, and Christopher Gelpi, 1992. System Uncertainty, Risk Propensity, and International Conflict Among the Great Powers. *Journal of Conflict Resolution* **36** (3): 478–517.

Huth, Paul K., Christopher Gelpi, and D. Scott Bennett, 1993. The Escalation of Great Power Militarized Disputes: Testing Rational Deterrence Theory and Structural Realism. *American Political Science Review* **87** (3): 609–23.

International Studies Institute of the Philippines, 1985. *Muslim Filipino Struggle for Identity: Challenge and Response.* Selected Documents for the Conference on the Tripoli Agreement. September 12–13.

Isaac, R. Mark, and Vernon L. Smith, 1985. In Search of Predatory Pricing. *The Journal of Political Economy* **93** (2): 320–45.

Jaggers, Keith, and Ted Robert Gurr, 1996. *Polity III: Regime Type and Political Authority, 1800–1994.* 2nd ICPSR version. Ann Arbor, MI: Inter-university consortium for Political and Social Research.

Jung, Yun Joo, John H. Kagel, and Dan Levin, 1994. On the Existence of Predatory Pricing: An Experimental Study of Reputation and Entry Deterrence in the Chain-store Game. *The Rand Journal of Economics* **25** (1): 72–93.

Kacowicz, Arie, 1994. The Problem of Peaceful Territorial Change. *International Studies Quarterly* **38** (2): 219–54.

Kahler, Miles, and Barbara F. Walter (eds.), 2006. *Territoriality and Conflict in an Era of Globalization.* Cambridge: Cambridge University Press.

Kennan, John, and Robert Wilson, 1993. Bargaining with Private Information. *Journal of Economic Literature* **31** (1): 45–104.

Kinder, Donald, and Thomas Palfrey, 1993. On Behalf of an Experimental Political Science, in Donald Kinder and Thomas Palfrey (eds.), *Experimental Foundations of Political Science.* Ann Arbor, MI: University of Michigan Press.

King, Gary, and Langche Zeng, 2001. Explaining Rare Events in International Relations. *International Organization* **55** (summer): 693–715.

King, Gary, Michael Tomz, and Jason Wittenberg, 2000. Making the Most of Statistical Analyses: Improving Interpretation and Presentation. *American Journal of Political Science* **44** (2): 347–61.

Kreps, David M., 1990. *Course in Microeconomic Theory.* Princeton, NJ: Princeton University Press.

Kreps, David M., and Robert Wilson, 1982. Reputation and Imperfect Information. *Journal of Economic Theory* **27**: 245–79.

Laitin, David, and James Fearon, 2001. Minorities at Risk Database and Explaining Ethnic Violence. National Science Foundation. grant proposal (apsanet.org.)

Lane, Max, 2003. West Papua: Papuans "Marginalised in our Own Country." www.greenleft. org.au/2003/555/29524, September 24.

Lebow, Ned, 1985. Deterrence Reconsidered: The Challenge of Recent Research. *Survival* **27** (1).

Legge, J. D., 1972. *Sukarno: A Political Biography*. New York: Praeger Publishers.

Lekic, Slobodan, 1999. The Legacy of East Timor: Other Indonesian Provinces feel Stirrings of Separatism. *The Montreal Gazette*, November 7.

Leng, R. J., and C. S. Gochman, 1984. Dangerous Disputes: A Study of Conflict Behavior and War. *American Journal of Political Science* **26** (4): 664–87.

Lieberman, E., 1994. The Rational Deterrence Theory Debate. *Security Studies* **3** (3): 384–427.

Lieberman, E., 1995. What Makes Deterrence Work? Lessons from the Egyptian–Israeli Enduring Rivalry. *Security Studies* **4** (4): 833–92.

Lloyd, Grayson, 2000. Indonesia's Future Prospects: Separatism, Decentralisation and the Survival of the Unitary State. *Current Issues* **17** (June 27), 3.

Luard, Evan, 1986. *War in International Society*. London: I. B. Tauris and Company.

Mackinder, Halford, 1919. *Democratic Ideals and Reality*. New York: Henry Holt.

Majul, Cesar Adib, 1985. *The Contemporary Muslim Movement in the Philippines*. Berkeley, CA: Mizan Press.

Mandel, Robert, 1980. Roots of the Modern Interstate Border Dispute. *Journal of Conflict Resolution* **24** (3): 427–54.

Marshall, Monty G., and Ted Robert Gurr, 2003. *Peace and Conflict, 2003: A Global Survey of Armed Conflicts, Self-Determination Movements, and Democracy*. College Park, MD: Center for International Development and Conflict Management, University of Maryland.

Marshall, Monty G., and K. Jaggers, Polity IV Project: Political Regime Characteristics, and Transitions, 1800–2003. College Park, MD: Center for International Development and Conflict Management, University of Maryland.

McAmis, Robert D., 1974. Muslim Filipinos, 1970–1972. In Peter G. Gowing and Robert D. McAmis (eds.), *The Muslim Filipinos: Their History, Society, and Contemporary Problems*. Manila: Solidaridad Publishing House.

McDermott, Rose, 2002. Experimental Methods in Political Science. *Annual Review of Political Science* **5** (June): 31–61.

McKelvey, R. D., and R. R. Palfrey, 1998. Quantal Response Equilibria for Extensive Form Games. *Experimental Economics* **1** (1): 9–41.

McKenna, Thomas M., 1998. *Muslim Rulers and Rebels: Everyday Politics and Armed Separatism in the Southern Philippines*. Berkeley, CA: University of California Press.

McKenna, Thomas M., 2004. Muslim Separatism in the Philippines: Meaningful Autonomy or Endless War? *Asia Source*, www.asia.source.org/asip/mckenna.cfm.

Mercer, Jonathan, 1996. *Reputation and International Politics*. Ithaca, NY: Cornell University Press.

Milgrom, Paul, and John Roberts, 1982. Predation, Reputation, and Entry Deterrence. *Journal of Economic Theory* **27** (August): 280–312.

Miller, Ross M., and Charles R. Plott, 1995. Product Quality Signaling in Experimental Markets. *Econometrica* **53** (4): 837–72.

Moller, Herbert, 1968. Youth as a Force in the Modern World. *Comparative Studies in Society and History* **10** (April): 237–60.

Morgan, T. Clifton, and Sally Campbell, 1991. Domestic Structure, Decisional Constraints, and War: So Why Kant Democracies Fight? *Journal of Conflict Resolution* **35** (2): 187–211.

Morgenthau, Hans, 1978. *Politics Among Nations*. New York: Alfred A. Knopf.

Morton, Rebecca B., and Kenneth C. Williams, 2007. Experimentation in Political Science, in Janet Box-Steffensmeier, David Collier, and Henry Brady (eds.), *The Oxford Handbook of Political Methodology*. New York: Oxford University Press.

Muller, Edward N., and Mitchell A. Seligson, 1987. Inequality and Insurgency. *American Political Science Review* **81** (2): 425–51.

Muller, Edward N., and Erich Weede, 1990. Cross-national Variation in Political Violence: A Rational Action Approach. *Journal of Conflict Resolution*, **34** (4): 624–51.

Murdock, Lindsay, 2000. Indonesia is Crumbling, Wahid Fears. *Sydney Morning Herald*, August 8, 1.

Mydans, Seth, 2006. In Tsunami's Wake, Old Foes in War Now Wage Politics. *New York Times*, December 11.

Nalebuff, Barry, 1991. Rational Deterrence in an Imperfect World. *World Politics* **43** (3): 313–35.

Neral, J., and J. Ochs, 1992. The Sequential Equilbrium Theory of Reputation Building: A Further Test. *Econometrica* **60** (5): 1151–69.

Newman, David, 1999. Real Spaces, Symbolic Spaces: Interrelated Notions of Territory in the Arab–Israeli Conflict, in Paul Diehl (ed.), *A Road Map to War: Territorial Dimensions of International Conflict*. Nashville, TN: Vanderbilt University Press.

Noble, Lela G., 1981. Muslim Separatism in the Philippines, 1972–1981: The Making of a Stalemate. *Asian Survey* **21** (11, Nov), 109–114.

Ochs, Jack, 1995. Games with Unique Mixed Strategy Equilibria: An Experimental Study. *Games and Economic Behavior* **10** (1): 202–17.

O'Neill, B., 1987. Nonmetric Test of the Minimax Theory of Two-person Zero Sum Games. *Proceedings of the National Academy of Sciences* **84** (7): 2106–9.

Orme, John David, 1992. *Deterrence, Reputation, and Cold-War Cycles*. London: Macmillan.

Ostrom, E., J. Walker, and R. Gardner, 1992. Covenants With and Without a Sword: Self-governance is Possible. *American Political Science Review* **86** (2): 404–17.

Palfrey, Thomas R., 2005. McKelvey and Quantal Response Equilibrium, in James Alt, John Aldrich, and Arthur Lupia (eds.), *A Positive Change in Political Science: The Legacy of Richarde D. McKelvey's Most Influential Writing*. Ann Arbor, MI: University of Michigan Press.

Pisani, Elizabeth, 1990. Anti-Javanese Rebellion Grows in Sumatra. *The Independent*. Jul 25.

Powell, Robert, 2002. Bargaining Theory and International Conflict. *Annual Review of Political Science* **5**: 1–30.

Powell, Robert, 2006. War as a Commitment Problem. *International Organization* **60** (1), 169–204.

Press, Daryl G., 2001. Power, Reputation, and Assessments of Credibility During the Cuban Missile Crisis. Paper presented at the 97th Annual Meeting of the American Political Science Association, August, Boston, MA.

Press, Daryl G., 2005. *Calculating Credibility: How Leaders Assess Military Threats*. Ithaca, NY: Cornell University Press.

Rabasa, Angel and Peter Chalk, 2001. *Indonesia's Transformation and the Stability of Southeast Asia*. Santa Monica: The Rand Corporation.

Ramos, Fidel V., 1999. *Developing as a Democracy*. New York: St. Martin's Press.

Richardson, Lewis Fry, 1960. *Statistics of Deadly Quarrels*. Chicago, IL: Quadrangle Publications.

Ricklefs, M. C., 2001. *A History of Modern Indonesia Since c. 1200*. Stanford, CA: Stanford University Press.

Roberts, John, 2004. Ambon Communal Violence Flares Up Amid Indonesian Presidential Poll. *World Socialist*, www.wsws.org, June 15, 1.

Rosenthal, Robert W., 1981. Games of Perfect Information, Predatory Pricing, and the Chain-store Paradox. *Journal of Economic Theory* **25** (1): 92–110.

Ross, Michael, 2005. Resources and Rebellion in Aceh, Indonesia, in Paul Collier and Nicholas Sambanis (eds.), *Understanding Civil War: Evidence and Analysis*, Vol. 2. Washington, DC: The World Bank.

Roth, Alvin E., and Françoise Schoumaker, 1983. Expectations and Reputations in Bargaining: An Experimental Study. *The American Economic Review* **73** (3): 363–372.

Rudolph, Joseph R., and Thompson, Robert J., 1985. Ethnoterritorial Movements and the Policy Process: Accommodating Nationalist Demands in the Developed World. *Comparative Politics* **17** (April): 291–311.

Saideman, Stephen M., 1997. Explaining the International Relations of Secessionist Conflicts: Vulnerability vs. Ethnic Ties. *International Organization* **51** (4): 721–53.

Sambanis, Nicholas, and Branko Milanovic, 2004. Explaining the Demand for Sovereignty. Unpublished manuscript. New Haven, CT: Yale University.

Sambanis, Nicholas, and Annalisa Zinn, 2004. From Protest to Violence: An Analysis of Conflict Escalation with an Application to Self-determination Movements. Unpublished manuscript. New Haven, CT: Yale University.

Santos, Soliman M. Jr., 2005. Peace Negotiations Between the Philippine Government and the Moros Islamic Liberation Front: Causes and Prescriptions. East–West Center Washington Working Papers, No. 3.

Sartori, Ann E., 2005. *Deterrence by Diplomacy*. Princeton: Princeton University Press.

Schelling, Thomas, 1966. *Arms and Influence*. New Haven, CT: Yale University Press.

Schmalensee, Richard, 1981. Economies of Scale and Barriers to Entry. *Journal of Political Economy* **89** (6): 1228–38.

Schmalensee, Richard, 1983. Advertising and Entry Deterrence: An Exploratory Model. *Journal of Political Economy* **91**: 636–53.

Schwarz, Adam, 2000. *A Nation in Waiting: Indonesia's Search for Stability*. Boulder, CO: Westview Press.

Selten, Richard, 1978. The Chain-store Paradox. *Theory and Decision* **9** (April): 127–59.

Shadish, William, Thomas D. Cook, and Donald Campbell, 2002. *Experimental and Quasi-experimental Design*. Boston MA: Houghton Mifflin College Division.

Shimshoni J., 1988. *Israel and Conventional Deterrence*. Ithaca, NY: Cornell University Press.

Sicat, Gerardo P., 1972. *Economic Policy and Philippine Development*. Manila: University of the Philippines Press.

Slantchev, Branislav, 2003. The Principle of Convergence in Wartime Negotiations. *American Political Science Review* **97** (4): 621–32.

Smith, Alastair, and Allan C. Stam, 2001. Bargaining and the Nature of War. Unpublished manuscript. New York: New York University.

Smith, Anthony, 1991. *National Identity: Ethnonationalism in Comparative Perspective*. Reno, NV: University of Nevada Press.

Smith, Anthony, 2001. *Nationalism*. Cambridge: Blackwell Publishing.

Smith, Anthony L., 2002. Aceh: Democratic Times, Authoritarian Solutions. *New Zealand Journal of Asian Studies* **4** (2): 68–89.

Snyder, Jack, 1991. *Myths of Empire: Domestic Politics and International Ambition*. Ithaca, NY: Cornell University Press.

Snyder, G.H., and P. Diesing, 1978. *Conflict Among Nations*. Princeton, NJ: Princeton University Press.

Spence, Michael, 1973. Job Market Signaling. *Quarterly Journal of Economics* **87** (August): 355–74.

Steinberg, David Joel, 2000. *The Philippines: A Singular and a Plural Place*. 4th edn. Boulder: Westview Press.

Stremlau, John, 1977. *The International Politics of the Nigerian Civil War, 1967–1970*. Princeton, NJ: Princeton University Press.

Sundali, J., A. Israeli, and T. Janicki, 2000. Reputation and Deterrence: Experimental Evidence from the Chain Store Game. *Journal of Business and Economic Studies* **6** (1): 1–19.

Sundali, J. A., and D. A. Seale, 2004. The Value of Cheap-talk and Costly Signals in Coordinating Market Entry Decisions. *Journal of Business Strategies* **21** (1): 69–94.

Symonds, Peter, 2000. The Historical Roots of the Confrontation Brewing in West Papua. World Socialist website, December 7.

Taylor, John G., 1991. *Indonesia's Forgotten War: The Hidden History of East Timor.* London: Zed Books.

Thoenes, Sander, 1999. Indonesia Sends Riot Troops to Dissident Province: President Fears Domino Effect. *The Financial Times.* May 8, 3.

Tilly, Charles, 1978. *From Modernization to Revolution.* Reading: Addison-Wesley.

Tingley, D., and S. Wang, 2008. Strategies and Beliefs in Sequential Games of Two-sided Incomplete Information: An Experimental Study. Paper presented at Experimental Political Science Conference, New York University.

Toft, Monica Duffy, 2001. A Theory of Territory, Indivisibility, and Ethnic Violence. Unpublished paper, JFK School of Government, Harvard University, Cambridge, MA.

Toft, Monica Duffy, 2003. *The Geography of Ethnic Conflict.* Princeton: Princeton University Press.

Tomz, Michael, 2005. *The Influence of International Agreements on Foreign Policy Preferences.* Palo Alto, CA: Stanford University.

Tomz, Michael, 2007. *Sovereign Debt and International Cooperation: Reputational Reasons for Lending and Repayment.* Princeton, NJ: Princeton University Press.

Touval, Saadia, 1972. *The Boundary Politics of Independent Africa.* Cambridge, MA: Harvard University Press.

Triesman, Daniel, 2004. Rational Appeasement. *International Organization* **58** (2): 345–74.

Urdal, Henrik, 2004. The Effect of Youth Bulges on Domestic Armed Conflict, 1950–2000. Working Paper 29740, International Peace Research Institute, Oslo.

Van Evera, Stephen, 1998. *Causes of War: Power and the Roots of Conflict.* Ithaca, NY: Cornell University Press.

Vanzo, John P., 1999. Border Configuration and Conflict: Geographical Compactness as a Territorial Ambition of States, in Paul Diehl (ed.), *A Road Map to War: Territorial Dimensions of International Conflict.* Nashville, TN: Vanderbilt University Press.

Vasquez, John A., 1993. *The War Puzzle.* Cambridge: Cambridge University Press.

Vatikiotis, Michael R. J., 1998. *Indonesian Politics Under Suharto: The Rise and Fall of the New Order.* New York: Routledge.

Walker, Mark, and John Wooders, 2001. Minimax Play at Wimbledon. *The American Economic Review* **91** (5): 1521–38.

Walter, Barbara F., 2002. *Committing to Peace: The Successful Settlement of Civil Wars.* Princeton, NJ: Princeton University Press.

Walter, Barbara F., 2003. Explaining the Intractability of Territorial Conflict. *International Studies Review* **5** (4): 137–53.

Walter, Barbara F., 2004. Building Reputation: Why Governments Fight Some Separatists but Not Others. *American Journal of Political Science* **50** (2, Spring): 313–30.

Walter, Barbara F., 2006. Information, Uncertainty, and the Decision to Secede. *International Organization* **60** (1): 105–35.

Waltz, Kenneth, 1979. *Theory of International Politics.* Reading, MA: Addison-Wesley Publishing Co.

Ward, Michael D., and Kristian Gleditsch, 2002. Location, Location, Location: An MCMC Approach to Modeling the Spatial Context of War and Peace. *Political Analysis* **10** (summer): 244–60.

Wenstedt, Frederick L., and Paul D. Simkins, 1965. Migrations and the Settlement of Mindanao. *The Journal of Asian Studies* **25** (1): 83–103.

Woods, Jackie, 2000. Megawati Bad News for Papua Independence Hope Activist Says. August 10. (www.converge.org.nz/pma/wpapua5.htm.)

Woodward, Susan L., 1995. *Balkan Tragedy: Chaos and Dissolution after the Cold War.* Washington, DC: Brookings Institution Press.

Yegar, Moshe, 2002. *Between Integration and Secession: The Muslim Communities of Southern Philippines, Southern Thailand, and Western Burma/Myanmar.* Lanham, MD: Lexington Books.

Yeltsin, Boris, 2000. *Midnight Diaries.* New York: Public Affairs.

Index